Yesterday:
Memoirs of a Russian-Jewish Lawyer

די יודישע אמונה איז אנ'אלטער שמועד אייזען, אן וועלכען
עס זענען צוקלאפט געווארען אלערליי האמערם, שווערע
האמערם פון שונאים...   א.א. גרוזענבערג.

O. O. GRUZENBERG
Courtesy of Encyclopaedia Judaica

Yesterday: Memoirs of a Russian-Jewish Lawyer

O. O. Gruzenberg

Edited and with an
Introduction by Don C. Rawson
Translated by Don C. Rawson
and Tatiana Tipton

UNIVERSITY OF CALIFORNIA PRESS
Berkeley • Los Angeles • London

University of California Press
Berkeley and Los Angeles, California

University of California Press, Ltd.
London, England

© 1981 by
The Regents of the University of California

Printed in the United States of America

1 2 3 4 5 6 7 8 9

Library of Congress Cataloging in Publication Data

Gruzenberg, Oskar Osipovich, 1866–1940.
  Yesterday: memoirs of a Russian-Jewish lawyer.

  Translation of Vchera.
  Includes one chapter from Gruzenberg's
Ocherki i rechi.
  Bibliography: p. 223
    1. Gruzenberg, Oskar Osipovich, 1866–1940.
  2. Lawyers, Jewish—Russia—Biography.
  I. Title.
Law   345.47′0092′4 [B]   80–39850
  ISBN 0–520–04264-6

Contents

CONTENTS

Acknowledgments

The preparation of this volume was made possible by a grant from the Program for Translations of the National Endowment for the Humanities, an independent federal agency; and by a faculty leave from Iowa State University.

Special thanks are extended to Professor Vladimir Grebenschikov of Carleton University for reading the entire manuscript and making valuable suggestions on the translation; to Professor Deborah Lipstadt of the University of California at Los Angeles, for providing information on Jewish history and customs; to Mrs. Alexandra Pregel for sharing her recollections of O. O. Gruzenberg and supplying leads for locating materials; and to Mr. Jerry L. Jones for assisting with legal terminology.

D. C. R.
T. T.

Translators' Note

This translation of O. O. Gruzenberg's memoirs comprises all of *Vchera: vospominaniia* [*Yesterday: Memoirs*] (Paris, 1938), except for the several biographical sketches of professional acquaintances that Gruzenberg appended to the main text. The chapters have been slightly rearranged in order to provide a more chronological sequence. The chapter on the Soviet of Workers' Deputies is taken from O. O. Gruzenberg, *Ocherki i rechi* [*Essays and Speeches*] (New York, 1944), which was published by a group of Gruzenberg's friends after his death.

The transliteration of names generally follows the usage recommended in J. Thomas Shaw, *The Transliteration of Modern Russian for English-Language Publications* (Madison, 1967). Thus, System I is used for names appearing in the text: ё = yo, й = y, ю = yu, я = ya, кс = x, –ый = –y, –ий = –y, –ия = –ia; and System II for names appearing in bibliographical references: ё = e, й = i, ю = iu, я = ia, кс = ks, –ый = –yi, –ий = –ii, –ия = –iia. Personal names having a non-Russian origin are rendered according to the nationality to which they belong. Thus, for example, Witte, Herzenstein, Lucis, and Spasowicz, rather than Vitte, Gertsenshtein, Lyuts, and Spasovich. Place names in non-Russian territory within the Empire, such as the Baltic provinces, are given according to their official Russian designation in the early twentieth century; but the first time they appear in the text, they are followed by their local usage. Thus, for example, Vilna [Vilnius], Verzhbolovo [Virbalis], and Libava [Liepaja].

Since Gruzenberg's writing reflects the distinctive oratorical style he used as a courtroom lawyer, some passages in his memoirs lack the necessary phrasing to convey the transitions of mood and ideas that he would have provided in vocal discourse by voice inflections, pauses, and changes of pace. Generally, we have tried to preserve in translation the structural characteristics of his writing; occasionally, we have inserted minor connective words and phrases for the sake of clarity and readability.

Gruzenberg's footnotes are preserved as he wrote them, and are indicated by asterisks; editorial comments and elaboration are presented in brackets and separate editorial footnotes are numbered to distinguish them from the author's.

D. C. R.
T. T.

Editor's Introduction

Oskar Osipovich Gruzenberg, one of the most prominent defense lawyers in late tsarist Russia, prepared these memoirs as an émigré in western Europe after the Bolshevik revolution. In them he offers a valuable commentary on the Russian judiciary during a significant period of its history, when it occupied the anomalous position of being a largely independent institution in an otherwise autocratic political system. But for the curious reader Gruzenberg provides much more, particularly through subtle themes relating to problems of personal identity, both as a partially Russified Jew during an era of mounting anti-Semitism in the late nineteenth and early twentieth centuries, and as a liberal critic of the autocracy whose efforts were eclipsed by the radicals after the 1917 revolution.

Especially crucial during his early years was Gruzenberg's position as a Jew, whose hopes and frustrations reflected fluctuations in official Russian policy toward the Jews, as well as developments within Russian Jewry itself. Official policy paralleled the traditional attitude among Russians that the Jews were intruders in their land. Though historians have shown that in ancient Russia there was little discrimination against Jews, the emergence of a sense of national and religious distinctiveness among the Russians, beginning in about the eleventh century, contributed to a gradually increasing enmity. By the sixteenth century, the government had banned Jews from entering Russian territory, partly because of its general distrust of foreigners but more so because of religious prejudice against "the crucifiers of Christ." In the early eighteenth century, imperial edicts decreed that those Jews found living in the western borderlands should be banished beyond the frontier and refused reentry. While a few Jews still managed to migrate into

these border areas, Russia did not acquire a sizable Jewish population until the partitions of Poland in the late eighteenth century,
when almost a million Jews in eastern Poland, as well as Lithuania,
Belorussia, and the western Ukraine (all of which had been under
Polish rule), became residents of the Russian empire. Since banish-
ment no longer served as a feasible policy, the government tried
to confine the Jews to its western provinces—the so-called Pale of
Settlement (see accompanying map). Even within this area it
closed many localities to Jewish settlement, including Kiev, the
principal city of the Ukraine.

At the beginning of the nineteenth century, liberal currents filtering into Russia from western Europe ameliorated the status of
Jews, as the government removed the burdensome double taxation
previously imposed on them and permitted a few Jewish merchants
and artisans to reside temporarily, for business purposes, in the
interior of Russia. The government also admitted Jewish children
to Russian schools in order to prepare them for a more active role
in the general life of the country—though with the expectation that
in the process some of them would accept Christianity, an objective
recognized by most Jewish parents, who continued to send their
children to Talmudic schools.

During the reform era that marked the early part of the reign of
Alexander II (1855–81), residence restrictions were relaxed even
more. By the mid-1860s, the government had issued laws permitting prosperous Jewish merchants to reside permanently outside
the Pale and in Kiev. Similarly, the government abolished residence
requirements for Jews holding medical and advanced university
degrees, as well as for skilled Jewish artisans. Like most of Alexander's reforms, this legislation had practical motivations, since it
included only Jews especially useful to Russian society because of
their commercial, technical, or intellectual capabilities, all of which
were in short supply. But regardless of the rationale, many Jews
recognized that for those who qualified, these policy modifications
provided greater opportunity than had ever before existed.

Important, too, was the fact that the government once again encouraged Jews to enter Russian secondary and higher institutions
of learning. Though it still assumed that these educated Jews
would more readily be assimilated into Russian life and would
perhaps adopt Christianity, the policy found greater acceptance by
Jews than it had earlier in the century. The reason for the change
was an internal development in Judaism known as the *haskalah*, or

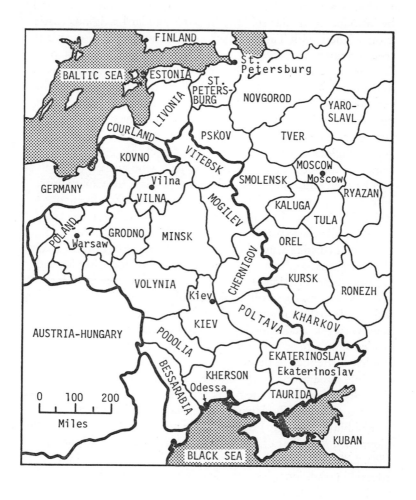

enlightenment. The movement began in the late eighteenth century as a reform tendency in Jewish education, which stressed the need to raise the intellectual level of the Jewish people, particularly by introducing secular subjects into the standard religious curriculum of the Jewish Talmudic schools. By the middle of the nineteenth century, the advocates of the *haskalah* had gone a step further, emphasizing the advantages of shedding Jewish customs and attending Russian schools in the hope that, by integrating into the Gentile world, the Jews would have a better chance of gaining civic equality. During its early stages the movement encountered strong resistance from many Jews, who valued the tradition of a solely religious education in the Talmudic schools. Later, its opponents expressed the fear that those Jews who availed themselves of a Russian education would abandon Judaism for Christianity. However, by the 1860s, the *haskalah* movement was influencing a sizable minority of young Jews, mainly from affluent and cultured families, who were eager to gain a Russian education and embrace a Russian way of life. Few of them spoke of the equality they sought as a right or a prerequisite to assimilation, but instead regarded emancipation as the result—almost as a reward—for their willingness to Russify. Like members of most minorities long vulnerable to the authority wielded by the dominant society, these Jews were not accustomed to thinking in terms of rights, but tended simply to accept, usually gratefully, whatever concessions might be extended to them.

While some young Jews followed the *haskalah* route without difficulty, others found the break with traditional Judaism a traumatic experience. The Jewish writer and publicist Moses Lieb Lilienblum (1843–1910) described the crisis poignantly in his autobiography, *The Sins of Youth* [*Hattot Ne'urim*], published in 1876. Lilienblum had been raised in the Talmudic mold and steeped in traditional Judaism. In his early twenties he began to read *haskalah* literature, which made a great impression on him, and soon he was ready to cast off what he regarded as "the dead world of the Talmud." Despite the pleading of friends and family, he left his wife and small children, and went to Odessa to study in a Russian gymnasium, or secondary school, in preparation for the university and a career in law. But it was a formidable transition, and in his autobiography he lamented his decision. Having chosen this "enlightened" path, he recognized how poorly prepared he was to proceed because of the "bad education" of his youth. He had fled his past without an adequate means of reaching his destination. As he recalled the simple life in the village, he questioned whether the *haskalah* had been worth the sacrifice. "Once I lived with illusion instead of truth," he confided, "but I did not know that it was illusion. I thought it was the truth. That is why I was happier then than now."[1]

In contrast to Lilienblum, Gruzenberg was an excellent example of those young Jews who seemed adequately equipped to travel the road to assimilation. He had been born in 1866 in the Ukrainian city of Ekaterinoslav (now Dnepropetrovsk), two hundred and thirty miles southeast of Kiev. Though his grandfather was a rabbi and a traditionalist, his father became a prosperous merchant and an adherent of the *haskalah* movement, who arranged for his six children to grow up feeling that Russification was a natural process. Not only did he make certain that they learned Russian as their primary language (rather than Yiddish), but he obtained permission to move his family to Kiev in 1876, where he enrolled his sons in a Russian gymnasium to prepare them for the university and professional careers. For the young Gruzenberg these years at the gymnasium and university were exhilarating, filled with intense study and academic achievement.

However, his memoirs reveal the psychological problems involved in this endeavor. Imbued with the idea of taking his place in the Russian world, he had also been taught not to forsake his Jewish heritage. This double imperative resulted in a disturbing identity conflict. Instead of achieving a synthesis of being both Jew and Russian, he found himself in the dilemma of feeling that he was neither. Because he had been raised without the customary Jewish education and adherence to Jewish cultural and religious traditions, he did not feel a close connection with the Jewish people; and because he could not be fully accepted into the mainstream

---

[1] An excerpt of Lilienblum's autobiography in English translation appears in Lucy S. Dawidowicz, *The Golden Tradition: Jewish Life and Thought in Eastern Europe* (New York, 1967), 120–29. After the anti-Jewish pogroms of 1881 (see p. xviii), Lilienblum was even more convinced that the *haskalah* would never result in equality. Consequently, he turned to Jewish nationalism, which within a few years evolved into Zionism, with its emphasis on emigration as the only acceptable alternative to the suppression of the Jews in Russia. He concluded that even for those Jews who were psychologically able to assimilate into Russian society the logical consequence was conversion — the complete loss of identity as a Jew — which negated the essential philosophy of emancipation.

of Russian life without converting to Christianity, he was to some extent an outsider among the Russians. In either case, he lacked a sense of belonging.

In an especially introspective portion of the memoirs, Gruzenberg recalls the struggles of his youth in defining his identity, in particular his relationship with Judaism. Though he had great difficulty in forming a spiritual bond with the Jewish people and repeatedly insisted that his personal destiny was not tied to theirs, he finally arrived at the conviction that he had a practical obligation to the common Jewish people, whose vulnerability to persecution summoned capable Jews in the Gentile world to come to their assistance. As he concludes in his memoirs: "It may be that you do not acknowledge the voice that is yours by blood; it may be that from the days of your childhood the Russian element has been closer to you. But do you really not know that 'the crucifiers of Christ,' those who supposedly despise the people among whom they live, rarely receive help from anyone who is not a Jew?" Gruzenberg probably did not completely discern the motives that led him to this conclusion. Certainly he possessed a strong sense of social justice, stemming from his own encounters with discrimination, but he seems also to have felt a need to act generously toward those Jews who were less fortunate than he, perhaps because he harbored traces of guilt for having left traditional Judaism in quest of personal success. However intertwined his motives, he at least managed to clarify his relationship with the Jewish people. Though he might never feel the security of "belonging," he could find some satisfaction in serving as a guardian of their interests.

Having made this commitment, Gruzenberg still faced the frustration of attempting to enter Russian professional life during a period of rising anti-Semitism, which accompanied the late nineteenth century surge in Russian nationalism. Just as he finished his law studies at Kiev University in 1889, the government issued a decree that non-Christians were to be admitted to the bar only with the personal approval of the Minister of Justice, which meant a virtual ban on Jews. The best he could hope for was to become a lawyer-in-training, an assistant to an established member of the bar, with little prospect of becoming a full-fledged member himself.

Gruzenberg's consternation over this unexpected development typified the concern of an entire generation of young Jewish intellectuals who witnessed the narrowing of possibilities for their entering Russian society: the exclusion of Jews from the bar, discrimination in the other professions, quotas for Jewish students in secondary schools and institutions of higher learning, and a renewed prejudice against Jews in general. Disillusioned, one of them wrote, "When I remember what has been done to us, how we have been taught to love Russia and Russian speech, how we have been induced and compelled to introduce the Russian language and everything Russian into our families so that our children know no other language than Russian, and how we are now repulsed and persecuted, then our hearts are filled with sickening despair from which there seems to be no escape." [2]

The general mood of frustration brought varied responses. Some young Jews converted, though often with an attitude reminiscent of Daniel Chwolson, whose appointment as a professor at St. Petersburg University in the 1850s required that he accept Christianity. When asked if he had converted out of conviction, he reportedly replied, "Yes, I was convinced it was better to be a professor in St. Petersburg than a *melamed* [a teacher of small children in a local Jewish religious school] in Eyshishkes." Others penitently found their way back to Judaism, either to immerse themselves in the Talmud and embrace the old traditions or to promote Jewish nationalism and eventually Zionism. Still others, including Gruzenberg, elected neither to convert nor to retreat, but to persist in the difficult task of pursuing careers as Jews in the Gentile world.

Gruzenberg remained a lawyer-in-training for the next sixteen years, until the revolutionary events of 1905 caused the government to relax a number of its more stringent policies, among them the one regarding admission to the bar. Fortunately, as a lawyer-in-training he was permitted to plead cases under the nominal supervision of his patron, and he steadily developed his proficiency as an advocate.

During his career, Gruzenberg felt a kinship with other prominent Jewish lawyers whom he knew, such as Sliozberg, Winaver, and Hessen; but he also sought the approval and friendship of non-Jewish members of the bar. On the whole, his colleagues, like other educated persons in Russian society, tended to be less anti-

[2] S. M. Dubnow, *History of the Jews in Russia and Poland* (Philadelphia, 1916–20), vol. 2, pp. 326–27.

Semitic than either the general populace or the government. Thus, despite the restraints he encountered, Gruzenberg felt reasonably comfortable in Russian judicial life. Seldom did he display a "we-they" attitude in distinguishing between himself as a Jew and the Russian legal profession. Rather, he assumed the attitude of those liberal intellectuals, both inside and outside the profession, who perceived the principal "we-they" dichotomy as being the division between educated society as a whole and the state.

Though Gruzenberg did not choose to become an integral part of the Jewish community during his career, he maintained his sense of responsibility to the Jewish people. From his own experiences he recognized that the hopes for Jewish equality, which had been so bright in the 1870s, were rapidly dimming. Along with its emphasis on nationalism and Russification, the conservative press had aroused public opinion against the Jews as an alien blight on Russian society. The recent argument that "useful" categories of Jews, such as merchants, artisans, and professional persons, could contribute to the general welfare of Russia now gave way to the accusation that these very Jews, as they became successful in their respective fields, were exploiting the Russian people. Jews were also identified with the nascent revolutionary movement of the late 1870s, which had resulted in the assassination of Alexander II in 1881. Though there had been only a few Jewish participants in the radical groups, both the press and high-ranking bureaucrats warned that the Jews were a dangerous element in Russia whose activities should be stringently curtailed. In addition to new legislation restricting the number of Jews who could enter institutions of secondary and higher education and the professions, a wave of public agitation against the Jews swept across Russia, culminating in the pogroms, which began in 1881 and reached their peak in the first decade of the twentieth century. Legal recourse against these violent attacks on Jewish life and property was difficult, since the police often failed to apprehend the culprits, and the courts in many instances tended to hand down light sentences for serious offenses. Thus, it was with only limited success that Gruzenberg and other lawyers sued for damages in behalf of victims of the pogroms. Probably the greatest benefit of these trials was to bring the plight of the Jews to the attention of conscientious members of Russian society.

Gruzenberg was more effective in countering legal charges

brought against Jews by anti-Semitic opponents. Twice he defended Jews accused of using Christian blood for ritual purposes. The first of these trials took place in 1900, when a court in Vilna [Vilnius] convicted a Jew, David Blondes, of wounding a Christian girl in order to obtain blood for use during Passover. Since the court imposed only a light prison sentence, local Jewish leaders expressed their willingness to accept the verdict, rather than to contest the case and risk the possibility of a more severe sentence in a second trial. However, Gruzenberg, who had followed the case from St. Petersburg, was of a different mind. He insisted on challenging the verdict, and, when it was nullified by a higher court, he acted as defense counsel during the retrial. Blondes' acquittal in this trial was a tribute to Gruzenberg's ability and persistence, and brought his first widespread recognition within the legal profession, as well as within the Jewish community.

An even more dramatic episode was the Beilis trial in 1913, which attracted international attention. In his memoirs Gruzenberg discusses some important aspects of this case, in which he served as chief counsel for Mendel Beilis, a Kievan Jew, charged with the ritual murder of a Christian boy. During a grueling five-week trial, the imperial government tried to manipulate the case to assure a conviction, but Gruzenberg and his associates effectively refuted the charges brought by the prosecution. When the jury found Beilis innocent, it was, as Gruzenberg rightly notes, not only a victory for the defense and the Jewish people, but an irrevocable blow to the regime.

Still another kind of anti-Semitic discrimination into which Gruzenberg's memoirs provide personal insight was the fury unleashed against the Jews during World War I, especially after Russian losses began to mount and the authorities endeavored to justify the defeats by blaming "disloyal" elements within Russia. Besides deporting thousands of Jews from the western provinces to the interior because they were considered sympathetic to the invading Germans, and holding many others hostage in order to ensure the loyalty of those Jews remaining in the war zones, the Russian military command frequently brought charges of treason against individual Jews, allegedly for collaborating with the enemy. Gruzenberg repeatedly came to the defense of Jews accused (usually on the flimsiest of evidence) of espionage and other treacherous crimes.

Over the years, Gruzenberg added his voice to those calling for full emancipation of the Jews in Russia, insisting that they be granted equal rights in gaining an education, entering the professions, owning property, and choosing their place of residence. The notion that Jews despised the Russian people, he argued, was a myth; the majority of the Russian people, if freed from anti-Semitic propaganda, he was convinced, would willingly accept Jews into their society. He also had some words of caution for Jews. Though he himself occasionally contributed articles on Jewish literature to Jewish publications, such as the newspaper *Budushchnost* [*The Future*], which his brother Semyon edited in St. Petersburg, he warned against Jewish exclusiveness. He persistently encouraged the integration of Jews into Russian society, maintaining that this need not diminish their ethnic identity.

Eventually, Gruzenberg's hopes for Jewish emancipation were realized. On March 21, 1917, the Provisional Government, which had replaced the autocracy after the February Revolution, abolished all religious and ethnic restrictions in Russia, thus granting Jews and other minorities equal rights as citizens. It was undoubtedly gratifying to Gruzenberg that a delegation representing Jewish organizations throughout the country selected him to deliver a speech to the Petrograd Soviet of Workers' and Soldiers' Deputies, lauding the emancipation and pledging Jewish cooperation with the Russian people in their collective future.

Gruzenberg entered the Russian legal profession during a distinguished period of its history—the half century following the judicial reform of 1864. Prior to the reform, the Russian judiciary had been conspicuously arbitrary and inequitable. Procedures were complicated, and officials were often uneducated and prone to corruption. The government had long recognized the desirability of a more effective administration of justice, but the necessary impetus did not come until the reform-minded Alexander II succeeded to the throne in 1855. With the emancipation of the serfs in 1861, the need for a uniform judicial system became even more apparent. S. I. Zarudny, a member of Alexander's committee for drafting the judicial reform, later remarked, "Under serfdom there was no real need for an equitable administration of justice. The only true judges were the landowners, who themselves were ruled over by a higher arbitrary justice. The regulations of February

19, 1861, brought an end to these deeply rooted procedures. Even our higher officials recognized that the time had come when Russia, like any well-regulated state, urgently needed a speedy and equitable administration of justice."[3]

The drafting committee attempted to establish a judiciary that was not only comprehensive enough to administer justice to the entire population but that was also independent. Drawing on western European judicial practice, which had been greatly influenced by the writings of Montesquieu and other theorists in the eighteenth century, the committee drafted Article 1 of the Basic Principles of the Statutes of Judicial Institutions to read: "The judicial power is separated from the executive, administrative, and legislative power." The statutes specified that all judicial proceedings must go through the courts, and that no punishment could be inflicted for an offense unless it had been adjudicated in court. Further, the statutes indicated that while judges would still be appointed by the Minister of Justice, they would no longer be regarded as officials of the government; and, except for misconduct, they would not be subject to removal.

The statutes also enabled a more consistent and effective administration of justice by providing equality before the law and speedy litigation. They placed preliminary investigation of cases in the hands of examining magistrates, and the hearing of minor cases under the purview of justices of the peace. More serious cases they entrusted to trial by jury, one of the most important innovations of the 1864 reform, which gave representatives of the people an integral function in the judicial process.

Over the years practice did not always match intention, for the government frequently interfered with the judiciary. Though the Ministry of Justice upheld the principle that judges were appointed for life, it could impede advancement, and transfer judges to less desirable posts. At times it brought pressure to bear on judges to obtain convictions, particularly in political cases. Gradually it withdrew various categories of cases from trial by jury, most notably cases involving crimes against "state order and public tranquility," which it placed under the jurisdiction of the military courts. In addition, it often circumvented the courts by exiling political dissidents through administrative decree. But despite these

---

[3] G. A. Dzhanshiev, *Epokha velikikh reform* [*The Epoch of the Great Reforms*] (St. Petersburg, 1907), pp. 612–13.

pressures and manipulations, the judiciary proved immeasurably more equitable than before 1864, and maintained much of the independence intended by the reform.

The new statutes also had a salutary effect on the members of the judiciary. Some degree of apathy and corruption continued, but especially among the younger men it became a matter of conscience and pride to administer justice. An emphasis on education and training resulted in more competent judges, as well as more scrupulous prosecutors. Moreover, the reform, by guaranteeing litigants in civil suits, and the accused in criminal cases, the right to be represented by counsel, gave new significance to the role of the defense lawyer. Prior to 1864, the function of legal counsel was restricted to submitting written briefs and petitions in behalf of a client, together with written evidence, to be used by the court, which decided the case in closed session, without even the defendant present. The statutes of 1864 transformed this old inquisitorial system into one based on oral argumentation by permitting a client's counsel to plead his case in open court.

While any Russian citizen could legally represent another in court as a "private attorney," it rapidly became the practice for cases to be handled by members of the newly created bar. Admission to the bar required formal training in a law school or faculty of law at a university, followed by a five-year probationary period as a lawyer-in-training. By the 1880s, the Russian bar had become a creditable institution, devoted to maintaining high professional standards and preparing its candidates for an effective role in court.

The legal profession also provided opportunities for specialization, both in criminal and civil law, as well as in particular procedures. Gruzenberg, for example, became an expert in cassation proceedings—a process he frequently discusses in his memoirs— which had been borrowed from the French practice, and involved review of a lower court's verdict by the Senate, the highest judicial body in Russia, or, in a case covered by military law, by the Main Court-Martial. Unlike appeal procedures, which also had a place in the Russian system (see chart on p. 208), cassation did not deal with the substance of a case, such as the content of the evidence or even the reasoning of a lower court in reaching its verdict. Instead, it focused on procedural questions, such as deficiencies in the indictment, improper application of the laws, or the introduction of presumably inadmissible evidence—in short, judicial errors.

After submitting a complaint to the criminal or civil cassation department of the Senate or to the Main Court-Martial, the counsel for the defense appeared to argue the complaint. If the cassation court reversed the verdict of a lower court, the case was remanded for a retrial, either to another court or to a different section of the court that had originally heard the case.

Gruzenberg enjoyed exceptional success in cassation cases. He had a thorough knowledge of judicial procedure and a keen memory of previous decisions of the Senate or Main Court-Martial, which he could cite as precedents. He was persuasive before the bench, basing his pleadings not so much on legal technicalities as on a careful analysis of a case in order to show that judicial error in a lower court had indeed resulted in an unjust verdict.

At the same time, Gruzenberg understood the adversary principle in courtroom proceedings, both in cassation cases and in cases he defended at a lower level. He appreciated the fact that along with argument there was counter-argument, that the courtroom was the site of a judicial contest. In this respect, his colleagues were right when they referred to him as "an advocate by calling." It was obvious that he relished the drama of courtroom combat and responded energetically to its demands. He was by nature a fighter, competitive and determined, driven by a strong ego and inclined to be brusque with adversaries, judges, and even colleagues. Occasionally his impulsiveness caused him to make injudicious remarks in court, but usually he disciplined the intensity with which he pleaded a case so that his forceful manner strengthened his arguments.

One of Gruzenberg's major concerns as a defense lawyer was the protection of the rights of the individual, particularly against the authority of the state, a concern widely shared by others in the Russian legal profession during this period. The concept of individual rights had not traditionally been a part of Russian jurisprudence, for the laws and legal procedures had long been directed toward enabling the state and society to function smoothly as a whole, rather than toward guaranteeing individual liberties. The new philosophy, rooted in eighteenth-century Enlightenment thought, which had reached Russia as part of the westernization process, emphasized that while the state might exercise political sovereignty, it must not encroach on the personal rights of members of society through an arbitrary use of power. Since the authority of the state in Russia remained strong, the tendency within the emerging group of independent lawyers, following the judicial reform of 1864, was to take the side of the individual.

Appropriately, some of Gruzenberg's best known cases were in defense of persons accused of crimes against the state. He defended Maxim Gorky against charges of preparing insurrectionary literature at the time of the Bloody Sunday incident in January, 1905; Leon Trotsky and other participants in the first Soviet of Workers' Deputies, when they were tried in 1906; and P. N. Milyukov, the leader of the Constitutional Democratic Party, who was indicted for publishing the Soviet's manifesto in his newspaper, *Rech* [*Speech*]. In addition, Gruzenberg defended other, less prominent persons in political trials, customarily without charging a fee, his reasoning being that he had a duty to protect the individual against the authority of the state.

Gruzenberg's commitment to the defense of individual rights and his moderate opposition to the autocracy led him to join the Constitutional Democratic (or Kadet) Party, organized by Milyukov and other liberals in 1905. Even though, as one of Gruzenberg's colleagues recalled, he was too independent and self-willed to be a disciplined member of a party and too impulsive and impatient to be a party leader,[4] he agreed with the Kadets' emphasis on civil liberties and constitutional government. Because of his legal training and dedication to the rule of law, this seemed a natural political orientation. As a member of a restricted minority, he was also attracted to the liberals' tendency toward pluralism and their belief in religious and ethnic tolerance.

Gruzenberg's liberal persuasion contributes to a subtle and perhaps unconscious theme in his memoirs, particularly as he defends his position as a critic of the tsarist regime who welcomed its fall in February, 1917, but was in turn swept aside by the Bolsheviks when they came to power in October. Shortly after the fall of the autocracy, he was appointed by the Provisional Government to be a judge in the criminal cassation department of the Senate, a role with which he had become familiar during his career as an advocate. Within a month after the Bolsheviks replaced the Provisional Government, they abolished all existing judicial institutions and organized new ones, which Gruzenberg

[4] A. A. Gol'denveizer, *V zashchitu prava* [*In Defense of the Law*] (New York, 1952), p. 244.

and many of his colleagues felt were not sufficiently independent
of Bolshevik political control to provide the freedom necessary for
them to function either as lawyers or judges. At the time, Gruzenberg supposed that this would not be a permanent arrangement.
In December, 1917, he was elected to the Constituent Assembly,
previously scheduled by the Provisional Government and permitted by the Bolsheviks, though they received only a minority of
the votes in the national elections. Along with many other delegates, Gruzenberg held to the hope that the assembly would draw
up a constitution for a multi-party government with an independent judiciary. On the opening day of the assembly, January 5,
1918, he was ill, and friends prevailed on him to stay at home
"until tomorrow." But he soon discovered that the Bolsheviks, who
dissolved the assembly at the end of its first session, intended that
there would be no tomorrow.

Excluded from both judicial and political life, Gruzenberg debated his future. After settling briefly with his brother Matvey, a
lawyer in Tiflis [Tbilisi], he moved to Kiev, the city of his youth,
and then to Odessa. Finally, in the spring of 1921, he emigrated
to Berlin, later going on to Riga and eventually to Nice, where he
lived until his death in 1940. In exile, he had the task of coming
to terms with the fact that the revolution had not only exceeded
his own intentions but had made him superfluous to Russia's new
society. It may be that he did not perceive the irony of the situation:
he had had a greater role under the tsarist government, whose
demise he had earnestly awaited, than under the post-revolutionary
regime.

This irony was compounded by the fact that before the revolution he had been among those liberals who held the view that in
the struggle against the autocracy they had "no enemies on the
left." As already noted, he served as chief defense counsel in the
trial of Leon Trotsky and other members of the first Soviet of
Workers' Deputies in 1906. He next encountered Trotsky in the
summer of 1917 during a political meeting in Petrograd, at which
Trotsky delivered an eloquent speech against the Provisional Government. When Trotsky approached Gruzenberg and asked how
he had liked the speech, Gruzenberg jokingly replied that he was
impressed that Trotsky had not lost his erudition, but that as a
judge in the Senate he was ready to sentence Trotsky to a term of
hard labor. "Ah," Trotsky retorted, "you want to correct the mistake you once made in defending me." In the months and years

that followed October, 1917, the turn of events no longer was a joking matter for Gruzenberg.

Along with many of his liberal contemporaries in exile, he had ample time to reflect on his position as a liberal. Why had the liberals in Russia not proved more successful? Did their ineffectiveness mean that their role had not been a valid one? These, of course, are questions that have been debated at great length by scholars and political figures alike. Most historians of the period interpret the role of the liberals in the context of prevailing trends in Russia, though they disagree on the significance of these trends. On the one hand are those who view Russian liberalism as having been a natural and integral part of the country's historical development. Some who take this point of view argue that Russia would gradually have reached the liberals' objectives of an open and pluralistic society had it not been for the massive dislocations of the war, coupled with the government's monumental mishandling of it, which antagonized practically all segments of the population. Armed with more concrete arguments but reaching similar conclusions, others maintain that the liberals proposed an adequate alternative to autocracy but failed in 1917 because of specific errors of policy and tactics. According to this argument, the liberals miscalculated in supporting the war, which was becoming increasingly unpopular, as well as in delaying social reform, especially land redistribution, supposing that deferring such action until the convocation of the Constituent Assembly was in accord with popular desires. Some scholars also argue that a set of fortuitous circumstances in 1917 enabled the Bolsheviks almost to stumble into power, their chief strength being their willingness to take risks at opportune moments. In any case, those who emphasize the role of the war, tactical errors, or historical accident in accounting for the liberals' lack of success, still maintain that in substance they offered a valid alternative to tsarist rule.

In contrast, some scholars argue that liberalism never had a chance in Russia: it was simply a Western European importation, whose emphasis on parliamentary government and moderate social reform, while appealing to certain Russian intellectuals, offered little in meeting the enduring needs and aspirations of an impoverished and oppressed populace. In a similar vein, others contend that liberalism was poorly adapted to a people accustomed to authoritarianism and lacking the political experience that accompanied the evolutionary constitutional development in Western

Europe. The result was that liberalism could not satisfy the Russian people's impatient demands for rapid social and economic change. Some also argue that backward Russia required an authoritarian transformation in order to modernize at a rate that would enable it to catch and keep up with the other major powers, a process that would have been impeded by a parliamentary government. And, of course, the Marxist view holds that only a radical proletarian revolution could have satisfied the dictates of history. Most of these scholars agree that the popularity of the liberals during the 1905 revolution and their prominence in the first two Dumas was largely an illusion—a momentary victory resulting from tsarist concessions calculated to undermine the demands of the liberals, which did not at all mean that the liberals could ultimately provide an alternative to the old regime.

The conclusions formed in all of these arguments must to an extent remain speculative, in some cases because they are based on theoretical models of political transformation or modernization, and more generally because they depend on certain philosophical assumptions about the role of determinism and contingency in history. For similar reasons, Russian liberals who were active in the period under consideration have usually supplied only nebulous explanations of their function during the final years of the old regime and the revolution. Their task has also been complicated by the urge—perhaps the need—to justify their position, which is not to say that such an endeavor is illegitimate, but that it has often led to ambiguities in their arguments. For example, the Kadet leader P. N. Milyukov maintained before the revolution that liberal constitutional government for Russia was practically a historical necessity; yet he employed an equally deterministic interpretation after the revolution to conclude that historical forces had propelled the revolution from its moderate beginning to a radical conclusion, his contention being that in the general pattern of revolution there is an instinctive fear in the populace that the revolution will end too soon, and because of this popular demand for extreme solutions the moderates are cast aside.

In his memoirs, Gruzenberg expresses much the same attitude. The liberals, with their emphasis on civil liberties and constitutional government, had the best solution to the problems facing Russia, he felt, but the autocracy had created so vast a reservoir of popular indignation that, once released, it carried the people to intemperate demands for alternatives. Gruzenberg touches on this point in his reference to the apprehension he shared with Vladimir Korolenko shortly before the fall of the autocracy, as they discussed the likelihood of violent outbursts once the revolution began. He elaborates the point in his description of the revolutionary fervor of the peasant-soldiers in 1917, which only Trotsky and other Bolshevik leaders were able to harness. What he implies is that the liberals, while hoping for and contributing to the end of the old regime, were not responsible for the extremes of the revolution. This was the fault of generations of oppression, a circumstance illustrative of the principle that the more thwarted the aspirations of a people, the more sweeping are its demands.

This interpretation leaves Gruzenberg in the ambivalent position of defending the liberals while also sanctioning the radicals. Though he disagreed with many of the policies of the Bolsheviks once they came to power, he ascribes to them a certain legitimacy by placing their victory, together with the liberals' demise, in the context of transcendent, often uncontrollable, historical forces.

Still, whatever inconsistencies appear in Gruzenberg's rationalization of the political role of the liberals, his memoirs convey another message far less ambiguous. They suggest that in assessing Russian liberalism one should look beyond the political sphere and recognize the important function liberalism fulfilled in judicial life. Because of the relative independence of the judiciary under the old regime, and despite recurrent governmental pressures, conscientious liberals in the legal profession achieved considerable success in promoting the cause of individual liberties and applying the principles of justice. Indeed, one of the values of the memoirs is the understanding they provide of such persons and activities.

Gruzenberg's memoirs contain a variety of recollections about his experiences as a lawyer, a liberal, and a Jew in late tsarist Russia. But throughout his writing there runs a vital thread: the sense of justice that pervaded his life and career. In an early chapter of the memoirs, he recalls that at the time of his decision to enter the legal profession, he resolved to "master the iron whip of the law." Like others in the profession he regarded the law as an instrument for protecting members of society from the arbitrary imposition of authority. In some instances, he directed his attention toward certain groups. As a Jew, he was especially aware of the discrimination against religious and ethnic minorities that prevailed in Russia, and he insisted that the rights of these minorities be scrupulously upheld by the judiciary. In a broader sense, he supported the rights of individuals whatever their background. While he did not deny the role of law in guarding society and the state from injury by individuals, he was more concerned that the law should serve to defend individuals from injury by society or the state. This principle had a particular significance in autocratic Russia, but it also speaks at any time to all who respect human dignity and justice.

D. C. R.

Chapter 1

Early Expectations

The first word that reached my consciousness was Russian. Songs, tales, nannies, childhood games with friends—all these were Russian.

I fell in love with this marvelous language. In expressing affection, it is bewitching and as soft as silk. In denoting struggle, it is touched with frost, passionately restrained. When it appears as the printed word, it is simple and transparent, incapable of concealing the slightest falsity.

Beginning in the fourth class at the gymnasium, I studied the Russian language, especially folk works—the *byliny*,[1] tales, and songs—with love and persistence. At that time our literature teacher at the Fourth Kiev Gymnasium was a Great Russian, N. I. Ivanov, an expert in his field. He was an anti-Semite, but like most Russians he did not act maliciously toward any particular Jew. In articles he published during the 1880s in *Notes of the Nezhin (Demidov) Lyceum*,* he only complained that the Jews were corrupting the Russian language.

I was overjoyed when, soon after one of these articles appeared, he summoned me, a sixteen-year old pupil in the seventh class, to the teachers' office and in his characteristically stern manner growled, "Look here now, I have a lad in the fifth class who's a capable fellow, but he's lagging behind. Give him a hand with his literature. The tutoring will help you, too. After all, I hear you're not living very sumptuously."

A year later, just before the final examination, he came to me

[1] [Old Russian epic poems.]
* At that time the Lyceum had a historical-philological curriculum; subsequently it became a law school.

again. In that same stern manner, but with smiling eyes, which shone with a paternal tenderness I had forgotten after four years of being an orphan, he affectionately informed me, "A few days ago we notified the district curator about those in your graduating class who have distinguished themselves. In the subject I teach, you were the only one I could designate. I wrote that you have studied Russian literature with exceptional devotion."

He looked away from me and asked, "Well, what have you decided? In what field will you continue your studies?"

In what field? What should I answer. In my mind burned passages from the folk tales, in my ears rang the rhythmic music of the *byliny*, but in my heart gnawed the annoying thought: Where do you think this love of yours can get you? Who needs it? You'll only look ridiculous and pathetic if you persist. You won't be allowed to teach, even in a grammar school. Or do you intend to pay the price of admission to a Russian teachers' office by deserting your faith?

My face flushed, as if from the lash of a whip. Certainly not. I had not thought of doing this even in my weaker moments.

Ivanov looked at me askance, and, having guessed my unspoken answer, he firmly grasped my hand and quickly left.

Soon afterwards, I enrolled in the faculty of law. Why? Was it that I liked the fields of study this faculty offered? Except for the Russian gospel of the 1880s—political economy—I had only a vague idea about the subjects I would study. No, it was something else that attracted me. During my last winter as a student in the gymnasium, I spent some time with a young lawyer, who was just beginning his career in the criminal court. Behind the luster and beauty of the forensic contests, I recognized with my whole being the terror of loneliness, the alienation of those whom the law has snatched from among the hundreds of thousands of their fellow citizens, those whom it then arrays in prison garb, places in the confines of the courtroom dock, surrounds with guards, and confronts with judges and prosecutors in their resplendent uniforms and jurors in their frock coats, suits, and jackets. I sensed, too, the mood of the spectators, aroused by an insatiable craving to watch someone experiencing genuine fear and suffering, the cost of which is a mutilated life.

Something terrible seethes in the courtroom, something elusive, but definitely tangible. Later, I identified it as a cruelty engendered by suspicion. An isolated event is pulled from a person's life, from his past, from his present, and everyone concentrates on it, without any desire to understand that the whole person is no less a fact than any of his deeds.

All against one! The entire state, the entire world! Who, then, is for him? Who will protect him? One person—only one: the counsel for the defense.

It is imperative, I thought, unquestionably imperative for me to master the iron whip of the law, in order to lash out at those judges who forget their impartiality and to drive off those prosecutors who revel in their badgering. In the autumn of 1885, I entered Kiev University.

The next four years of university life were a thoroughly intoxicating time for me. From the break of day I was continually drunk—drunk without a single drop of wine, but with the dreams of the poet I had been reading late the night before; drunk with rapturous wondering before the capriciously unfolding expanse of life, so green and fresh, where my path lay distinctly marked, narrow though it might be, but still mine; drunk with the sweet anxiety of listening for the soft steps of happiness stealing close, for the incessant whispering that it will come today—now. And everywhere the sun, the towering sun, which never seemed to set. But all the same, it was a pity to miss even a single ray. Later, I thought, I shall give it back. As I am able, I shall repay. I shall keep nothing to myself. But for the present, I must absorb, I must drink in everything.

Our family managed to get along. My father's former wealth, which had enabled us to live not only comfortably but luxuriously, rapidly melted away in the hands of clever liquidators after his untimely death. For the sake of our family's well-being, my sister, brother, and I hitched ourselves to the load and pulled it along the bumpy road of life. The three of us gave lessons, and our earnings were just sufficient to settle six brothers and sisters, with my mother as head of the family, in two rooms and to provide a diet of some soup with a bit of meat in it on good days and a glass of tea with some bread on lean ones. Like the celebrated medieval monk, we could then say that we were basking in fasting and delighting in privations. But we felt terribly rich.

Russian books, Russian friends and acquaintances, all that marvelous world of youthful dreams and unselfish enthusiasm captured us completely, sent us whirling along, and lifted us high above the earth. We had our own special calendar. We calculated

3

time according to literary events and meetings. *This* was before the appearance of the article by Shchedrin or the one by Mikhailovsky, and *that* was after Nadson's visit to Kiev or shortly before or after a particular story or lecture.

I descended to earth only when I was walking from one lesson to another. But even then I threw back my head, so that I could more comfortably view the sky, still high above and filled with promises of good.

Those who were staid and steadfast said of me: What will come of a boy who never looks beneath his feet? Silly people. What could I have seen there? Only my worn-out boots, which no shoemaker would have attempted to repair. And beneath them? The impoverished earth, even more impoverished than my boots— the earth, filthy and afflicted with blood and tears.

Chapter 2

Experiences of Childhood

An older person should not tell the story of his childhood. He will introduce bits of wisdom and touches of irony into the story, smooth over the sharp lines, touch up the wrinkled face, and in the best of cases turn out to be an old man made up as a child.

Even Tolstoy did not present a childhood in his book by that title. People like his *Childhood* because he described it better than any of the other great artists. In one of the more vivid scenes, Nikolenka sticks a quill up the nose of his sleeping tutor, Karl Ivanovich, who sneezes and wakes up. Would Nikolenka himself have really told about this incident in the way that Tolstoy wrote about it? In Nikolenka's story the ecstasy no doubt would have resounded with ingenuity and courage, along with a bit of anxiety over whether or not Karl Ivanovich would complain. A small boy plays a clever prank the same way a youth writes what in his opinion is a good poem. Even before the ink is dry, he rushes off to solicit the praise of a favorite friend.

Another reason that one should not tell the story of his childhood, it seems to me, is because everything is already too well known. One puts a coin into the machine and out drops a chocolate bar. A parade of trite feelings and trite words. Even the punctuation marks are reduced to exclamation points and ellipses, because the reader will know what is meant anyway.

Instead of telling a story that cannot be told accurately, I shall dwell only on those fragments that, like thorns, cannot be eradicated from my memory.

First, from the Ekaterinoslav period of my childhood, when I was in my seventh year.

5

It was summertime, early in the morning, and the sun was not yet hot and blazing down, but was sparkling with delicate, soft-yellow sprays of light. After my mother left the house, I climbed up on a chair, leaned my elbows on the window sill, and looked down the street. Our nurse was nearby, but she did not interfere with me, only watched to make sure that I did not lean too far out the window.

Suddenly to the right, from the direction of the boulevard—the main street intersecting the city—I could hear the sharp, vigorous, double-noted beating of a drum: "tra-tra," without the shorter, cushioned roll of a "ta-ta-ta."

The cook came running, together with the maid and a friend of the family who happened to be staying with us at the time.

"Most likely haulin' off Schwartz," conjectured our all-knowing cook. "He burned down his mill just to grab the insurance."

In a few minutes a high wagon appeared, like nothing I had ever seen before. It was completely black. Atop it was a platform, which was also black. On the platform, on a short, narrow bench, with his back to the driver, sat a thickset old man with a full, gray beard, his hands bound behind him. In front, on either side, and behind the wagon, there were soldiers, many soldiers.

And the drums, without ceasing, spat out their malicious "tra-tra" into the face of the old man.

"Oh, mercy on us!" wailed the cook.

The nurse grew pale, her shoulders quivering, her teeth chattering. Suddenly she broke herself loose, seized my hand, pulled my cap down over my eyes, tied a shawl around me (despite the summer heat), and ran out onto the street, into the crowd.

Everything—the wagon, the soldiers, the crowd—slowly made its way up the hill, but this did not take long. Then, the cavalry square. And on it a scaffold.

The old man was untied. A short ladder was set up, and he was helped down from the wagon. With heavy step, his chains clattering, he climbed up onto the scaffold. Waiting there, along with the "executioner," were two officers. The senior officer issued an order to his subordinate, who read in a loud staccato. As if from a bursted bag of woes, the numbers of the pertinent laws spewed forth, only to be concluded by the clearly understandable words: ". . . deportation to hard labor for eight years." The junior officer fell silent. Then the drums again, over and over.

The old man was fastened to the high, black pillory. He stood there ever so long, not in terms of time, but of torment. He stood alone, pierced by hundreds of curious eyes.

Perched in the arms of my nurse, I looked at the old man, at his crestfallen, but unclosed, eyes. At the time I did not understand their expression, but I have always remembered them. Later, over the years, I have guessed their riddle. Those were the eyes of a fallen beast of burden, beaten down, frightened and pleading.

From somewhere in the paralyzed crowd, women shrieked, and some young bullies whistled. Finally the command rang out: "Untie him!"

The old man was unfastened. His eyes had changed. They were no longer pleading, but now were filled with hatred, a dark hatred. He straightened up, braced himself, and looked as if he had grown taller.

He was nudged toward the steps. He looked back, as would a wolf. I understand now how he wanted to cry out, "You've gotten even with me! Are you satisfied? Is my sentence enough for you? You extortioners!"

He left the scaffold with an insolent, thumping step, as if showering his thumps on everyone around him. He was seated in the prison coach and taken away.

This was the exhibition at the pillory, and hence the popular expression: "To put on the pillory" or even "To pin to the pillory." This appendage to the main punishment—hard labor or deportation—had even found its way into the legal code (Art. 963 of the Code of Criminal Procedure, 1864 edition), and had survived the entire "epoch of the Great Reforms," being abolished only in 1880.[1]

I recall another incident. This time I was ten years old. Our family had moved from Ekaterinoslav to Kiev, where our first

[1] [Article 963 described in detail how a "civil execution" should be conducted. The convicted person was to be taken to the place of "execution" in prison garb, with an inscription across his chest, indicating the nature of his guilt; he was to be transported on an open, black wagon, surrounded by a military guard; and, after the reading of the sentence, he was to "be put on a black pillory (literally, be exhibited on a black pillar of disgrace) on a scaffold, and remain in this position for a period of ten minutes," whereupon he was to be transported to the place of confinement. *Sudebnye ustavy, 20 noiabria 1864 goda: Ustav ugolovnago sudoproizvodstva* [*Legal Code, November 20, 1864: Code of Criminal Procedure*] (St. Petersburg, 1866), Part 2, 343–44.]

apartment was on the Kreshchatik in the Shirokov building. Although this entire area had been densely built up, our courtyard was a spacious one, and it belonged entirely to us children. Adults did not bother us, nor did they linger there.

The youngsters in our courtyard were a delightful bunch (but then, of course, there are no bad children—only bad parents, who ruin them). Among the children there were four I especially liked: two blue-eyed little boys, a little girl, and their father, a shoemaker, Vasily, who was indeed a most playful, a most ingenious and perpetually amiable child. He was small, with light hair, a little, wedge-shaped beard, and a high forehead, around which, for some reason, he always wore a leather band. I especially liked his blue eyes, which were uncommonly kind, with just a touch of good-natured mischief. There was only one thing that was troubling about them: their constant luster, their unhealthy luster.

The adults dealt with Vasily disdainfully. "A drunkard!" they said. "But then, is there ever a shoemaker who is not a drunkard!" What nonsense! If people did not intoxicate themselves with alcohol, tobacco, love, or ideas, what fool would agree to live?

During Holy Week, on the night between Friday and Saturday, a great misfortune befell our courtyard. We were awakened by a discordant cry, a woman's howling and lamentations. We rushed out into the courtyard. Dawn was just breaking. Almost all the residents of our building were there.

What had happened was that some "gold diggers" had come to clean out the cesspool. They unscrewed the lid, and one of them, carrying a bucket, was lowered into the cesspool on a rope. He shrieked and fell across the surface of the cesspool, unfortunately in such a way that it was impossible to drag him out. A second "gold digger" was lowered to help him, but immediately choked from the stench and did not even utter a scream. The other "gold diggers" lost their heads and began to yell and call for help.

As we came running up, Vasily was also just arriving, along with his wife and children. He shifted from one foot to another, as if trying to decide what to do. Then he rushed forward, pushing people aside. His eyes had a strange look in them, as though they were no longer of this world, and they were fixed on only one point—the cesspool. His wife let out a scream, one such as she would never have the inner strength to utter again.

"Vasya, don't! Vasya, have pity on the children! Have pity on me!"

8

But by this time, Vasily was hearing nothing. He was pushing the crowd aside. No one dared stop him. He paused briefly in front of the cesspool, crossed himself with a broad, sweeping motion, and leaped into it, in order to rescue someone he did not even know.

Soon two fire wagons arrived. The firemen, equipped with poles and hooks, fished out the three bodies and laid them in a row. Throughout the courtyard, the stench from them took one's breath away. Vasily's wife and children rushed to his body and fell down at his side. Tearing myself away from my mother's arms, I also rushed up. Vasily's wonderful blue eyes, which I loved so much, were pasted over with sewage.

After awhile, the police chief's runabout flew into the courtyard. As always, our gallant police chief, von Hubbenet, stood there, his feet planted on the foot board, his arm resting on the shoulder of the driver. As always, he was drunk, although his trade was far removed from that of a shoemaker. And, as was always the case in those years of political terror, two Cossacks followed along behind him with their lances poised.

His authoritative command rang out, "Cossacks, out with your whips! Don't lash anyone. Just break up the crowd!"

The crowd fell back, but it did not disperse. It merely huddled against the buildings. The police chief found himself in front of the three stinking bodies. He winced, but his voice did not vary.

"A fine bunch," he said. "When the police ask for help to put out a fire, to pump water, you all scatter. And here, on such a solemn day, you come out to clean a cesspool. Cover the bodies. And you, officer, make out a report."

The crowd grew bolder. It crept up to the covered bodies. I was also irrepressibly drawn. I raised the covering a little, so I could take one last look at the insult done Vasily, at the two chunks of dung that sealed his eyes.

The police, having completed their work, took away the bodies.

Chapter 3

Adolescence

Then came adolescence with its proud rejection of childhood and its eagerness to press on to youth.

My adolescence had a sad beginning. I had just finished the examinations for passing on to the fifth class and was starting to enjoy the summer at our *dacha* outside of Kiev, when we got a telegram from my father in Ekaterinoslav, where he had gone on business for about ten days. The telegram read: "Bite of poisonous insect has required operation on lip. Have weathered crisis but am ill."

We rushed to the railroad station. The local trains ran frequently, and in less than an hour we were in Kiev. Without stopping at home, we transferred to the first train leaving for Kharkov. It turned out to be a complicated trip with several transfers, and we dragged along for two days and nights. We arrived in Ekaterinoslav just at daybreak. As we were crossing the bridge, we met one of my father's senior employees, whom we had telegraphed during the trip.

"Didn't you get my telegram?" he asked. "It's all over. We've already buried him. The police wouldn't let us wait for you to get here, because he died of Siberian plague.[1] A few stops before Ekaterinoslav, Iosif Davidovich[2] felt a fly bite him. A pustule appeared on his lip, and the next day he was sick in bed. We called

[1] [A Russian name for anthrax, an infectious disease of livestock, which is occasionally transmitted to human beings, usually by contaminated hair or wool but sometimes by insects.]

[2] [The name Iosif, by which the employee referred to Gruzenberg's father, was the more formal equivalent of Osip, which the father used, as indicated by the patronymic in his son's name, Oskar Osipovich.]

the doctors, who decided they needed to operate. They cut up his lip, but it didn't help. On the day before he died, they caught on that it was Siberian plague. He never lost consciousness and was hardly ever delirious. All the time he talked about you and the children. His last words were: 'Poor Malka (Matilda), poor children—they'll be in poverty.' Then the blood came gushing out, and he was gone."

A couple of hours later, when it was completely light and possible to go to the cemetery, I stood by the grave and from a slip of paper read my first orphan's prayer.

In a few days, my mother and I returned to Kiev, where five other children awaited us at home. A well-provided life came to an end, and one of poverty began. But it did not frighten us. Millions of people lived in eternal hunger and cold. In what way were we better than they?

Three years before his death, my father had sent us to the gymnasium, where I entered the second class and my brother the first. But the joy lasted only a few weeks. My father had bought us each a blue uniform with imitation silver buttons and collar braid, as well as a cap, fashioned on the Austrian military model, with a high top and an extended visor. At night, first my brother and then I, each thinking that the other was asleep, would light a candle-stub and admire our new, military-style clothing. However, my uniform soon lost its charm, especially since I managed to get it spotted with something sticky. From then on I hated any new piece of clothing and felt a fiendish delight whenever the first stain appeared. There! No more need now to take care of this idiotic garment with its outstretched arms.

Just like all the others who were my age, I did not like the gymnasium. We were harassed entirely too much for trifles. I suffered many unpleasantries because I used to carry my knapsack in my hands, instead of on my shoulders. The director kept watch by the window facing the street, and woe to you if he should notice that the knapsack was not on the shoulders. He would immediately rap on the glass with his bony finger. And you would have to come back and sit in an empty classroom for an hour or two "without dinner."[3]

[3] ["Without dinner" was a set expression meaning that a student was not permitted to leave the classroom during the dinner recess. Dinner in Russia was the main meal of the day, usually taken in the early afternoon.]

After my father's death, the gymnasium became abhorrent to me for a special reason. A year before my father died, I heard him talking with a friend.

"Where were you yesterday?" asked the friend. "I couldn't get hold of you all day long."

"Yesterday was the anniversary of my father's death. I went to pray for him."

"Well, I didn't expect this. You—praying! Surely you don't believe in all this nonsense. Besides, it's been twenty years since your father died."

My father answered, "I promised him."

"Do you think your father will be offended if you don't keep the promise? Why, your sons aren't going to run to the prayer house on account of you."

My father looked at me and said, "That would be a pity—one ought to remember his parents."

I remembered my father's words, and though I had never liked religiosity, because of its theatrical character, I overcame my feelings all the same. During the first year after a father's or mother's death, one is supposed to pray for the repose of the soul for eleven months, three times a day—once in the morning, a second time at sunset, and a third when the stars are out. All these prayers have to take place in a gathering of no fewer than ten persons.

The closest prayer house to our home was one used by artisans. During the day and late in the evening, it was not very difficult for me to run over to it, but what trouble I had with the morning prayer! The artisans—small proprietors—began their working day before five o'clock in the morning; then, after having worked a few hours, they would go to the prayer house. It was impossible for me to finish my prayers before eight-thirty; and, as if to spite me, classes in the gymnasium also began at that time. Therefore, I had to be late every day.

At first, my teachers responded to my tardiness with a somewhat coarse but good-natured humor. "You must be working as a cook and running down to the market in the morning," they would say.

Then they began to keep me in the classroom for two hours "without dinner." When even this did not help, I had to stand on the platform beneath the clock during the noon recess. For me this was the most offensive punishment, because the pupils of the preparatory class for the gymnasium and various other "small fry," as we haughtily called them, would giggle, stick out their tongues, and tease, "Sen-try . . . sen-try . . . he's a per-ma-nent sen-try!"

Then, on Sundays and holidays, I was locked in the detention room. Of all the punishments at school, the detention room was considered to be the most severe, but for me it was the easiest. No one bothered you there, and out of boredom you prepared your lessons well.

Worst of all was the fact that even my friends now began to reproach me. "This is terrible!" they would say. "You get up early, and you only live fifteen minutes away from school. You must be a slowpoke, or else you've got your nose stuck in the paper when it's time to leave. Shame on you."

I would snap back angrily, "Keep quiet! Why don't you worry about yourself."

I did not dare tell the truth even to my friends. Out of a sense of kindness, in order to protect me from the undeserved punishments, they would certainly have told the teachers. The latter would have commended me for my devotion, which was sincere toward my family, though only a pretense in regard to religion; but this would have been so base—to profit from the loving memory of my father.

During my three trips a day to the prayer house, I met an officer of the guard, who had converted to Judaism. A closeness developed between us, inasmuch as it is possible between an adolescent and an older man of fifty years or so. He was living in the prayer house, eating whatever people gave him and sleeping on a narrow bench without bedding. He spent entire days praying and reading the sacred books in the ancient Hebrew language. Those who were experts said that he knew this difficult language perfectly.

The Jews revered him for his sanctity, but felt him to be somewhat of a burden. They were afraid that they might be accused of making converts to "the Jewish heresy."

Once he stopped me after the evening prayer and suggested that we take a stroll in the yard. With some embarrassment, he began to talk about himself. He had been an officer in one of the regiments of the guard. He served well and got along nicely with his friends, although he often skipped their jovial get-togethers. Then, suddenly he became depressed. Such a strange profession, he thought, to spend one's entire life preparing to exterminate others like yourself. He began to study the Gospels and was surprised that he had not noticed before how they consisted almost entirely of quotations from the Old Testament and the prophets. Even the moving Catholic prayer for the dying, *De Profundis,* was composed from the works of the prophets. From then on he devoted himself to learning the ancient Hebrew language. This strange behavior bothered his superiors in the regiment, and he was asked to resign. His commanding officer informed others about him, some of whom needed to know and some of whom did not. Soon priests were coming to admonish him. Then he was incarcerated in a monastery. Here he became more and more incensed, as every day first one preceptor and then another tried to make him change his mind. Once it went so far that he grabbed a knife from the table, and crying, "You'll not budge me," he chopped off his finger. After this, he was set free.

And so, in his search for the true faith, he ended up self-incarcerated in a poor Jewish prayer house.*

Starting with the seventh class at the gymnasium, we were formed into self-development groups. The reports we prepared in these groups were rather good, considering the fact that we were only adolescents. Revolutionary proclamations even got into our meetings. We gradually became conscious that not only we school-boys felt oppressed by our prison, but that anyone who had ideas and sensitivity regarded the entire structure of tsarist Russia as a prison, in which the worst cells, manned by guards of proven coarseness, were set aside for ethnic minorities.

However, there were two events that had a greater impact on us than the revolutionary leaflets: the closing of the journal *Otechestvennye zapiski* [*Notes of the Fatherland*] and the execution of two boys.

I was indifferent to the fact that, along with the closing of *Otechestvennye zapiski,* Saltykov-Shchedrin lost his teaching post.

---

* Many years later, when I was reading Tolstoy's *Father Sergy,* I remembered the officer of the guard who was a "practicing Jew," and I wondered if it was not he who served as the prototype. However, I quickly realized that my amiable conversation partner was not capable of such meanness as Tolstoy attributed to his own hermit. Most likely Tolstoy was fascinated by Flaubert's *The Temptation of St. Anthony.* Just as Schiller used to place a basket of rotten apples near him while he worked so that that their smell would inspire him, Tolstoy sometimes based his creative work on someone else's mediocre compositions.

I had never been fond of him. One could sense a *barin*[4] in him. He knew how to crack jokes and make fun, and he was good at scrapping with the authorities, but he did not really love anyone or anything. For him the whole of Russia, with its agonizing history, was only the huge city of Glupov.[5]

But to close the journal nourished by the blood and tears of Nekrasov, even though he had died, was another matter.[6] My generation felt a closer kinship with Nekrasov than with Pushkin. Nekrasov was Russian through and through. Even his occasional flaws in character were Russian. If some catastrophe were to occur and all of Russia's books were destroyed with the exception of Nekrasov's works, one could still discover and come to love Russia on the basis of these alone.

He was a tragic figure in spite of his outward success. Surely it is tragic to write while still a child: "Dear Mama, please accept this feeble effort and see if it is fit for anything." And before his death, not to be able to hold back the lamentation: "For two hundred days now, for two hundred nights, I have endured this agony." And, then, to turn to his wife and friend, with the helpless plea: "Do not curse the day when you began to love me and heard me say that I loved you. My grave is near. I'll make amends for everything. I'll atone for it all with death."

Some kind of curse hangs over Nekrasov, for to this day people laud him mainly for his slogan: "You may not be a poet, but you must be a citizen." The fact is, however, that he was an excellent lyrical poet, second only to Pushkin and better than the cold rhetorician Tyutchev. Anyone with sensitivity would not be ashamed of shedding tears upon reading Nekrasov's introduction to his poem *Red Nose Frost*, or many of his lines from *A Knight for An Hour*, or his reply to the anonymous author (Polonsky) who sent him the verses, *It Cannot Be*. To ignore the memory of such a poet and destroy the journal he had brought into being was to despise the spiritual values of one's country.

The other event, unbelievable in its cruelty, was the hanging of

---

[4] [See p. 24.]

[5] [In one of his major works, *The History of a City*, Saltykov-Shchedrin satirized Russia, with its idleness and hypocrisy, as the city of "Glupov," the name being derived from the Russian word meaning "foolish" or "silly."]

[6] [Nekrasov and Saltykov-Shchedrin co-edited *Otechestvennye zapiski*, a leading Russian radical review, from 1868 until Nekrasov's death in December, 1877. Saltykov-Shchedrin continued to edit the journal, which was eventually suppressed by the government in 1884.]

the two boys, Lozovski and Rozovski.[7] They were attempting to rescue a friend who was being held under armed guard. If those guarding the friend had killed Lozovski and Rozovski on the spot, one might have explained it as a rash act committed under duress. But to kill the boys by verdict of a court-martial, and then not even during a time of foreign or domestic warfare with all its madness—such barbarism cannot be justified. After this, it was with horror that I would pass the white, two-storied building of the Kiev Court-Martial, a building so elegant and peaceful in its appearance. I could not understand how well-educated people, who cherished their own children, could be so callous to the grief and tears of the mothers of these two boys.

The city was filled with the terrible tale, as told by the jailers, of the last moments of the boys' lives. When they came for the boys, Rozovski kept repeating in bewilderment, "Oh no . . . this isn't possible . . . it's a mistake . . . I'm sick to my chest, and the doctor told me to use an herb drink instead of tea. . . ."

No, this was not punishment—it was a crime!

[7] [The names of these two Polish boys were actually Lozinski and Rozovski. They were hanged on March 5, 1880. Tolstoy recounts their execution in his novel *Resurrection*.]

Chapter 4

My Jewish Heritage

Revenge is a foul thing, and one should forgive all injuries; but it is not possible to forget how the laws in Russia brought tyranny and persecution to the Jews. To forget how my aged mother was degraded—she who had never hurt anyone in her entire life—would mean to forget that if life is worth anything at all, it is only when it is not enslaved.

One winter night in 1886, shortly after two o'clock, we were awakened by knocks on our door and window. I jumped out of bed and opened the door. Into the room burst a police officer, two policemen, a bustling red-headed man, most likely a detective, and the yard keeper.

"What's the matter? What do you want?"

"What do we want! Can't you see? This is a roundup."

A roundup! In they came, like headhunters, going wherever they pleased.

My brothers and I began to dress quickly. Two of the "hunters" rushed into the adjoining room, where my mother and both sisters were hurrying about, looking for their clothes, not yet having realized what was happening.

"Let's see your residency papers! Come on, move!"

We handed them our passports, matriculation certificates, identification cards.

"Hmmm ... students ... well, you have a right to live in Kiev. But what about this old woman?"

"This is our mother. By law, we not only have a right to keep her with us, but even an obligation."

"Keep her in Berdichev," wisecracked the policeman to the laughter of his retinue.[1]

"All right, old woman, get going. And be quick about it!"[2]

"Don't you dare speak to her that way," I intervened.

"Hey, you student, don't get excited. This isn't a university."

I followed along, as my mother was led out into the street. Two or three persons were being removed from every yard. There were men and women of all ages, and even some youngsters. Policemen surrounded them and drove them along, while relatives followed, crying and screaming.

The frost crackled, and it was snowing lightly. The lonely street lights blinked unwillingly, as if to say that since they could not light everything, why bother at all.

And they—the "criminals"—were taken away to the police station, accompanied by jokes and jeers. After a short interrogation, my mother was shoved behind a partition, where prostitutes caught that night without permits were milling about, along with women thieves apprehended at their work. There in the filth, cold, and drunken disorder, she spent a night and a day, until a wealthy man, whose patronage we solicited, opened the door to freedom for her.

What did I experience that night? What did I resolve? I can state it concisely. After this agony, I saw in everyone who fought against autocratic tyranny and its cruelty an ally, a brother, to whom I was indebted and to whom I was obligated to help in time of trial.

In the fall of 1888, during my last term at the university, I was visited by God.

Slowly and painfully, my child was dying.[3] As soon as the

[1] [The intent of the policeman's reply was a sarcastic suggestion that rather than in Kiev the mother should be "kept" in a town like Berdichev, some distance away, which had traditionally been permitted a predominantly Jewish population, mainly of the mystical Hasidic sect. Consequently, Berdichev had become a common target of abuse by many Russians and Ukrainians.]

[2] [In giving this command, the policeman uses the familiar form of address, in the second person singular, rather than the polite form, in the second person plural, another insult to Gruzenberg's mother.]

[3] [Gruzenberg had married Rosa Gavrilovna Golosovkar in the spring of 1887 in Kiev. Besides their first child, who died in infancy, two others, Sofia and Yury, were born and survived to adulthood.]

shadow of death touched his face, our dwelling began to fill with
strangers, wearing long side locks and dressed in long robes, dirty
with grease. They walked from room to room, bustling about and
giving orders in a language I barely understood.

The eldest of them, sad and solemn, approached the bed of the
infant (who in seven months had completed his difficult journey
on earth) and bending low over him announced in a dispassionate
voice that his father and mother and all his relatives begged his
forgiveness. The child must have forgiven us, for he was immediately placed in an elongated black box and carried out into the
remoteness of that bleak November day.

In front of the box, a skinny little Jew, covered with a thick
beard, scurried back and forth. Rattling a cup, which held some
copper coins, he insistently cried out, "Charity saves from death!
Charity saves from death!" The poor people believed this and
hurriedly dropped in their coins.

I walked along among clusters of people who until then had
been strangers to me. I listened to, but did not really hear, their
sad words of comfort, falling heavily, as if swollen from the rain.
At the cemetery they sang something and tried to persuade someone about something, but, having failed, they meekly lowered
the tiny, naked body into the grave and began to cover it with
the wet soil, which made a sucking sound as it left the spade.*

During the funeral my closest Christian friends quietly moved
aside to make room for those whom death had brought into my
home, and I began to realize that the latter had a claim on me. This
realization kept growing day by day, maturing and strengthening,
until after a few months I became convinced that the claim was
an enormous one, which could not be denied, though neither could
it be comprehended. And I, who loved independence and refused
to tolerate anyone's authority over me, sensed that there was no
escaping the dominion of these strangers, that along with the body
of my child they had also taken my soul.

Who were they, these people? Why had they been entitled to

---

*According to Jewish law, it was not permissible to bury someone in a
casket or shroud, for "naked came I from my mother's womb, and naked
shall I return." In time this custom was largely abandoned, being
preserved only among Orthodox Jews. [Despite Gruzenberg's comment,
the usual custom, even among Orthodox Jews, was to bury a person in a
plain, white shroud, this practice dating from instructions given by
Rabbi Gamaleil in the first century.]

come to me at so crucial a moment and take me captive without any resistance? What right did they have?

I started reading books. Openly and explicitly, they told me the history of the Jewish people and illuminated all the turns of their tortuous path. Yet, it was a strange thing, for although these books stirred me, they did not win me over. Indeed, there had been blood, agony, and tears, but these have flooded the paths of all peoples, not just the Jews. How does one weigh or calculate which of these peoples suffered the most, or wept the most, or tired the most under the burdens of life?

The past beckoned me with its millions of bodies, stretching their bony arms toward me, looking at me from the empty sockets of their eyes, and rattling their toothless jaws: "You are ours, ours! Remember the covenants of your ancestors, and see that you keep them!"

Still, I asked myself if I was obligated to bind my life to the millions of graves throughout the ages—my life, which had been miraculously set afire and was being constantly tossed about, ready to expire at any moment—my life with its own designs, its own truths, its own dreams.

No, it was not to the grave that I was obligated, but to life. I would not walk with the dead. Significantly, I was soon to find that what the dead could not accomplish, the living did.

The following year I had occasion to spend about two months of the winter in a village next to a Jewish settlement. A small settlement. Tiny houses molded out of clay. In the windows torn paper instead of glass. Here and there smoke rising from the chimneys, like a powerless revenge against the angry frost.

In Kiev, residents watched the stock exchange bulletins that announced the rising and falling values of the stocks; but here a small clump of people, dressed in rags, gathered around the thermometer hanging outside the window of the apothecary and noted with alarm that the temperature had fallen three degrees. Another three degrees! Lord, wasn't it cold enough yesterday to suit you? Must you add to your generosity? This was the stock exchange bulletin of the poor.

Then market day arrives. From the surrounding villages, the peasants bring all kinds of poultry and rough-milled flour. The horses are unharnessed and their shafts raised up. The poor, hungry Jews weave their way among the peasants, hoping they will be able to get something out of their bargaining. They haggle violently, squabble, and get kicked. The market comes to an end, and they have gained nothing, not even enough for herring heads for their wives and children. Again they implore the peasants, but the latter, having lost patience, chase them away. "Get out of here! The market can do without *Zhids*!"[4] Dejected, they twist their dilapidated homemade canes in their hands; and, heads lowered, they trudge home, with empty hands and equally empty stomachs.

A woman wrapped in rags and selling pickles fails to make anything either. During the entire time of the market, she does not sell more than three dozen pickles. Next to her, a little boy, her grandson, is shivering from the cold. With a hungry longing, he cannot take his eyes off the bewitching tub of pickles. The grandmother has long ago noticed the yearning eyes of her little pet, and with a sacrificing motion she pushes a pickle into his hand and sticks her finger, which has probably not been washed since Passover, inside his mouth, so that he will get all the brine off it.

"Ah," adds the grandmother tenderly. "My little lover of delicacies."

And I ask myself: As you study the law, the rules of jurisprudence, the various articles of the laws, do you really think that by means of these you can alleviate human sorrow? Look how terrible it is:

> The hungry poor, covered with filth,
> The timid poor, the beaten poor. . . .
> They perish during the day,
> At midnight, and after midnight.
> They perish and no one comes to help.
> They perish without the slightest of support,
> Without a sympathetic heart, without a friendly voice.
>
> NIKITIN, *The Tailor*

It may be that you do not acknowledge the voice that is yours by blood; it may be that from the days of your childhood the Russian

---

[4] [Both *Evrei* and *Zhid* meant Jew in Russian. The first of these words was inherited from the Hebrew through Byzantium and the Greek *evraios*; the second was derived from the Latin *judaeus* and made its way to Russia probably either by way of the Balkans or else through Germans who were in contact with Romanic peoples north of the Alps. (The *j* became the Slavic *zh*, and the initial Slavic usage *Zhud* eventually became *Zhid*.) *Evrei* survived as the formal, and in time official, designation for a Jew in Russia, while *Zhid* gradually acquired a pejorative connotation and was commonly used to express anti-Semitic feelings.]

element has been closer to you. But do you really not know that "the crucifiers of Christ," those who supposedly despise the people among whom they live, rarely receive help from anyone who is not a Jew?

You who at the age of thirteen, along with all your family, came to know poverty and concealed it because of pride—can it be that you will turn away from the needs of an entire people, so as not to defile yourself by appearing to be a Jewish "nationalist?" Have you really forgotten the reproachful voice of the prophet: "If you are not for us, who is? And if not now, when?" [5]

[5] [This quotation comes from the sayings of Hillel, one of the sages, rather than from the prophets. For the entire saying and commentary on it, see Morris Schatz, *Ethics of the Fathers in the Light of Jewish History* (New York, 1970), 59–66.]

Chapter 5

The Peasantry

And what should be said of the peasantry, which I watched daily in the village?

The first time we actually met was inside a spacious office. About five peasants came in, and at once the room seemed crowded. Each was wearing clothing from all four seasons of the year—spring, summer, fall, and winter—in order to keep from freezing. The boots on their feet were made of stiff leather, with heels held on by heavy nails, which accounted for the nicks in the office floor. They came in and planted themselves by the doorway, no doubt so they could retreat into the hall with less embarrassment should they be ordered away.

Bent down from their heavy labor and somber in their appearance, for they had never known lasting joy, the peasants were continually oppressed by dismal thoughts about the bleak earth, which so inadequately nurtured them. They did not trust any of the townsfolk. Everywhere they saw some sort of trap or plot. Their speech was tangled and filled with deliberate hesitations, almost like a stutter. And yet, they spoke fluently with their own kind without having to search for words.

Of course, a people that created such wonderful poetry from the meager adjectives and still more meager participles at its disposal could not be tongue-tied.[1] Even the great literary masters did not always emerge victorious from their struggle with these parasites of the language. But the peasants succeeded.

---

[1] [Colloquial Russian often used subordinate clauses, short-form adjectives, and attributive nouns instead of participles and long-form adjectives, which generally had their origins in Old Church Slavonic and were employed mainly in formal writing.]

Certainly they were not tongue-tied, when even the peasant women, humiliated and mortally beaten, composed songs about their fate, the equal of which cannot be found among the best of poets. One need only recall this plaintive verse:

When the water flooded the guelder-rose and raspberry,
It was then my dear mother gave birth to me.
With little heed she gave me to wed
To a land that was strange . . .
To a land that was far. . . .
A strange land withers without a wind.
A strange father and mother lay waste without blame.[2]

And the song continues to the mournful closing lines, which tell how three years of marriage have transformed the girl into an old woman, whom even her own mother cannot recognize.

The peasant was the wisest of the wise, but he pretended to be a fool, content to let the *barin* chatter away. He regarded as a *barin*[3] anyone other than a peasant, and he got along quite well without the *barin*. He would call the priest to baptize and to bury, though only for the sake of outward appearance, for nowhere were there as many sects as among the Russian peasantry. Everything he needed for his modest life, he created himself. All that he received from the culture of the gentry were a smelly kerosene lamp and some cotton cloth, which was likely to fade.

In 1905–1906, peasant uprisings encompassed three hundred districts in forty-seven provinces. Over one thousand manors were pillaged, pedigreed cattle slaughtered, valuable libraries and paintings burned, and musical instruments destroyed. It was typical that in the proclamations issued during those days, the peasants demanded not only that all the land be turned over to them, but also that the landowners be removed. As the peasants said, they did not want the landowners to remain as an eyesore. This was the inevitable tragedy, for, as Proudhon observed, if a rod bent severely in one direction is to be straightened, it must be bent severely in the other.

[2] [In Russian, this song has a complex meter and intricate sound combinations with partial rhymes.]

[3] [Even the more formal definitions of *barin* are imprecise, generally referring to a person belonging to the privileged strata of pre-revolutionary Russian society, especially the landed gentry.]

This same kind of pillaging, rather than an actual revolutionary movement, occurred again in 1917–1918.[4]

In its concealed hostility toward the intelligentsia, the peasantry resembled the police officer who once dumbfounded me with his cynical, yet rather witty, reply. This happened in the early nineties, shortly after I began working as an attorney. I was on my way to court, when suddenly from around the corner a crowd of people appeared, about a hundred of them, surrounded by a chain of police inspectors, district officers, and local policemen. Among those arrested, I noticed a friend of mine, a fellow lawyer. Waving his hat at me, he shouted, "Help me out! I didn't do a thing!"

I asked one of the police officers, "Where are you taking them?"

"Where?" he replied. "To where the workers of the world unite —to jail!"

Neither will I forget the disturbing response of a young fellow from the country, who was working after the busy season as a cabby in "Pieter."[5] This happened on October 17, 1905, the day of the "granting" of the constitution, such as it was. The weather was uncommonly sunny for the nasty Petersburg autumn, and the Nevsky Prospect was entirely flooded with people. No one could drive, or even walk, along it. Red flags were everywhere. On the balconies of public buildings, as well as private homes, "orators" were shouting enthusiastically. What they were saying did not really matter, for words were powerless to reflect the general sense of exhilaration.

The cabby, turning part way toward me, said with a sneer, "See what a good time the gentry's having."

"What do you mean—the gentry? It's not just the gentry that's having a good time. I bet you're happy, too."

"What's there for me to be happy about? I've got to give three-and-a-half rubles to the owner, no matter what. And that eagle-

[4] [Arson and pillage in the countryside seems to have been less prevalent in 1917-1918 than in 1905-1906. Generally, the peasants directed their efforts to forming village committees, which in quasi-legal fashion redistributed the land of private estates into smaller peasant holdings. Although this action did not constitute a unified movement nor assume the character of insurrection, it had definite objectives in land allotments, and was not merely a destructive outburst.]

[5] [A popular short form of St. Petersburg, stemming from the Dutch name that Peter the Great initially applied to his new capital at the beginning of the eighteenth century.]

eyed pharaoh of a policeman will take down my number if everything's not exactly right. So, it's all going to be just like it was
before."

The peasant always ate poorly, and as a reward heaven frequently sent him a bad harvest. Then he ate goose-foot plants and
weeds—and died. Then also the tender-hearted townsfolk set off
for the country, as if on an expedition, and fed the people; and
the newspapers described the famine, though it was impossible for
someone whose stomach was full to understand the hunger pangs.

Emperor Alexander III became irritated whenever the press
mentioned a "famine," as if the word had simply been invented
by those who had nothing to eat. He issued an imperial order that
the word "famine" be replaced by the expression "crop failure,"
and the Main Administration for Affairs of the Press immediately
distributed a strict circular to this effect.

There is no need to deceive oneself: there have always been two
Russias. One Russia proclaimed either "God Save the Tsar!" or
"Down with the Autocracy!" This was the Russia with its jailers
and with its sacrificial intelligentsia, whose members were willing
to have their personal lives shattered, in order to build the people's
happiness out of the splinters. In return, they were reproached,
because their deeds did not live up to their words. What a reproach!
It is well that their deeds did not match their words, because
whenever in the course of Russian history the two did coincide,
nothing resulted except the notorious "word and deed" of the
Sovereign, with all its inhuman tortures. For the sake of our
country's destiny, it was best that some served through courageous
word, while others served through liberating deed.

The other Russia, outwardly humble and seemingly submissive,
was physically close by but spiritually far away, irreconcilable and
probably irreconcilable for a long time to come. This other Russia
was Peasant Russia.

Having created a great state, this teeming peasant force, because
of its incomprehensible humility, was content to be the object of
political and social power, rather than the subject.

In a fit of despair, Alexander Blok, the finest poet since Nekrasov,
wrote the following irate lines about Russia:

> What have you ever known? When have you ever trusted God?
> What have your ballads ever had to say?

The Chud worked all the wonders, and the Merya[6] mapped
The trails, the roads, the posts that mark the way.

What, indeed, have your ballads had to say? Well, this, for
example:

With voices booming the pilgrims called,
And the tower-tops came tumbling down;
On the chamber walls the plaster crumbled,
And the bottles in the cellar shook.
Religious Verse of the Forty Pilgrims and One

The peasantry had its own tsars: Emelka Pugachev and Stenka
Razin. And it was expressly Emelka and Stenka, not Emelian Ivanovich and Stepan Timofeevich. Among yourselves you do not call
those you love by their patronymics.

The anthem of the peasantry was not "God Save the Tsar!"
but "Down Along the Mother Volga." This anthem was not dedicated to the Tsars and Tsaritsas. Rather, it proclaimed, "In the
stern sits the master—the master Stenka Razin." That same master who, with his unarmed, naked, barefoot army, almost reached
Moscow.

Political fools and hypocrites ought not attempt to represent the
Russian revolution as alien to Russia. The Russian revolution
was the most national of all the national revolutions, and its se-
verity was national in character as well.

Where tears have long been flowing, the inevitable retribution
is in blood.

[6] [The Chuds and Merya were ancient Finnish peoples, skilled in
craftsmanship and trading, who inhabited an extensive area in northern
Russia, which was gradually settled by the Slavs from about the ninth
century.]

Chapter 6

Kiev University

The best part of my life was connected with Kiev University, even though I entered it under the new statutes of 1884, which provided for academic police—inspectors and subinspectors—and required that students wear uniforms. My greatest joy was that I could use my time as I saw fit and attend whatever lectures I wished.

The university was a small town in itself, with a population of over six hundred persons. It had large, airy lecture halls, arranged like amphitheaters. And instead of a detention room for those caught smoking, such as there had been at the gymnasium only three months before, the university had a huge room especially set aside for this purpose. The smoke was so thick that one could almost cut it. It was impossible to see faces (which was just as well, since not all faces, particularly the eyes, are pleasant to look at anyway), but the voices rang out clearly, like the myriad sounds of an orchestra tuning up its instruments.

During the first two months, I attended lectures from all four years of instruction, so I could get to know the law professors, the four most outstanding of whom were M. F. Vladimirsky-Budanov, V. I. Demchenko, D. G. Talberg, and N. K. Rennenkampf. Professor Vladimirsky-Budanov was particularly loved and respected. He was a scholar in the European tradition. His lectures on the history of Russian law were concise and saturated with rich content, without a single superfluous word. Even the lazy students diligently attended them. We were entranced by everything about him: the introspective gaze, oblivious of everyone; the precise word, encompassing an idea the way a fine glove encompasses a hand (whereas the speech of most of the professors was more

like a bulky mitten); the intimate voice, which seemed to have
been created for friendly conversation. His anthology of the mon-
uments of ancient Russian law, together with his commentaries
on them, is priceless. No book its equal has been published to
this day.[1]

Demchenko was a substantial lecturer, who knew his subject
well. He was an old man, amiable and benevolent.

Talberg, a professor of criminal law and legal procedure, was
also a gifted scholar, who loved his subject. Unfortunately, he did
not have sufficient time to reveal the potential with which he had
been endowed. While still a young man, he had become ill with
a serious form of consumption. He continually suffered from
chills, and his brief span of life was spent in a constant battle
against fever.

Our rector and professor of encyclopedia of the law[2] and the
philosophy of law, N. K. Rennenkampf, was a marvelous lecturer.
However, his low morals, lack of self-respect, and insuperable
tendency for intrigue nullified his talents. I do not know how it is
in the exact sciences, but in literature and the humanities, whether
juridical or historical, a morally depraved person can hardly
create anything of significance. Just as even an electric light cannot
adequately penetrate the soiled glass of a lantern, so a full measure of talent cannot be revealed in an unscrupulous soul.

But then, perhaps I am being unfair toward Rennenkampf for
personal reasons. I had applied for a scholarship, which, according
to the rules of the university, required that a candidate be examined
at a special colloquium in two subjects. In the second year of
studies these subjects were the history of Russian law and encyclopedia of the law. In Russian law the colloquium went well,
and in encyclopedia of the law Rennenkampf showered me with
compliments on the way to the door and assured me that the
scholarship was mine. At that point, someone had to open the door.
Naturally, I should have done this and let the old man go out
ahead of me, just as one would have done for an older friend.
But the thought suddenly struck me that this was not the thing

[1] [M. F. Vladimirskii-Budanov, *Khristomatiia po istorii russkago prava*
[*Anthology of the History of Russian Law*] (3 parts; Kiev, 1873–75).
This widely used anthology had passed through five editions by 1915.]

[2] [Encyclopedia of the law was the name given an introductory course
in jurisprudence, which summarized the theoretical basis of law, standard
legal procedures, and contemporary juridical scholarship.]

to do, for at the moment, I was a petitioner, and he was the source of mercy. And so, I stepped back. Rennenkampf turned toward me and threw me an angry glance. Three or four days later, I learned that my scholarship had not materialized, only because I had not opened the door. No, he was not a man of stature.

The students in my class were nice enough, but they did not trouble themselves very much with studies. With few exceptions, those who were more gifted and more impatient were expelled from the university during the first two years, some because of their participation in student disorders, some because of "politics."

I took particular delight in imagining what we would be like in a few years. I envisioned that this person would shave all his life; a second would acquire a distinguished set of side whiskers; a third would have an exquisite little beard; a fourth would have a full beard, thick and matted. The first would be an implacable public prosecutor; the second—a presiding judge, with a bent for giving incriminatory instructions to the jury; the third—a defense attorney for big bankers who prey on the public; and the fourth —an examining magistrate for particularly trivial cases in some out-of-the-way district.

We had all sorts of people, but only a few—too few—who were kind and compassionate. Consider, for example, how they brought a friend to ruin.

We attended lectures in some courses together with students who had entered the university under the old statutes. They were allowed to wear civilian clothes and to finish their studies according to the old regulations. One of them set out to publish some lectures, if I am not mistaken, in Russian law. He collected money from us, about one hundred fifty to two hundred rubles. The publication of the lectures dragged on, and the students were becoming irritated. In spite of the delay, he showed up at the university. He stepped to the rostrum, dressed like a beggar, with dull eyes, a small, badly-matted beard, and an earthy-gray complexion, like someone who is starving.

"So far," he began, "I've only brought three pages per person. I ran out of time. I'll bring the rest in a few days."

He barely finished these words when the auditorium filled with the howling of a hundred voices. "What do you mean only three pages? There ought to be at least forty. You've squandered our money!"

Almost everyone was shouting and cursing chaotically. His face became an even darker gray. "Friends, let me explain," he stammered. "If you don't want to wait, I'll bring back the money day after tomorrow. I'm no thief. I just got things mixed up."

"Aha! He's admitting that he squandered it!"

"I'll give it back!"

"Where will you get it? Go on, get out of the university! Turn in your withdrawal right now! We don't need any thieves!"

"Friends, let me a say a word. I'm not as bad as you think."

"Don't you dare call us friends. A thief's no friend to us!"

Wordless, he kept motioning with his hands, as if he were swimming against a giant wave. It rolled over his head. He emerged, and the wave of savage cursing swallowed him again.

It became frightening. I jumped up and began to shout, "You're sorry that you lost your money, but you're not sorry for him! You beasts, you're worse than he is!"

My voice was lost in the general uproar. One of the students next to me glared at me angrily, "Take it easy! Do you want your face punched in?"

I rushed toward the rostrum, but I could not get near it. A bunch of students was in front of it, threatening the embezzler with their fists.

In a few minutes the watchmen arrived, along with a perplexed subinspector. They surrounded the cornered young man and led him out into the hall. Behind them came a brutal throng of students, whistling and hooting. They engulfed the sad procession. Faces, which an hour ago seemed quite good-natured, could no longer be recognized. Nevertheless, it was clear that as soon as they went out into the street, they would cool off and scatter.

But what would become of *him*? Something told me that he could not bear such disgrace. He was not a shameless person, but merely an unfortunate one. A shameless person would not have tried to justify himself. After the first few curses, he would have shrugged his shoulders in contempt and left the rostrum.

No, this was more than he could bear. I knew that I must go to his home, so that he would not be left alone, at least during these first few hours. I went to the office to get his address, but all the employees had left their work and were huddled together, excitedly discussing the "scandal." Only after about twenty minutes did I manage to obtain the information, and then it turned out that

31

I had to go to the very edge of town. When I got there, my heart skipped a beat, for by the gate stood a policeman and a cluster of people.

I walked into the yard. Inside the shabby little house, in a tiny room, which was even more shabby, stood a kitchen table, a single chair, and a bedstead, its metal bars bent from age. There, on the straw mattress with its dirty pillow at one end, lay our friend. His face was calm and restful. In his temple was a small hole, and under it, on his cheek, a bit of blood.

Chapter 7

St. Petersburg

In the fall of 1889 I passed the examinations of the State Juridical Commission, which had just been established.

"This is the last examination in my life," I shouted merrily to my friends, throwing my lecture notes on police law[1] out the window. The last examination? Hardly. From that time on, there were endless, merciless examinations, one after another, without a break. And I was poorly prepared for them.

A few days after the examination, while at the university, I happened to meet our professor of public law, A. V. Romanovich-Slavatinsky. He was a jovial fellow, who liked to joke. Grimacing, he told me, "Too bad. Yesterday we discussed the proposal of Dmitry Hermanovich (Talberg) to keep you at the university and send you abroad to prepare for a faculty position. Too bad it can't be done. By keeping you we would be setting a precedent unparalleled in the history of the law faculty here at the university. And, by taking the necessary step of converting to us, you would only be adding to the already rather numerous precedents of the Jewish enlightment."[2]

He chuckled, "Now, it's up to you." And, giving me a roguish wink with his only good eye (he had lost the other one in a childhood accident), he hurried on along the corridor.

I went out into the university gardens. The setting sun was

[1] [Police law was another name for administrative law, which encompassed all aspects of governmental regulations on such matters as internal migration, residency permits, police protection, education, religion, industry, trade, transport, and other public and private activities.]
[2] [The Jewish enlightenment refers to the *haskalah* movement. See pp. xii–xv.]

hastily fingering the piles of fallen leaves with its golden feelers. Couples, soon to separate, were strolling aimlessly along the damp paths, exchanging silent glances of sympathy with one another for the love that so abruptly had come to an end. In the distance, behind the greenhouse, a woodcock was whistling in praise of the university marsh.

I breathed deeply the damp air of the late autumn, and without bitterness, in fact almost merrily, I thought to myself, "A faculty position ... criminal law ... another of the countless dissertations on the freedom of the unfree will ... the search for the secret of a merciful cruelty in administering punishment (like devising a recipe for the preparation of hot ice). Never mind all that. I'll manage. It's far more interesting to be fighting in the courts anyway. At least one finds less hypocrisy there, whether from the prosecutor, who abhors the crime, as defined in the latest circular from the authorities, or from the defense counsel, who is concerned about his client, whom he has been entrusted to represent. No problem. I'll manage."

But then, five or six days later, on the ninth of November, I read in the local newspaper a dispatch from St. Petersburg: "Admission to the bar and to the profession of private attorney of persons of non-Christian faiths may be carried out only with the permission of the Minister of Justice."

I read and re-read the stunning dispatch. I kept changing the words around, trying to find some ray of hope. But it was clear: there was none.

What was I to do? Provided with recommendations from my professors, I decided to seek my fortune in Petersburg. I reasoned that if I did not manage to become a lawyer-in-training (though nothing was said about this position in the prohibitory law), I would take up journalism.

Fortunately, the Petersburg Council of the Bar, as well as its supervisory body, the Chamber of Justice, interpreted the new law literally. And so, I became a lawyer-in-training to the talented and sensitive lawyer Peter Gavrilovich Mironov.

The designation of lawyer-in-training in itself granted no rights for conducting legal suits; it was only an apprenticeship in the legal profession. However, in criminal cases the law permitted any citizen who had not been legally deprived of his rights to conduct the defense.

I held this position for *sixteen years*, despite the recommendation presented to the Minister on my behalf by the St. Petersburg Council of the Bar at the end of the five-year probationary period. Significantly, during these years, not a single Jew was approved.

Yet, this was all a personal matter and how insignificant compared with the proud and poignant feeling emanating from St. Petersburg, that city so unique in all the world. Some presumptuous foreigner wrote of it: "How can one live in a city where the streets are always wet and the hearts are always dry?"[3] As for the streets—and this is as far as his perceptions went—his remark was correct, but not for the hearts. The creative Russian spirit did not care about the tsars and their governments, but about building a new and better life. In St. Petersburg, two forces worked constantly toward this end: the intelligentsia and the workers. Nothing pacified them, and they feared nothing but their own conscience. They could be bent, but they could not be broken, for it is impossible to force someone to crawl on his hands and knees after he has straightened himself to his full height.

In St. Petersburg, there were three landmarks sacred to all of Russia: the monument to Peter, Senate Square, and the square of the Kazan Cathedral. Peter whipped a decaying Muscovy into shape; on Senate Square, the Decembrists kindled an inquenchable protest against autocracy; and on the square of the Kazan Cathedral, students and workers shed their blood.[4]

In his *Literary Memoirs*, P. V. Annenkov describes how Herzen, Granovsky, Ketcher, Nekrasov, and others once spent the summer in Sokolovo, near Moscow. He notes: "This circle, whose most important representatives now gathered for a time in Sokolovo, resembled a *knightly* brotherhood, a militant *order*, which did not have any written regulations, *yet knew all its members*, scattered

---

[3] [In this sense, dry (*sukhoi*) means barren or unproductive.]

[4] [In addition to the modernization policy of Peter the Great in the early eighteenth century and the unsuccessful revolt by a group of young army officers, drawn from the educated gentry, in December, 1825, Gruzenberg probably refers to the demonstration staged by dissident students, other radical intellectuals, and discontented workers, all calling for greater individual liberties, on December 6, 1876. This demonstration, broken up by the police, was remembered by those in the opposition movement as the first dramatic example of united action between the intelligentsia and the common people. (Another memorable demonstration in front of Kazan Cathedral occurred on March 4, 1901. This one was composed mainly of students and writers, protesting government restrictions at the universities; it was also brutally dispersed by the police.)]

35

over our vast land."[5] That is it precisely: a knightly order! It manifested itself everywhere.

I shall be specific and relate in sequence how Petersburg unfolded before me.

First of all, I got to know the courts and the legal profession. Of all the reforms of Alexander II, the most significant (not counting the emancipation of the serfs, which stands apart) was the judicial reform. In evaluating the judiciary created by this reform, as in the case of any judicial institution, one must judge it by its magnitude and not by its annoying blemishes, which did not change its essence. I can say without exaggeration that the courts in Russia were unmatched in Western Europe. Prior to the law of March 18, 1906, which transferred political cases to the Special Tribunals of the Chamber of Justice and entailed the appointment as judges of all kinds of obsequious careerists, the Russian judges were selfless and dedicated figures.

Their salary was miserable, however. Any excise inspector in the liquor business received much more. In addition, the work was extremely laborious. No judge dreamed of an eight-hour working day. He put in at least fourteen hours, and frequently eighteen. In criminal cases being tried before a jury, court was recessed only after midnight, in order to reduce the number of times the jury had to stay overnight in the court building. Upon returning home, the judges still had the task of checking the records of the proceedings and drawing up the verdicts in their final form.

It was no easier in the civil cases. The courts in the capital frequently sat until two or three o'clock in the morning. When the judges returned home, there was the same bother with the records of the proceedings and an even more difficult and complicated statement of the rationale involved in the decision.

In the fifty-year existence of the courts following the Judicial Statutes of 1864, there were only a few instances of violations of judicial duty for the sake of personal gain, and these were among justices of the peace who had been poor choices of the zemstvos and municipal dumas.[6]

[5] [P. V. Annenkov, *Literaturnye vospominaniia* [*Literary Memoirs*] (Leningrad, 1928), 423–24.]

[6] [The zemstvos and municipal dumas were rural and municipal organs of local self-government, created in 1864 and 1870 respectively, as part of the reforms of Alexander II. In addition to supervising primary schools, hospitals, public health and veterinary services, and road maintenance,

I recall a cartoon in a Berlin humor magazine, many years before my move to St. Petersburg, in regard to the arrest of the greedy multimillionaire Ovsyannikov, who had been charged with setting fire to his mill in order to collect the insurance. The Germans, who did not concede that genuine justice might exist among the "Russian savages," condescendingly joked: "In St. Petersburg a millionaire, Ovsyannikov, worth eight figures, was arrested. Soon we shall read that a millionaire worth seven figures was released." However, what they actually read was that the multimillionaire was convicted and sent to Siberia.[7]

The Petersburg legal profession of my day did not consist of "Balalaykins" (one of Saltykov-Shchedrin's expressions), that is, of persons having consciences for hire.[8] In Petersburg, there was a working force of almost two thousand persons, including the lawyers-in-training. Their life, with minor exceptions, was difficult and worrisome.

There were only a few prominent criminal lawyers, whose names were well known. This was due to the fact that a criminal law practice was very exhausting and wore out the nerves quickly. It meant that one was always in public view, undergoing a continuous examination, dealing under stress with impromptu situations (for one could not foresee everything no matter how well he prepared), and weltering in people's tears and grief.

No other profession, not even medicine, provided such a huge proportion of free aid: defenses appointed by the court, constant legal consultations in offices for legal assistance to the poorest segment of the population, and free advice in one's home—all of which frequently demanded great effort.

There was also the work of leading judicial conferences for lawyers-in-training. The trainees were divided into three groups, each headed by a lawyer of outstanding knowledge and experience, either in criminal law, civil law, or administrative law. Attendance at these conferences was mandatory. After completing five years

---

the zemstvos, as well as the municipal dumas in St. Petersburg and Moscow, elected justices of the peace, who tried minor cases at the local level.]

[7] [The trial of S. T. Ovsyannikov took place in St. Petersburg in November-December, 1875. It is described in A. F. Koni, *Sobranie sochinenii* [*Collected Works*] (8 vols.; Moscow, 1966–69), *1*, 37–45, 514–16.]

[8] [Balalaykin was a character in several of Saltykov-Shchedrin's satires. He was an unscrupulous young lawyer, who represented a type of person who would engage in almost any devious activity for money.]

of service and upon filing an application to the bar, each lawyer-in-training had to submit a certificate from the leaders of these conferences that he had attended them for two years, completed three written papers, and conducted ten criminal defenses before a jury.

Benevolent contributors within the profession also provided financial means for young lawyers to travel to district sessions of the criminal court in order to conduct defenses.

I owe much of my legal success to my patron, P. G. Mironov; to A. Ya. Passover; to the noted professor of criminal law, Senator N. S. Tagantsev; and to the assistant presiding judge of the St. Petersburg Circuit Court, D. F. Helschert. If it had not been for their support, I would have been compelled to abandon law, for I would not have been able to support our large family. The kind disposition of these men toward me was all the more touching since my temperament, particularly my bellicose character and my inability (or rather unwillingness) to smooth off the sharp edges, frequently made me unbearable. Often I was involved in "incidents" with the presiding judges or the prosecutor's office; and once, in a letter to a person being held under arrest, I went so far as to call the all-powerful Minister of Justice, N. V. Muraviev, a "pedlar of justice, who is entering a disgraceful page into the glorious history of the Russian court."

However, all the disciplinary proceedings brought against me were eventually dismissed, except the one in the well-known Beilis case, in which the defendant was charged with ritual murder. Being outraged by the false witnessing of Lieutenant-Colonel Ivanov of the gendarmes, I declared in court that he was a "dishonest witness." Disciplinary proceedings were brought against me in the Kiev Circuit Court, where the offense was committed. My associates and I myself were certain that I would be removed from the legal profession, since the Minister of Justice Shcheglovitov, on the way to his estate in Chernigov, visited the circuit court in Starodub, where, in conversation with the judges, he mentioned that I would be expelled for the grievous insult in court to Lieutenant-Colonel Ivanov. A dispatch to this effect even appeared in the Petersburg newspaper *Den* [*The Day*].

On the day that my case was to be heard, I arrived in Kiev, and, having changed clothes in the railroad car, I set off for the general meeting of the Circuit Court. I made this long journey, thinking

ST. PETERSBURG

that there would not be many hunters waiting to devour the bird
whom they so recently had looked in the eye.

As it turned out, there were more than sixty judges. The hearing
proceeded solemnly and sluggishly. I sat down on a chair by the
rostrum. Later I was told that I had broken the custom, according
to which, out of respect for the court, those against whom disciplinary action was being taken were supposed to remain standing
the entire time.

I did not want to look for excuses, nor would there have been any
point in doing so. I only insisted that Lieutenant-Colonel Ivanov
had indeed given false testimony under oath. I pointed out that
perhaps it is sometimes impolite to call things by their names, but
that my harsh appraisal of Ivanov's lie was not so much a juridical
question as one of etiquette, such as could be found in Hermann
Hoppe's *Good Manners.**

The prosecutor did not even mention expulsion in his argument,
but recommended only that I be forbidden to practice for six
months. And even this demand he mumbled disconcertedly, with
a note of hopelessness in his voice.

In the end the affair resulted in nothing more than a warning.

Certainly one does not need to be ashamed of the legal profession
that existed in Petersburg, Moscow, or Russia as a whole. What
a pity that the names of the principal creators of the Russian legal
profession, whom I encountered while they were still alive, are
gradually fading into oblivion. They should be impressed in the
memory of society, as should the fact that in a country where,
as Aksakov remarked, only silence could be heard and speaking
in public was like committing a public indecency, exemplary legal
discourse developed quickly.

The king of the courtroom orators was W. D. Spasowicz.[9] He
entered the legal profession as one of the best, and to the end of his
days that is what he remained. He was a Pole by birth, and his
speech never sounded Russian but like a translation from Polish.
It was filled with an unusual, peculiar beauty, and sounded like
pearls falling onto a silver platter.

*A naive book about how to behave in "fashionable society," favored
by wives of petty officials and of pretentious members of the *meshchanstvo*.

[9] [During his career, Spasowicz was widely referred to as "the king of
the Russian bar," hence Gruzenberg's designation of him.]

39

Then there was P. A. Alexandrov, who traded his job in the office of the Chief Prosecutor of the Senate for the humble duties of a lawyer. He was the distinguished defense counsel for Vera Zasulich, who, for political reasons, had made an attempt on the life of the Petersburg police chief, F. F. Trepov.[10] Alexandrov possessed the mind of a philosopher and speech as sharp as a razor.

There was also the uncommonly clever P. A. Potekhin, a native of Kostroma. Like most of those who came from that area, he was a pugnacious and ruthless polemicist. Heaven help those who might provoke him; he would crumble them and reduce them to ashes.

Another prominent lawyer was V. N. Gerard, an elegant and handsome man, who fought energetically, while appearing to treat his adversary with affection and tenderness.

I also recall A. M. Unkovsky, an elderly public figure, who was not distinguished by any special talents, but was steadfast and dependable, as well as free from greed. His only weakness, resulting from his friendship with Saltykov-Shchedrin, was a constant need to be witty, which at times took considerable effort on his part.

In contrast, another wit, V. I. Zhukovsky, possessed a true Russian humor: biting, but not malicious. Moreover, he was unconcerned with chasing after pretentious words, which generally conceal an empty soul. Zhukovsky, like S. A. Andreevsky, had willingly sacrificed his splendid position in the prosecutor's office in the capital by refusing to appear as the prosecutor against Vera Zasulich. This refusal was the result not of political considerations but rather moral ones, because the police chief, Trepov, had overstepped the law by flogging a political prisoner.[11]

Upon becoming a member of the bar, Zhukovsky found himself in a helpless situation. He disliked criminal defenses, and he limited himself to the role of civil plaintiff in criminal cases. He was overly scrupulous and never took up arms against a weak or a casual offender. There were instances when, after becoming convinced in court that his client was not in the right, he hemmed

---

10 [The widely publicized Zasulich trial took place in 1878. After a brilliant defense, Zasulich was acquitted.]

11 [The prisoner, Arkhip Bogolyubov, had failed to remove his cap when Trepov walked through the prison yard. Trepov ordered that Bogolyubov be given twenty-five strokes of the rod, which prompted Zasulich to enter Trepov's office and fire a revolver at him, wounding him seriously.]

and hawed, feeling more foolish than a Molchalin.[12] People began to avoid him, for, after all, life does not take into account one's
conscience, and, having accepted the harness, one has to pull.

With his characteristic lack of malice, Zhukovsky once described
his situation in a conversation with me. "The trouble is with my
wife," he said. "There is no way to please her. When I was a
prosecutor, I would come home after a trial, and my wife would
say, 'Well, how was it?' 'He was acquitted.' 'Of course!' she would
say. 'With someone like you, acquittal is inevitable.' I became a
defense attorney. 'Well, how was it?' 'He was convicted.' 'Of
course!' she would reply. I don't understand her at all. An acquittal
was bad—so was a conviction. But then, why should I blame a
sweet woman. It's not she, but life itself that's such a quarrelsome
old nag."

In the eyes of society, the only equal to Spasowicz was A. Ya.
Passover. After graduating from Moscow University, Passover had
been sent abroad to prepare for a professorship. He greedily
"gnawed the granite of knowledge." He could not lock himself
into a narrow specialty; and thanks to his exceptional abilities, he
became a master in all areas of jurisprudence. Upon his return to
Moscow, he realized that academic life had shifted sharply to the
right and that a Jewish jurist would never find a teaching position.
However, during the first years of the reform, the judiciary was
not affected by ethnic prejudices, and Passover ended up in one of
the towns on the Volga as a splendid assistant prosecutor. But
even the judiciary soon fell victim to lower standards and lost
whatever taste it had for Jews. Passover transferred to a law practice in Odessa. From the time of his arrival, he occupied a prominent position, but he did not care for the social level he found in
Odessa. So, he left for England, where, thanks to his perfect
knowledge of almost all the European languages, he was admitted
to the bar. As a passionate Anglophile he was enamoured with
English culture for the rest of his life, but still he was drawn to his

[12] [In a series of sketches during the 1870s, Saltykov-Shchedrin satirized
a type of people whom he called the "Molchalins." These were petty
officials who had sacrificed their personal qualities in order to ingratiate
themselves with their superiors. So as not to offend, they would choose
their words carefully or remain silent, even if it was embarrassing to do so.
The literary precursor to these Molchalins was a subservient character
named Molchalin in Griboedov's play, *The Misfortune of Being Wise*
(1823); the name Molchalin was derived from the Russian word
"molchat," meaning "to keep silent."]

own country. He registered with the bar in Petersburg and at
once became known as an indisputable legal authority. He was
showered with cases and huge sums of money. However, this did
not satisfy him. His real calling was scholarship. Since he was not
permitted into a university, he created one of his own through the
judicial conferences. The deep content and brilliant form of his
legal arguments in regard to the papers that were presented attracted crowds of young lawyers. They hardly listened to those
giving the reports, but waited impatiently for what Passover had
to say.

Like a generous man of wealth, he lavishly distributed ideas
and words; yet not a trace of them ever found its way into print.
When he was reproached for this omission, he answered with a
scoff, "My professional position frees me from intellectual pursuits.
Why should I take four books that others have written and make
from them a fifth one of my own—and a poor one?"

During a celebration in honor of Passover, Spasowicz character-
ized him thus: "You, Alexander Yakovlevich, are a stingy knight.
You bury your countless treasures in the cellar. Why not share
them with us?"

His appeal was in vain. Passover had an invincible passion for
intellectual hoarding. His enormous library was as fine a private
library as could be found. He spared no resources on it. An eccentric
who did not trust antiquarians, he once traveled to America for
the sole purpose of locating a copy of a rare book that he lacked.
He lived alone and acquired a reputation as a self-centered person,
who cared nothing about others. This was not true, however. He
was exceptionally kind and sensitive, but because he was embarrassed by his kindness, he concealed it. I knew this from experience.
After brutally criticizing one of my papers in his customary way,
Passover came to see me.

"I came to let you know," he said, "that in the next few days a
wealthy man from Odessa, by the name of Shpolyansky, will visit
you. He has been arraigned for his conduct as a contractor to the
Navy Department. His case will be heard in the Sevastopol naval
court, and according to my calculations it will last about a month
and a half. Here is your chance to provide for yourself for two
or three years. Be sure not to miss this opportunity, and set such-
and-such a fee." And Passover named a huge figure.

"For goodness' sake, Alexander Yakovlevich," I protested. "What

fool would give such money to a beginning attorney, still on pro-
bation and not widely known to the public?"

"What fool? The one who trusts my judgment."

Even my closest friends did not conceal their surprise about the
exorbitant fee that Passover instructed me to charge.

During the last years of his life, Passover became even more of
a recluse than he had been previously, now opening his doors only
to young people. Thus passed his long life, which gave rise to so
many false opinions of him. Despite the outward appearance that
he was whirling with success, he was actually unhappy. His exceptionally skeptical mind had eaten away all the self-deceptions
and enchantments with which life is adorned.

There were other notable lawyers who came somewhat later,
such as S. A. Andreevsky. He was a poet among the jurists and
a jurist among the poets—not the kind of person I admire, but still
a man of strong moral fiber.

A close contemporary of his was N. P. Karabchevsky, whose
rating as an orator was debatable, but who left no question about
his merits in the area of conducting a courtroom examination,
whether in questioning witnesses or in submitting statements on
specific judicial procedures. Here he was an innovator. With the
spontaneous instinct of an Asiatic—he was the son of a Crimean
police chief named Karapchi, who had adopted the name of
Karabchevsky at the time of his baptism—Nikolay Platonovich
understood that it is impossible to shift the center of gravity to the
lawyer's summation. It is impossible because the judges—and the
jury even more so—have formed opinions long before either side
presents its final arguments, and therefore it is difficult for a lawyer
to dissuade them with his summation. Karabchevsky made clear
his views on debatable points in the case while he was still questioning the witnesses. His questions were almost always fragments
of his forthcoming summation, which is the reason they were
longer and more complex than the answers of the witnesses. Later,
when he made the summation, it did not sound like something
new, because he had already borrowed heavily from it during the
examination. In return for this oratorical sacrifice, the interests
of the defendant were greatly benefited.

P. G. Mironov also brought strength to his defenses before a jury.
He infected its members with his kindness and compassion—a
feeling that one should pardon a transgressor, because a great feat

43

and a crime have much in common: it all depends on how the defendant's life had been shaped.

Among the celebrated Moscow lawyers, I had occasion to hear F. N. Plevako. He was a spontaneous orator of unusual strength. He never wrote out his arguments, but at most jotted down some choice individual phrases. This caused his arguments to have a much greater impact. They bore the impetuous character of improvisation and captivated his listeners with their unexpected twists—and frequently surprised Plevako himself.

I also made friends with some writers. Admirable people! They never slept themselves, and did not let others sleep either. A total violation of Article 37 of the Penal Statutes Administered by Justices of the Peace: "Inciting intellectual unrest and causing general anxiety by sounding alarm." Everywhere they broke out windows without worrying that those living inside would likely catch cold and cover the world with their sneezes. They broke the windows and wailed, "Wake up, you bumpkins! Life is a fascinating thing, which comes but once and only on condition that it be valiantly defended. Treat with care that which was built in the past, but destroy without hesitation whatever has served its purpose and only deadens life. Build anew with an impassive awareness that what you construct will itself be destroyed in time."

I met most of these writers at the home of Maria Valentinovna Watson. Two evenings a year, once on her birthday and again on her name day, literary and social figures dutifully made their appearance. The invited and the uninvited came, not only her friends but also their friends, whom she did not know personally. All the rooms of her small apartment on Ozerny Lane were packed with human bodies, pressing against one another and thirstily swallowing the air filtering in from the stairway landing and through the little casement windows, opened all around.

Even agents provocateurs, fulfilling the duties of their difficult work, found their way to her place, usually at about two o'clock in the morning, when due to the density of the crowd, no one presented himself to her any longer. It was at one of these receptions that I had the pleasure of meeting the provocateur Gurovich. He was a disgusting figure, who spoke gutturally and with a lisp, and who obsequiously fawned over everyone, unable to conceal the fact that at any moment his inborn and richly-nurtured insolence would burst into foul-smelling fireworks.

I have said that one could find good people everywhere in the judiciary. A sad exception, and even then only in part, was the Senate. Its First Department, which handled administrative cases,[13] consisted primarily of former governors who had thrown away their careers because of their unbounded arbitrariness. If a governor flogged the peasants while putting down agrarian disorders, if he harassed the populace with stupid and unreasonable fault-finding, he would be put out of the way in the First Department.

Petty tyrants also found their way into the Criminal Department of the Senate, which, generally speaking, maintained considerable eminence. One of these tyrants, who is well worth mentioning, was G. P. Repinsky. Given to shouting and swearing, he presided in the fourth section, which handled political and literary cases. To appear before him was torture, for he would abuse a person without provocation. In order to protect the defendants in a case, one had to endure his insults without a word. He showed no mercy toward anyone, not even toward the pride of the judiciary, W. D. Spasowicz.

I had occasion to witness one such savage scene. Spasowicz was preparing to address the court. He had scarcely approached the bench—in his old age his voice was weak—when Repinsky began to torment him.

"You're not standing where you're supposed to be. Stand to the right."

With some effort, Spasowicz moved over.

"Not there, more to the right."

The old man moved over again.

"No, not there either. Now you've gone too far to the other side. What a blockhead!"

Burning with injury and indignation, Spasowicz cried out, "Your Excellency, show me whatever point there is in the entire universe, where, if I were to stand, I could finally be heard by the Governing Senate."

Only once did Repinsky encounter an energetic rebuff, which threw him into complete confusion. One day, as I came into the Senate, I saw a disheveled old man, sitting by the wall of the huge lobby, from which one entered the courtrooms. He had a lawyer's insignia on his aged dress coat. Underneath he wore a night-shirt, tied with a black ribbon in place of a necktie, and on his feet he wore scuffed boots.

What a sight! I went up to him and got acquainted. It turned

[13] [See footnote on p. 33.]

out that he was living in a village, managing his grandfather's small estate; and with his legal knowledge, he was helping the peasants free of charge. He had defended in the Chamber of Justice some peasants accused of agrarian disorders. The verdict had been severe. He had written an appeal to the Senate and had come to argue it.

As I strolled around the lobby, I saw Repinsky approaching from the cloakroom, that room where a man goes in, but a god of thunder in gold-embroidered uniform comes out. I had not the slightest desire to meet him or to shake the two fingers he would graciously extend. I stepped behind the partition that had been erected to make an alcove for the lawyers. Suddenly I heard Repinsky's roar. I looked out from behind the partition.

"Get up!"

"Why should I?"

"Don't you see that a senator is going past?"

"Well, so what that it's a senator?"

"So what . . . ?" he said, taken aback. "Well—uh—well—you'll see so what."

And he pompously proceeded across the empty courtroom into the conference chamber.

I went to my colleague. "Let's go out onto the square for a moment. This is no time to stay here. He might send a guard to throw you out."

"I wouldn't think of leaving. Old as I may be, I can handle the guard. It's not for nothing that I do all sorts of work in the village. I've acquired good fists."

I stood beside him, thinking that a guard would feel embarrassed in my presence. After all, I enjoyed some recognition even in the Senate.

So we waited. A minute passed, then another, then several more. No one came, nothing happened. That was the end of Repinsky's "you'll see so what." The old tyrant had met his match.

Chapter 8

The Workers

It would be interesting to trace the transformation of a peasant into a factory worker and the changes that this transformation brought about in his personal life. However, this task is now beyond my power, for my ties with the external world have been severed, and only reminiscences remain.

What did my generation know about the worker, living as we did in a country with an impoverished industry, which had scarcely taken root? From books we had read, we knew about the Western European proletariat, which was emerging as a new class, but we had a hard time imagining it in the flesh.

In his remarkable article, "Year LVII of the Republic, One and Indivisible," Herzen wrote:

> From behind the half-demolished walls the proletarian appeared, the worker with his axe and blackened hands, hungry and barely clothed in rags, not as he appeared in books, or in parliamentary jabbering, or in philanthropic verbiage, but in reality. This "unfortunate and deprived brother," about whom so much has been said and who has been so pitied, finally asked where were *his* liberty, *his* equality, *his* fraternity. The liberals were surprised at the impudence and ingratitude of the worker. They took the streets of Paris by assault, covered them with corpses, and hid from their "brother" behind the bayonets of a state of siege, as they saved civilization and order.[1]

As a lawyer, I had occasion to handle legal affairs for workers, most often defending them in political trials. But even then I got to

---

[1] [A. I. Gertsen, *Sobranie sochinenii* [*Collected Works*] (30 vols.; Moscow, 1955), *6*, 53.]

know them only as individuals and could not discern their characteristics as a class.

I was somewhat more familiar with the life of the workers in the Sestroretsk arsenal, since I spent the summer months in Sestroretsk.

During the first summer, a three-member delegation—an old man and two younger ones—came to me for counsel. Because of the old man's devotion to his fellow-workers, as well as his active mind, erudition, and noble persistence, he was worth a dozen youths. We soon established a good relationship, and he frequently came to see me in town for advice on urgent questions, always adhering to the formality of bringing the other two members of the delegation with him. He chose to come on Sundays or holidays, without minding the bother of walking all the way from the distant Novoderevensk station.

The old man was exceptionally tactful. Once he and his companions picked an unfortunate day to come to see me, since Maxim Gorky was dining with us. They noticed him through the front door, which was open. As I joined them in the drawing room, the old man said to me, "No, it's not fitting for you to leave someone like that just for us. We'll come back some other time."

I objected that I had not left Gorky alone—my whole family was with him—and that there was no reason for them to spend their money traveling back and forth on the train, depriving themselves of their day off.

The old man held his ground and then gently inquired, "Would it be possible to see our Gorky a little closer?"

I invited them into the dining room, and they sat down. My wife asked them to have something to eat, but they did not touch a thing. The old man and his companions watched Gorky affectionately the entire time. Then they quickly arose. "You have things to do, and we don't want to bother you," said the old man in parting. "But we want to thank you for Gorky. We weren't wrong—he's just like we thought."

Nevertheless, one cannot regard these meetings as a means of comprehending the workers as a cohesive group. The meetings only provided an understanding of a few characteristics. I got to know the workers as a body during what was apparently the only workers' case in the history of the Russian court—the so-called "Maxwell Case."[2]

[2] [The Maxwell Case was tried in March, 1899, the result of a

Naturally, one may object that a single case cannot provide an exhaustive knowledge, for as the popular proverb tells us: "To know a person, one must eat a *pud* of salt with him."* However, if you know the individual traits of one group or another, no matter how disconnected these traits may be, the day comes when in your mind they intertwine in a single bundle, which you will not confuse with any other. Such a day arrives when the multitude, gripped by some deep emotional experience, appears as if it were a single person.

On the Schlüsselburg highway, leading from Petersburg, a workers' settlement of over 75,000 persons developed almost imperceptibly. Most of the residents lived in barracks belonging to the factories in which they worked, the various families having been allotted separate, tiny rooms.

These workers were peasants from the villages, with an insignificant number of the *meshchanstvo*³ from the outskirts of the city. However, the peasants had severed their connection with the village, having given their land allotments to family members or relatives. They seldom visited the village, and when they did it was only to get their passports in order.

A strong influence was exerted on the workers by Lenin's organization, the Union of Struggle for the Liberation of the Working Class. Thanks to this union, the workers had been taught a basic literacy, and they had begun to read carefully selected booklets and leaflets. In order to do this reading, they stole time from their nightly rest. I have rarely encountered among intellectuals, even in literary circles, such an insatiable craving for learning as that which gripped the workers.

The "Maxwell Case" attracted a wide range of public attention because of the unusual brutality that the police inflicted on the workers, simply because they went out on strike in defense of their few crusts of bread.

This strike took place, as did all the workers' strikes at that time, without damage to any machinery, without occupation of the

---

confrontation between striking workers and police the previous December.]

* Incidentally, it is doubtful that this bit of wisdom stems from the people. They value salt too much to waste a *pud* of it for the sake of knowing just one person. More likely this saying was invented by the salt producers. [One *pud* equals 36 pounds.]

³ [The *meshchanstvo* was legally and socially the lowest category of urban dwellers, consisting mainly of artisans, laborers, and petty traders.]

factory buildings, and without the slightest violence or offense
to any of the higher official personnel. The strikers did not raise
a hand.

Even the leaflets calling for the strike dealt solely with the
workers' occupational needs. They spoke about working conditions
in the weaving and spinning shops and about the cleaning of
machines during working time rather than after hours without
pay. They requested that workers be let into the factory even after
the whistle had blown, and that they have their wages deducted
for being late, rather than be fired. They also asked that the holidays abolished by the factory owners be restored. There was not
a word about political demands.

The Union of Struggle for the Liberation of the Working Class
tried to reduce the number of inevitable victims in conflicts between workers and the administration. It recognized that as soon
as the workers began to assert their working rights with any
vigor, they would necessarily clash with the political system and
would realize that unless the system were changed the contradictions between labor and capital could not be resolved justly.

However, the Okhrana[4] turned a simple strike into a bloody confrontation. Not content with having placed agents provocateurs
among the workers, it also sent one of its inspectors in civilian
clothes, who made his way into the crowd of workers in the street.
Four of the workers jumped him and beat him up. One of them
was arrested on the spot, and the other three hid in their barracks.
The arrested worker lost his head and gave the names of those
who were hiding. Despite the fact that it was late at night, a
Schlüsselburg district police officer by the name of Barach, in agreement with the police chief, decided to get into the barracks without delay and arrest the three hiding workers.

Barach had no rationale for this action. Apparently, he considered that his day of fame and glory had arrived, the day about
which any police officer with thwarted ambitions dreams. He reported the "workers' revolt" to the city governor, who gave orders
to take decisive action.

A savage episode ensued. In addition to the police on foot, a
detachment of over one hundred fifty police on horseback was dis-

[4] [The Okhrana (formally known as the *Okhrannoe otdelenie*, or Security
Section) was a division of the Department of Police, responsible for state
security. It employed numerous secret agents in its efforts to control political
and social unrest.]

patched to the Maxwell factory, along with an auxiliary squadron of gendarmes. A military siege began against unarmed people. The workers closed the heavy entrance gates, determined to defend themselves. A Russian may not know how to live, but he is unsurpassed in knowing how to die. His cheapest commodity is life. Here, take it, he seems to say, I'm sick of it anyway!

Barach decided to take the barracks by assault. He gave orders to break down the gates and begin the attack. The workers, who had occupied the staircase landings on all five floors, started furiously to fling at the police everything they could lay their hands on. The women workers in particular fought fervently and bravely. They shouted, "Workers aren't like *barins*. They don't betray their own people. We'll die, and so will you!"

I was not surprised by the behavior of the women workers. I had long known that when you seek a "real man," you find him only in a woman.

The victory, of course, went to the police. Barach rushed along every floor, wildly shouting, "Chop them up like cabbages!" And so, they were chopped up, so well in fact that many of those arrested had to be taken to the hospital. Most of the uninjured ones were exiled by administrative action. Only some twenty persons were handed over to the court, charged with forcibly resisting the authorities. Since the charge was soundly supported by evidence, the defense had little room to maneuver.

Among the defense counsels there were not only young lawyers but also older ones, who had no special liking for political and public defenses. The first to respond was the president of the Council of the Bar, P. A. Potekhin. An excellent thinker, splendid orator, and quick-witted polemicist, he had avoided a criminal law practice, because it was very exhausting and not materially rewarding. He quickly accumulated a large fortune in pleading civil cases and while still in his prime withdrew from practice, devoting himself to interests of his social circle and contributing to educational activity, as chairman of the school commission of the St. Petersburg Municipal Duma. However, his indignation at the unscrupulousness of the police and the helplessness of the workers was so strong that it overcame his political antipathy.

He was joined by N. P. Karabchevsky, a conservative in his manner of living, but a liberal, thanks to his temperament, in court. And then by F. I. Rodichev, an utterly sincere and extremely gifted man, noted for his outspoken oratory.

A few days before the trial, the defense lawyers met to discuss the assignment of roles and the individual defendants. It was clear that either Potekhin or Karabchevsky should take charge of the defense in court, not only because of their talent but also because of the esteem they enjoyed in legal circles and in society generally. I expressed my opinion on this matter and gave my reasons.

No sooner had I finished my argument than Potekhin said, "Neither I nor Nikolay Platonovich (Karabchevsky) should take charge during the trial. We are too old and worn out for this sort of thing. You are a fighter by the grace of God, and you are also convinced that there are no hopeless cases, only hopeless defense lawyers. You take charge."

I replied that each individual defendant was hopeless in the sense of being guilty, but there was hope in the case itself. If we could succeed in infecting the judges with our indignation, this might have an effect on the degree of punishment. By order of the Minister of Justice the doors of the court were to be closed, but our mouths were not. There were twenty defendants, and this meant they had the right to bring sixty persons into the courtroom without any explanation. But who to bring—this would be our business. We would select competent people from various social circles, which would result in a public trial not much different from one conducted in open court. That being the case, the more prestigious the leadership in the courtroom, the better.

"Well, there, you see," retorted Potekhin. "You've already figured it out, so you take charge of the case. Besides, you'll get individual defendants, just as the rest of us will." And my colleagues assigned Maria and Arseny Yastrebov to me.

There is no need to be hypocritical. A high appraisal of your strengths by senior colleagues is, of course, flattering; but what one pays for this appraisal by taking charge of a case in court is disproportionately high. To take charge means that one must: (1) be present in the courtroom during every moment of the trial; (2) know thoroughly every aspect of the case; (3) wrangle with the prosecutor constantly in regard to each of his statements and petitions; (4) be prepared, without consulting the law books, to present arguments on legal questions that arise during the hearing of the case; and (5) detect quickly the character of each of the defendants, in order not to offend their political beliefs by too zealous a defense.

I assembled all the defendants in the large chamber of the preliminary detention prison, in order to acquaint myself with their
views on the case and to determine what they were most concerned
about—themselves or the common good.

In spite of their prolonged solitary confinement, which is especially distressing for people accustomed to daily physical labor,
the defendants were feeling, if not cheerful, at least buoyed up
emotionally. None of them asked me about the nature or extent
of their impending punishment. Most of all they resented the fact
that a mountain had been made out of a molehill,[5] and that their
daily work had been disrupted.

With considerable agitation, Maria Yastrebova said, "Someone's got to show that to the police, workers aren't even human
beings and that they can treat us any way they please, worse than
cattle. An owner feels sorry for his cattle—they're worth money—
but there's no need to feel sorry for us workers. If there's a trough,
there are pigs. The defense lawyers don't need to worry about how
we feel, but about how we've been wronged. Here we sit locked
up. We don't get to see our children, and Barach is out walking
around and laughing to himself. At least, give him what he de-
serves in court."

"So that's the kind of woman you are! No wonder my colleagues
rewarded me with you and your husband. Well, then, we defense
lawyers don't need to feel sorry for you, though I thought some-
body was supposed to feel sorry."

"There's no need to feel sorry for us, because we don't feel
sorry for ourselves."

"As you wish. It's easier to defend someone without feeling
sorry. Tell me, Maria, how old are you?"

"Twenty-eight. And Arseny's nearly as old as I am. Why? Do
we look older?"

"Much older. It's strange. You are not drinking people—even
Barach doesn't say that—but you all look older than you really are."

"Working hasn't added to our earnings, but it's added to our
age."

"And do you read the booklets and leaflets put out by your
'Union'? They most likely urge you to revolt, don't they?"

"No, they don't do that, but now we can see for ourselves that
we can't get by without a revolt."

The day of the trial arrived. The St. Petersburg Chamber of

[5] [Literally, in Russian, "an elephant had been made out of a fly."]

Justice was trying the case with the participation of class representatives.[6] In view of the "significance" of the case, the Senior President of the Chamber was presiding.

Hardly had the trial begun when he announced that the case would be heard behind closed doors. One after another the defendants arose with a statement requesting that three persons for each of them be permitted to remain in the courtroom during the trial. This request was strictly legal and did not require any kind of discussion. The presiding judge, having heard the names of well-known public figures, said disconcertedly, "So that's it! And what does the prosecution have to say?"

The prosecutor, with a shrug of his shoulders, replied, "Inasmuch as the petition of the defendants complies with Article 622 of the Code of Criminal Procedure, I have no objection."

The presiding judge, utterly confused, announced, "The Special Tribunal rules that the petition of the defendants be denied."

A slight murmur swept the defense bench, not so much from indignation, as from surprise. This was too much. However, as for me, I felt a deep sense of satisfaction for the defendants, because whenever an obvious violation was permitted in a case in which an appeal to the Senate could not entail a reversal of the verdict, the court always attempted to favor the defense with an especially lenient verdict. The defense, then, was as secure as an acrobat performing a dangerous number above a safety net. While it would be annoying to fall, there was no risk of being badly hurt.

The indictment was read, the defendants were examined, and then Barach was called as a witness. He entered, chest stuck out, like a general at a pauper's wedding, who is aware that everyone's attention is fixed on him. Taking pleasure in his own fearlessness, he related in detail how he attacked the workers' barracks, how he took floor after floor by force, how the workers hurled pieces of broken benches and kitchen tables at him and dumped buckets of swill, and how he and his detachment kept going on and on to the very end.

[6] [Political cases involving violence against governmental authorities were generally tried by courts with class representatives, rather than by courts with jury. These courts consisted of four judges from the Chamber of Justice and three class representatives—a provincial marshal of the gentry, a district elder, and a city governor. While this composition preserved some character of public participation, it assured that the cases rested primarily in the hands of professional judges.]

The defendants were becoming agitated, and under their breath they began to reproach us. "Even here in court Barach is bragging and gloating over our injury and grief," they complained.

I quietly reasoned with them. "It would be easy to abuse Barach now," I said; "but this could get us defense lawyers thrown out of the courtroom. And we couldn't take you along with us. We'd be at liberty, and you'd be in jail. No, it wouldn't make sense to let Barach have the field of battle all to himself, and keep on with his gloating. Wait awhile and maybe we'll think of something a bit more clever." The workers trustingly settled down. They knew that we would not deceive them.

The defense now had its turn at examining Barach. He stuck out his chest even more, while throwing contemptuous glances at us.

"Tell us frankly," I directed the witness, "how did such a terrible affair come about? Is it possible that it was only because a couple of workers who had injured a disguised police detective were living in the barracks? You are an experienced policeman. So, you know that such matters are under the jurisdiction of a justice of the peace, who would have assessed a small fine or at most a few days under arrest. But you burst into a working families' barracks in the dead of night, called in mounted gendarmes and police, broke the workers' ribs, tormented them, and subjected the police and yourself to their blows. Under what auspices did this destruction take place?"

"Under the auspices of governmental authority, counsellor— authority which must not show mercy to rebels."

"Governmental authority is a great and noble thing, but it must be kept within the limits of the law; and the law prohibits what you did. You knew very well the names and addresses of the guilty parties, and you had no right to apprehend them. You should have limited yourself to sending a communiqué to the justice of the peace—and that would have been all. Why then bring governmental authority into this?"

At first the police officer became flustered, but then he insolently blurted out, "I beg you not to instruct me. I have my own superiors."

"Quite so. Now, would you mind telling us when your trial took place and if you have already served your sentence?"

"What trial? What sentence? This is ridiculous!"

"What trial? For exceeding your authority and causing bodily injury. What sentence? Why, at least prison."

The presiding judge interrupted, "Counsellor, you are insulting the witness. He is not subject to any trial or conviction."

Barach triumphantly added, "My superiors have expressed to me their gratitude."

"Your Honor, I request that it be entered in the record of the trial that you called my question about the application of the law an insult and that Mr. Barach testified that he had received the gratitude of his superiors."

The presiding judge replied reproachfully, though softly, "Well, now you've started all kinds of technicalities."

I lost patience and declared, "I request that it be entered in the record of the trial that you called my lawful request a technicality, to which I replied that keeping the defendants in prison is not a technicality, that the hunger and the injury inflicted on their families is not a technicality, that the judgment of the Special Tribunal is not a technicality, and that the defense does not consider the fulfillment of its responsibilities to be a technicality."

The presiding judge declared a recess. My associates grasped my hand with delight. The defendants were beaming. "Thank you," they said. "At last Barach has got everything he deserved."

"No, my friends, not everything. These are only the blossoms. The berries—or, more precisely, the berry—is still to come."

The secretary appeared and in a low voice said to me, "The presiding judge asks you to join him for a consultation."

I replied loudly, "Unfortunately, I cannot take advantage of his gracious invitation. I am still so upset that our talk would result in nothing but unpleasantness. He is cushioning Barach, as though he were a sacred relic, which must not be violated. And for me Barach is a common criminal, who has the brazenness to boast even here in court."

After several minutes the trial resumed. Barach approached the witness stand and said, "I ask to be dismissed."

"What does the prosecution have to say?"

"I have no further need of this witness. I think he could be dismissed from any further appearance."

"And the defense?"

I replied, "We ask to retain this witness until the end of the examination; and, furthermore, the defense petitions that he be

provided a special room with a guard posted at the door, in order
to prevent the possibility of his influencing witnesses from the
ranks of the police and gendarmes who have not yet testified."

"To put it more simply, you are petitioning that Officer Barach
be placed under arrest for at least three days."

"To put it more simply, Your Honor, I am petitioning, in the
interest of the defendants, that both the law and specific instructions from the Senate be observed."

"Bailiff, take the witness Barach to a separate room and post a
guard at the door."

The dumbfounded Barach suddenly lost his arrogant bearing.
He shot a hateful glance at me, to which I responded with an
affectionate smile, as if to say that I like wild animals only when
they are behind bars.

Four days later, the case was concluded with a light sentence.
Surprisingly, the Special Tribunal ruled that until the sentence
went into effect all those convicted should be released from custody, provided they made arrangements to post bail. We posted
bail, of course, and the defendants were immediately released.

Several days later, Maria and Arseny Yastrebov came to see me.
"Please don't turn down our gift," said Maria cheerily, as Arseny
shyly handed me a jewelry box containing a silver glassholder
embossed with gold and engraved with a lovely inscription.

"Listen here, what the devil is this! Workers really can't afford
such an expensive gift. It would take your wages for several days.
Why, you've gone hungry—or you will—to justify this much
expense."

"Now, what a silly idea that we went hungry! Can't bread and
tea make a meal?"

"I'll tell you what. I'll use this glassholder only when you come
to my place for tea. Let's start right now."

During tea we chatted. The Yastrebovs, adding to each other's
story, told me that on the day after the verdict, Barach summoned
all the defendants to the police station, stormed out to where they
had gathered, and said, "So, you're out walking around free?
With the Chamber of Justice encouraging you? Damned lawyers.
How did you get hold of them?"

Without waiting for an answer, he stamped his feet, turned his
back on them, and left, slamming the door behind him.

"But won't we soon be going to jail?" they asked me.

"Not for at least another six months. Your case will be tried again."

"How's that?"

"In the heat of the moment, the Special Tribunal made several serious errors. I'm sending an appeal to the Senate, and I'm certain that the verdict will be reversed and a new trial will be set. The sentence can't be increased, since the prosecutor is not submitting a protest. There's no hurry to set a new trial, now that you all are no longer in custody. This means that the workers can save up some money, so that while they are in jail their families won't be in need."

And that is exactly what happened. The Senate accepted our appeal. It reversed the verdict and returned the case for a new trial with different judges. At the second trial, I did not participate in the defense, since the case coincided with one I was defending in another province.

Chapter 9

"Robbers"

Sometimes I wonder why even people who are mean try to appear kind. Since there is not much demand for this commodity, why do they make such an effort? Still, I have met warm-hearted persons everywhere, even where I least expected to find them.

I remember one of my defenses as a young lawyer. A gang of dangerous thieves was being tried. Although they had been carrying weapons, they fortunately had never used them. In the legal code, such thefts were referred to as "robbery."

I was defending the leader of the gang, Chervinsky (whose name I remember because it was the same as that of a friend of mine), and his mistress. They were seated at opposite ends of the defendants' bench, according to the seriousness of their parts in the crimes.

Chervinsky was a handsome fellow, with an ironic smile and a polite, though rather disdainful, manner of speaking. He belonged to an old military family. When he was fourteen, he ran away from home, since the discipline of neither home nor school suited his taste. He admitted his guilt without reservation, but he refused to name his accomplices—over twenty persons were being tried along with him—and he zealously shielded his mistress.

During the examination of the witnesses, he seemed to be bored and did not interfere in the questioning. Only once did he flare up. A clever solicitor, who had become quite prosperous, was testifying. According to him, the thieves had broken open a desk drawer and taken over fifteen hundred rubles, which he said belonged to one of his clients.

Chervinsky rose to his feet. "I have a question for the witness. May I?"

"Go ahead."

"As I recall, you have a fire-proof safe, which I could not break open. Now, why would you keep your own money in the safe, but your client's money in the desk? I remember perfectly well that there was no money in the desk."

The witness hesitated, searching for an answer.

Chervinsky added hastily, "Ah, but then you're an honest man and I'm a thief."

The case went on for three or four days. While the foreman of the jury was announcing its findings on the numerous charges against Chervinsky, the latter listened indifferently. But when it came time for the verdict on the charges against his mistress, he became pale and agitated. When the mistress was acquitted on all counts, he turned toward her and joyfully made the sign of the cross, even though this verdict meant that they would be permanently separated.

When the judges retired to determine the punishment for those convicted, Chervinsky began to thank me fervently for my successful defense of his mistress. I cautiously remarked that it would probably be hard for him to be without her in exile. "However," I added, "she will willingly follow you."

"I won't allow it! Why should she perish with me in exile? I'm glad the jury freed her from me. The separation will be good for her. She'll grieve for a while and then forget. Maybe she'll meet some honest man, someone like that solicitor who robbed his client and used me to cover himself. Maybe she'll live a peaceful life. But I . . . I won't be tamed. I'll end up at hard labor."

There was another incident. Shortly after the February Revolution, I was appointed by the Provisional Government as chairman of the Special Commission for the Investigation of Corruption in the Navy Department. After about three weeks, a long telegram arrived from Odessa, saying that my presence was needed for dealing with the case of the commander of the port of Odessa, Admiral Khomenko.

In Odessa, I organized a large committee, consisting of representatives of all the parties, including the Bolsheviks, who sent a sailor with a revolver in his belt. Not only the officers, but also many of the sailors, warned me, "There'll be trouble. It's impossible to deal with him. He even brings his revolver to meetings

on the ship, and says, 'Here are my credentials!' What a bloody
robber!"

Nevertheless, he turned out to be a judicious and sympathetic
person. At the very first meeting, I called him and the other sailor
representatives into my office and said, "Let us be frank. I know
that the revolution does not indulge in tenderness, and employs
only one punishment—death! I've come here to examine a case
with you, not to take vengeance on the servants of the tsarist regime. If Khomenko is not guilty of the purely criminal charges
brought against him, he must be acquitted; and we must not be
influenced by any hostility toward him caused by the sternness he
displayed in his job. If you feel that you cannot handle your animos-
ity toward Khomenko, tell me, and I'll leave. I'll not be a party
to injustice."

I had hardly finished, when the "robber" answered, "Good
enough, we'll judge him fairly!"

"Excellent. And something else. All my life I have been a defense
counsel, but on our committee we have neither a prosecutor nor
a counsel for the defense. Thus, we must serve as both. Although
the admiral is intelligent enough, remember the saying: 'I can
easily unravel another's troubles, but I have no idea how to solve
my own.' We'll look into the case as though we were judging a
common sailor."

The work of the committee continued for a long time. Khomenko did not turn out to be the heroic type—he was timid and
also displayed a poor understanding of economic matters.

I watched the sailors. They took an active part in the interrogation of Khomenko, as well as of the witnesses, and none of them
tried chicanery or attempted to offend the self-esteem of the hated
admiral. However, I watched with amazement and indignation
as two of his subordinate officers settled old scores in their testimonies.*

---

*I should note here that while working on the Khomenko case, I was
visited at the committee headquarters by a senior lieutenant from the
Danubian front (where General Shcherbachev was commanding). I
reproduce almost word for word my conversation with this lieutenant.

"I have arrested a captain, second grade, and brought him here," he
announced. "He is an ardent monarchist, and he disturbs the younger
officers with his talk." I replied, "The special commission which I head
does not handle political affairs, but only investigates cases of embezzlement

Finally, after a long, thorough investigation of the accusations brought against Khomenko, the question of his guilt had to be decided. I formulated the charges and began to collect the votes on each of them, asking the members of the committee to comment briefly on the basis of their decision.

Suddenly the "robber" interrupted me. "Why waste time? We've agreed among ourselves that this . . ."—a strong word followed and immediately an apology that he let it slip—". . . that Khomenko should be acquitted. We don't have any hard facts."

And so, that was the decision we handed down.

The "robber" turned out to be very much like a judge.

There was still another incident that I have no right to forget. My wife, after suffering a serious illness in Petersburg, spent several months in Yalta. We wrote to each other daily. Then, abruptly her letters ceased. After a week, I sent a telegram to an acquaintance in Nikolaev, asking about the situation, but he told me that all communication with Yalta had been disrupted.

This worried me a great deal, and being excitable I failed to conceal my agitation as one should. The "robber" came into my office without knocking and caught me unawares.

"Why has the eagle become so sad?"

I told him and explained that the problem was that one could not get to Yalta and that I needed to fetch my wife as soon as possible, because no one knew what was going to happen there next.

"Is that all? Nothing to it. Tomorrow morning I'll take an automobile to Yalta and bring back your treasure."

"Good. I'm deeply grateful. We'll go tomorrow then."

"No, you won't be going with me. You'd ruin the whole thing. You know yourself what things are like these days. There's no way I could take a *barin* all the way there and back. But I could manage to take a woman, as long as she doesn't get too fancied up."

I took out my pocketbook. "Here is some money for my wife, and this is for your expenses. It's a long trip."

My "robber" became infuriated, and, raising his voice, said

---

in the navy. Allow me to ask, Lieutenant, whether you yourself have advocated a republic for long. Hasn't it only been since March?"

angrily, "You may be an eagle, but I'm not a crow! Would I really take money for a thing like this? Just write a note to your wife, so that she'll trust me."

Around town people began to talk. "This is madness, to trust your wife to a drunken sailor—and a Bolshevik at that. He'll rape her and kill her along the way."

I answered calmly, "I'm touched that you love my wife even more than I do, but I trust my sailor completely. I don't know why you call him a drunkard. He probably drinks, just as all sailors do, but for an entire month I haven't seen him drunk once."

In less than two weeks, the "robber" and my wife drove up in front of my daughter's house, where I was living. My wife went to clean up after the trip and only had time to say to me, "What a remarkable person this sailor is! Go and keep him company, so he won't feel offended."

The sailor was already sitting in the dining room, and my daughter was putting some food and wine on the table, and hurrying the cook with dinner.

Wearily, he said to me, "Wine and more wine. Is that any drink for a sailor? Tell your daughter to bring me some vodka."

My daughter quickly corrected her mistake. "Now, this is more like it. To your health, dear hosts! And excuse me, if I drink alone, but after all, eagles don't drink vodka."

"Today I'll drink it, too." I said, "We'll drink together as brothers." We embraced each other.

After quickly refreshing herself, my wife joined us and gaily began to tell us how the sailor appeared at her place in Yalta with my note. He took a look at her handbag and suitcase and said, "It's a good thing you don't have much luggage—just the handbag and suitcase. Get ready right away. I'll pick you up in half an hour. We can't lose any time."

"It was a hard trip," continued my wife. "Sometimes we went by water, and sometimes by rail or automobile. I remember that we arrived in Nikolaev about two o'clock in the morning. I didn't want to wake any of your friends, so we stopped at a hotel. It was overflowing with sailors and soldiers, and a lot of them were drunk. I immediately locked myself inside my room. An hour or so later, I came out to use the restroom. And there he was, marching back and forth.

" 'Why don't you go to bed?' I asked him.

"But he replied, 'See what kind of people are staying here. They look like they might break your door down.'

"And so he guarded me all night."

Now, twenty years later, I feel ashamed. I called a man my brother, and I cannot remember his first name. This is a quirk of an old man's memory, but I gratefully keep his image in my heart.

Chapter 10

The Trial of the
Soviet of Workers' Deputies

Revolution occurs not only because the masses, who have been driven to despair, come out, poorly armed, into the street, but also because the servants of the doomed regime lose all faith in it and are quickly paralyzed in their will to resist. This is exactly what took place when Louis XVI convened the Estates General to consider certain designated questions. Having almost immediately assumed a rebellious character, the Estates General, when ordered by the king to disperse, impudently replied to his representatives, "Tell *your* Sovereign that the people's representatives . . ." and so on.

One might think that after such an impudent challenge, a small detachment of troops would have been sent to disband the disobedient body and arrest its leaders. This is what one might think! But the government did not find the strength of spirit necessary to give a proper rebuff.

This same spiritual bankruptcy took hold of the brutal terrorist Robespierre and his associates. Something in their psyche weakened, something gave way, and all of them were overwhelmed by fatigue and hopelessness, despite the fact that they still had at their disposal a reserve of qualified personnel. They learned from experience the immutable law that the height of the revolutionary wave depends completely on the psychology of the masses. That which only yesterday appeared to be manifestly hopeless for the masses to achieve is realized today with seemingly incomprehensible ease, because tigers have turned into weak and harmless lambs.

The fate of the Soviet of Workers' Deputies also bore witness to this fact during the remarkable phenomenon of the Russian revolution of 1905–1906. The Soviet lasted only fifty-two days, but for this short period it possessed the strength of state power and dictated its will to the organs of legal government, which had begun to ail. During this time, there existed for Russia only the power of the soviets. The postal system, telegraph, press, railways, navigation—all submitted to the soviets and obeyed them.

I am not undertaking the task of writing the history of these fifty-two days. Rather, I shall try to characterize the leaders and determine whether they had real power behind them or acted only as a handful of professional revolutionaries pursuing their own goals under the shelter of a false flag. Were they a staff without an army? Or, conversely, did a sizable army actually push them into their positions of leadership?

It was unequivocally established in court that the Executive Committee of the Soviet of Workers' Deputies had been elected by authorized representatives of the mills and factories. What is more, these representatives numbered *over three hundred*. I considered it important to the case for them to appear in court, so that the militant force standing behind the Soviet would be evident. My petition to call them as witnesses was granted, for which the senior presiding judge of the Chamber of Justice, Maximovich, came under fire from the Ministry of Justice and was transferred to one of the old departments of the Senate.

However, even the new senior presiding judge, Krasheninnikov, found it impossible to get rid of these members of the Soviet, for he was bound by the previous ruling. This group provided considerable annoyance to the court. Upon arriving at the witness room, it first of all struck up some revolutionary songs. There was no way for the bailiffs to handle a crowd of three hundred persons. Moreover, when appearing on the witness stand, each of these witnesses began his testimony by reading a statement on behalf of the mill or factory workers. I shall cite, as an example, one such statement: "We, the workers of such-and-such a mill, declare to the Petersburg Chamber of Justice that we plead guilty to all the crimes with which our comrades have been charged and brought to trial in the case of the Soviet of Workers' Deputies. In their activities, they have only carried out our will. Therefore, we demand that the Chamber of Justice try all of us along with them."

Over one hundred and twenty thousand signatures had been collected on these statements, their authenticity being confirmed by the factory administration. There could be no argument, then, that this was a genuine workers' representation, rather than a camouflage.

During the first day of the trial (presided over by Maximovich), the defense gained the upper hand by managing to get some of the defendants released on a small amount of bail. However, all except one of them appeared on the second day anyway, in order to share the fate of their comrades.

The second day of the trial was presided over by Krasheninnikov, who replaced Maximovich. He was an exceptionally talented man, by nature neither malicious nor vindictive, but difficult to get along with, harsh and derisive. His questioning of the witnesses, during which he would trap them in minor contradictions, and his contemptuous ridicule were worse than a severe punishment. He also tried to prove that the Soviet was indeed a camouflage by the intellectuals and that the workers failed to realize the meaning and significance of the resolutions that had been adopted. He asked difficult questions of almost all the workers who appeared as witnesses, such as what a constituent assembly was and what significance it could have for settling their occupational needs. To my joyful surprise, the workers gave intelligent replies, which testified that they were fully conscious of these things.

The representatives of the parties—the Social Democrats and Socialist Revolutionaries (the latter in the person of N. D. Avksentiev)—had only a consultative voice in the Soviet and therefore did not participate in voting on the resolutions. Thus, in whatever way one might look at the role of the Soviet, there was no question but that it was a governing body consisting solely of workers, the like of which had not been known in western Europe. This phenomenon demonstrated irrefutably the unique giftedness of the Russian people, who understand intuitively that which to another people comes only through prolonged schooling.

The Soviet was unfortunate only in respect to its chairmen. The first of these was Nosar-Khrustalev, and the second was Trotsky. Nosar-Khrustalev had always been morally deficient, as was demonstrated by his career. The son of a poor peasant, he graduated from the gymnasium and university in spite of extreme poverty. He then registered as a lawyer-in-training and established a practice dealing with injury cases, without revealing, however, any lack of selfish motives in entering this field. He joined the Social Democratic Party, but did not become an active member. His un-scrupulous methods soon began to tell. In order to get into the Soviet, he managed to borrow identity papers from a simple-hearted worker named Khrustalev. Then, thanks to his education and persistence, he could not help but be singled out, and he obtained the post of chairman without any great difficulty.

As long as the revolutionary wave was running high, he, too, was prominent. But when the wave began to fall, without even the participants perceiving what was happening, he proved to be inconsequential. Although physically he was the leading defendant at the trial, in essence he was the least significant of all. There was a reason for this. At the preliminary gendarme investigation, he lost control of himself, acted cowardly, and named a large number of participants. Not wishing to compromise the Soviet, his comrades refrained from disavowing him openly, but only on condition that he remain obedient and submissive. He barely managed to meet this condition. When he ended up in exile along with the others, he felt very much alone. The only aid his comrades offered him was to arrange his escape. Having fled abroad, he did not want to be an ordinary member of the party, felt that he had been slighted, and tried to organize his own group. However, nothing came of this venture. Upon returning to Russia, he became involved in criminal activity, although the court spared him because he had once been a person of some consequence. He ended his life in a tragic fiasco by trying to establish an "independent republic" in one of the districts in Poltava province, for which he was shot by verdict of a court-martial.

After Nosar, Trotsky became chairman of the Soviet. Fate had played a nasty trick on him. Having endowed him with a multitude of gifts, it had given him an unbearable disposition. It is difficult for a defense counsel to pass judgment on his client, but the truth must not be ignored. By nature Trotsky was an individualistic anarchist, and his sojourn in the ranks of the Social Democrats was an intricate self-deception. He saw in those around him not colleagues but rivals, whom he must sweep out of his way at any price. Hence his absurd rivalry with Stalin, in whom he saw only short-comings, while consciously overlooking his indisputable merits.

Trotsky was a peripatetic, a person who had known many seas and harbors, whereas Stalin is possessed by a single love, having been committed from his youth to only one revolutionary idea:

the destruction of the old world.[1] He is capable of making wily zigzags, if tactically necessary, but he does not betray that which gives meaning to his life. Never before has the bourgeois world known such a relentless enemy, in comparison with whom Karl Marx and even Lenin were weaklings. He patiently awaits the hour when Europe, torn by war, will be powerless, when victors and vanquished alike will be reduced to dust. Then he will "slam the door" with such force that "the tower-tops come tumbling down, and the plaster falls from the chamber walls."[2]

I have often been puzzled as to how Stalin, with his non-Russian accent, could enchant everyone and everything into submission to him. It would be naive to explain his unparalleled success by craftiness or so inane a word as "luck." Everyone forges his own luck, but in this instance such gifted persons as the leader of the Socialist Revolutionaries, Viktor Chernov, or the Bolshevik Trotsky did not do a very good job of forging. Fate chose to cast Trotsky afoul of this man of iron—and his subsequent destruction was assured.

Surely no one would suspect me of being sympathetic toward Trotsky, for in meeting the demands of truth I have said uncomplimentary things about him. But there are also the demands of fairness, such as those that prompted the semi-official newspaper of the French Foreign Ministry, *Le Temps*, to give Trotsky his due credit in a short memorial of his death. It pointed out that Trotsky possessed tremendous merits in regard to his revolutionary activities.

An outstanding journalist and fiery orator, who gripped his listeners with his passion and drew the popular masses after him, he performed what was almost a miracle. As we know, the reluctance of the weary soldiers to continue the war served as a signal for revolution. The soldiers began to jeer their superiors heartlessly, to turn them into stable hands, even to murder them. All the attempts by the Provisional Government to reason with the soldiers proved to be in vain. They continued to murder the government's emissaries and ship them to "Dukhonin's headquarters," as some of the soldiers expressed it (in reference to the savagely killed chief

---

[1] [Gruzenberg probably wrote this chapter shortly after Trotsky's death in 1940, while Stalin was still in power, hence his use of past tense for Trotsky and present tense and future tense for Stalin in this paragraph.]

[2] [See the poem on p. 27.]

of staff of the Supreme Commander-in-Chief). Then the unauthor-
ized demobilization began. The soldiers would force their way
into a train, throw out the passengers, overcrowd the cars and even
sit on the roofs, from which they would tumble down while the
train was still in motion and sack the buffets at the stations. It
seemed that they would turn Russia, which was already bleeding
to death, into a wasteland. At this same time, I repeat, an incomprehensible miracle took place. Out of these rebelling slaves,
Trotsky managed to create the powerful Red Army, send it into
battle, and win victories.

Moreover, Trotsky was one of the emissaries sent by Lenin to
conclude the Brest-Litovsk peace treaty; and according to the testimony of the Austrian minister Czernin, he fought for every
inch of Russian soil, suffering acutely from the onslaught of various
self-styled representatives of self-determination.

One should also remember that Trotsky, along with Lenin and
Stalin, did not want to have anything to do with the Germans; and
the three of them were ready to continue the war. However, when
they asked for aid from the Allies, the latter replied with con-
temptuousness and guile. It was then that the sagacious Lenin, in
order to grant a respite to the exhausted land, accepted the "obscene" Brest-Litovsk peace, as he referred to it.[3]

But to get back to the court examination in the case of the
Soviet of Workers' Deputies. Having begun on September 19,
1906, it lasted almost a month, day after day, late into the night.
The judges, defendants, and defense counsels were worn out. The
tactics of the defendants—their militant behavior in court—invited
a threat of a sentence of hard labor. My task, since I had been
chosen by my colleagues to head the defense, was to get a sentence
of exile, from which only those who were lazy would not flee. I
used my influence to restrain the defendants, insisting that they
remain silent about the question of an armed uprising. However,
in addressing the court just prior to the final arguments, Trotsky
maintained that he and his comrades had called for an armed

---

[3] [Actually, when the Bolsheviks came to power in October, 1917, they
immediately issued their famous Decree on Peace, calling on all belligerents
in the war to begin peace negotiations. They also sent formal communications containing this proposal both to the Allies and the Central
Powers. None of the belligerents responded to the proposal, but the
Central Powers subsequently agreed to Bolshevik initiatives for a separate
armistice and peace treaty.]

uprising as the only means of overthrowing the tsarist regime. That is, Trotsky violated my plan for the defense. It was obvious that the other defendants would also follow this route in their closing statements and thereby place the Chamber of Justice in the position of having to sentence them to hard labor. I sought some means of keeping them from destroying themselves. Quite unexpectedly, I found the basis for doing so in a circumstance that in itself was rather insignificant.

I received, through a third person, two letters written by the former director of the Department of Police, Lopukhin. The first of these included a copy of his report to the Chairman of the Council of Ministers, Stolypin, about the pogrom agitation of the Department of Police, which had used a press confiscated from the revolutionaries to print leaflets on official premises, calling for pogroms throughout Russia. Furthermore, Lopukhin named a number of gendarme authorities and governors who had been engaged in these activities. In the second letter Lopukhin suggested that he be summoned as a witness to certify that only because of measures taken by the Soviet of Workers' Deputies had Petersburg been saved from a pogrom by the Black Hundreds at the end of October. I was aware that the Chamber of Justice, for obvious reasons, would not dare make Lopukhin's information public. Therefore, I filed a petition with the Chamber, asking that the information be released, the petition itself making public in its entirety the content of the written evidence I had presented. By this means I achieved my goal of acquainting the Chamber and the press with Lopukhin's disclosure. In addition, I filed a petition to call as witnesses both Lopukhin and the officials he had named.

Since the Chamber of Justice did not comply with either petition, I requested a recess in the proceedings, so that the defense could consult with the defendants about the situation arising from this denial. At the consultation, which lasted several hours, I insisted that both the defense and the defendants refuse to remain at the trial. My object in doing this is adequately explained in the following quotation from a book by D. F. Sverchkov (who was one of my clients), entitled *At the Dawn of Revolution*:

From the outset, Gruzenberg has disapproved of our demonstrative tactics, but now he takes the floor and resolutely speaks out in favor of our refusing to participate in court. I look at him with some amazement. At the end of his fiery speech, I go up to him and ask him to explain why he is joining our revolutionary tactics. He takes me aside and says, "Of course, I don't want you to leave the court for the reasons I mentioned. It's simply that I'm aghast at what you've been inviting on yourselves thus far, and I'm terribly afraid that in your closing statements you'll add enough to make certain that you'll get hard labor. You might be treated more leniently if you're not present at the trial."

In the end my opinion prevailed. However, while it was an easy matter for the defense to withdraw, the same was not true for the defendants. They were present in court not by their own volition but under duress. Therefore, I devised a plan. I would tell the Chamber why the defense was withdrawing, after which one of the defendants would file a request in behalf of the entire group that they be excused from further attendance at the trial. He would also explain that the defendants did not wish to achieve this objective by resorting to some means that they themselves considered reprehensible. That is, they would not act rudely toward the Chamber in order to be excluded from the courtroom.

When the trial resumed the following day, I told the Chamber that the defense felt compelled to relinquish the powers entrusted to it, since the Chamber's refusal to make public an important document and to call its author as a witness deprived the defense of the possibility of proving that the activity of the Soviet had been of service, inasmuch as it had averted a pogrom in the capital.

After I finished, one of the workers on trial named Zlydnev submitted a deposition, which had been drawn up in proper legal form. The Chamber of Justice accepted it and gave instructions for the defendants to be absent from the rest of the proceedings.

After this, the trial was quickly concluded in an empty courtroom with the defendants' bench deserted. It was a funeral in the absence of the deceased.

The sentence was a light one: deportation. Interestingly enough, three of the seven judges voted for full acquittal, these three being the provincial marshal of the gentry, Count Gudovich; the district elder; and one of the members of the Chamber.

As to the subsequent fate of those convicted, all who wished to do so fled from exile. However, the excellent physician Dr. Veit declined and instead built up an extensive medical practice in the locality where he had been sent.

Chapter 11

The Union of the Russian People

Karl Marx used to say, "All historical phenomena occur twice—the first time as tragedy, the second time as farce."

Sometimes, however, this sequence is reversed, which is what happened to Witte. As founder of an aristocratic terrorist society called the Holy Brotherhood, he did not suspect that this society would later be replaced by the Union of the Russian People, which would set about hunting him down with unremitting diligence.[1]

In his *Memoirs* (which are written as if he were using a wagon shaft rather than a pen—the only indication that they are his own work and not that of ghost writers), Witte boasts that he created the Holy Brotherhood.[2] An ambitious railway official, he conceived a brilliant idea of how to combat revolutionary terror. The prescription was simple: create an aristocratic terrorist society, one with connections even at Court. If a revolutionary kills a government official, send a fashionable terrorist secretly to kill the revolutionary. It was as simple as that.

He first explained this "brilliant" political plan in a note to one of his relatives on his mother's side, General Fadeev, who passed it on to a minister of the Imperial Court, Count Vorontsov-Dashkov. Within a few days it had come to the gracious attention

[1] [The ultra-conservative Union of the Russian People, which was organized in 1905, felt that Witte, as chairman of the Council of Ministers, was making too many concessions to the liberal opposition. Members of the Union attempted unsuccessfully to assassinate Witte in 1906.]

[2] [The Holy Brotherhood was organized shortly after the assassination of Alexander II in 1881. Witte's account of his role in its formation, as well as his mission to Paris, as described below, is found in his *Vospominaniia* [*Memoirs*] (2 vols.; Berlin, 1922), *1*, 113–19.]

of His Imperial Majesty Alexander III, who was renowned for his high morals and God-fearing disposition.

The work got off to a vigorous start, with General Cherevin and other pillars of patriotism at Court participating. A secret society, sanctioned by the Sovereign, was quickly organized under the modest name—the Holy Brotherhood. Those ordained to the task set to work at once, for after all, faith without works is dead. Sections were organized in the provinces; and Witte, as a reward for his services, was named to head the southern region.

The Holy Brotherhood had its own statutes and devised special signs and gestures by which fellow members could recognize one another. The activity of the society began with a mission to Paris by a former cavalry officer named Polyansky, who was also a paid agent of the Department of Police, for the purpose of assassination. The target of this "holy" act was a revolutionary then living in Paris by the name of Hartman, the author of an unsuccessful attempt on the life of Alexander II, which involved a plot for bombing the Imperial train on the Moscow-Kursk railway.

Polyansky seemed to be dawdling. Time was going by and money was running out, but Hartman remained alive and well. The Council of the Holy Brotherhood was worried about the lack of discipline, the laxity in fulfilling an official duty, in short, the total disarray. Witte was dispatched to Paris to inspect the situation. His meeting with Polyansky took place at breakfast on the veranda of the Grand Hotel. They exchanged the "holy signs." Polyansky sat down at Witte's table.

"I know," said Polyansky, "that you have come to kill me in the event that I do not kill Hartman. However, I am not to blame. I have prepared everything, but have been detained by instructions from St. Petersburg not to proceed with the assassination until I receive special orders." These instructions had been conveyed to him through the son of the former Russian ambassador to Greece, Zograffo.

At five o'clock the next morning, Witte set off with Polyansky for the Latin quarter, where he ascertained that the gate to the house where Hartman lived was being watched by two *apaches*,[3] who were supposed to start a fight with him and kill him. Hartman came out. The *apaches* followed him, but soon returned and angrily announced that they were tired of stalking their prey for nothing. Witte did not believe that the central office could have

[3] [Members of a criminal element in Paris, notorious for its violence.]

created so much confusion, but having joined Polyansky and Zograffo for dinner, he satisfied himself that such instructions had indeed been given. Moreover, Zograffo explained that he had been instructed to await the arrival in Paris of His Majesty's Adjutant-General Wittgenstein, who had been commissioned to "liquidate" this affair. Witte took offense, feeling that he was being ignored. He refused to stay and await the arrival of Wittgenstein, but instead returned to Kiev.

In this venture, the only result of which was a promotion for Witte, everything was in character. It was in character that all the horrified rhetoric regarding the bloodshed by the terrorists had only one moral: When they kill us, terror is deplorable; when we kill them, terror is beneficent. It was no less in character that the Sovereign and those around him, with their powerful governmental apparatus and legal constraints, with all their prosecutors, judges, police officers, and executioners, still resorted to clandestine terror and secret assassination—and this not even by their own hands but by those of mercenaries.

Who among those possessing a grain of conscience would dare reproach the terror of the revolutionaries, acting feebly and alone, with no other means of struggle against the cruel and implacable regime, which had refused even to move along the path of constitutional monarchy? The revolutionaries approached a terroristic act as if it were divine retribution or a moral obligation. But the autocratic idea did not produce one assassin inspired by his dreams. However, from that day on, Witte was guaranteed a successful career. Here was a young man who was not only capable, but capable of absolutely anything.

Witte's offspring, the Holy Brotherhood, was resurrected at the end of 1904 in the form of the Union of the Russian People.[4] As often happens, that which had been thoroughly forgotten now seemed altogether new.

A well-known representative of the Russian political police in Paris, P. I. Rachkovsky, decided to organize a party of rightist activists. In doing so, he copied the most prominent features of the Holy Brotherhood and the Socialist Revolutionary Party. At the head of the Union stood the Central Council, located in St. Petersburg. Under its auspices were established a special terrorist or-

---

[4] [Some plans may have been made in 1904, but the Union of the Russian People was actually organized in the fall of 1905.]

ganization called the Fighting Brotherhood, headed by a certain
Yuskevich-Kraskovsky, who had as confederates "Sashka" Polovnev, Alexandrov, Pimenev, Ryumin, Larichkin, and others. The
Department of Police and the Okhrana provided financial assistance, and the wealthy widow of the Petersburg merchant Pol-
uboyarinov and several prominent members of the aristocracy
donated additional money. (I am omitting names, since some of
them may still be capable of retribution.)

Sections of the Fighting Brotherhood were spread throughout
the major cities. The head of the Moscow section was Count
Buxhoevden, a special assistant to Governor-General Herschel-
mann. Boxhoevden worked closely with an Okhrana agent, Alexander Kazantsev, and together they provoked a politically naive
worker named Fedorov to assassinate a member of the State
Duma, G. B. Iollos. One should note in passing that Kazantsev
came to an unfortunate end. Fedorov, the murderer of Iollos, having subsequently perceived the true objectives of the Union of the
Russian People, then killed Kazantsev, who had recruited him
into the Union. Similar Fighting Brotherhoods were organized in
Kursk under the direction of Count Dorrer, as well as in Odessa
under the direction of Count Konovnitsyn.

Just before the dissolution of the First State Duma, the Central
Council of the Union of the Russian People, along with the heads
of several Fighting Brotherhoods, met and compiled a list of
thirty-three persons destined for immediate extermination. It was
in character that the list of those who were doomed did not contain
a single socialist, but only Kadets[5] and Jews. The Council correctly surmised that the revolutionaries could be dealt with by
courts-martial, but it was afraid that the Kadets might end up with
ministerial posts. Some of those slated as victims were Herzenstein, Iollos, Winaver, and Rodichev, all members of the State
Duma; and P. N. Milyukov and I. V. Hessen, who at that time
were not yet in the Duma. I was also on the list. The Brotherhoods
were divided into districts, and those members assigned to conduct the assassinations were issued credentials indicating their
status under the Okhrana. The governor of St. Petersburg at that
time, von der Launitz, authorized the issuing of these credentials,
in order to facilitate reconnaissance and other routine operations.

There was also a fighting unit concealed in the provinces, the
head of which was a physician's assistant named Belinsky, who

[5] [A nickname for members of the Constitutional Democratic Party.]

called himself "Colonel." This detachment was called to St. Petersburg by the Central Council, but not in time to participate in the
assassination of Herzenstein.[6] However, Belinsky was accorded the
high favor of being granted a private audience with the Emperor.
Afterwards, he bragged to the members of his Brotherhood that he
had reported to the Emperor about the aims of the fighting unit
in defending throne and fatherland, as well as the special operations
employed in conducting this defense. It is known for a fact that
the Emperor thanked Belinsky and graciously accepted gifts from
him for the heir to the throne—some Caucasian weapons (which,
incidently, Belinsky obtained without cost from the Caucasian
craftsmen who worked full-time in outfitting His Majesty's
Escort).[7]

I felt impelled to investigate the Union of the Russian People for
the following reason: several months after the assassination of
Herzenstein in Finland, I received a letter from a student member
of the Bund named Goldberg. He was being held in the Vyborg
prison in St. Petersburg, and he asked me to send one of my assistants to visit him there. At the meeting, Goldberg informed my
assistant, Gregory Fedorovich Weber, that another prisoner,
Larichkin, who was serving time for trying to smuggle liquor,
told him that the assassination of Herzenstein was the work of the
Union of the Russian People and that he, Larichkin, was one of
the participants in the assassination. He had now left the Union,
since it was not rendering him the slightest assistance. Larichkin
named the assassins and described in detail how the assassination
of Herzenstein had been organized and carried out.

On the basis of this information, the courageous and energetic
Weber managed to work his way into the lairs of the Union of
the Russian People, get acquainted with several of its more active
members, and obtain some highly valuable data. I found that the
material he obtained, although nothing in it had yet been officially
confirmed, was sufficient to begin legal proceedings. However,
I was apprehensive about going to the prosecutor's office, since I
was aware of two facts. The first was that a group of Petersburg
cabbies, affiliated with the Union of the Russian People and led
by the lawyer P. F. Bulatsel, had been granted an audience with

[6] [M. Ya. Herzenstein was assassinated while on vacation in Finland
in July, 1906.]

[7] [His Majesty's Escort was an elaborately outfitted guards' detachment,
traditionally composed of specially selected Caucasian and Cossack recruits.]

the Emperor, who received them warmly and dismissed them with the gracious words, "Unite and strive to do your best." Just what the cabbies should actually strive to do, I did not understand; but it was clear to me that a political prosecutor's office will always strive to please.

The second fact was that the governor of Odessa, General Grigoriev, who had had considerable trouble with the local Union because of his fair and impartial mode of operation, had been granted an audience with the Emperor. Grigoriev readily admitted to the Ministry of Internal Affairs that he intended to take advantage of the audience to inform the Emperor about the disorderly and deleterious activity of the Odessa section of the Union of the Russian People. Afterwards Grigoriev told about his embarrassment when he saw a small emblem of the Union of the Russian People on the Emperor's chest. The Emperor had worn it on purpose, in order to bring the silly man to his senses.

Under such circumstances, it would have been naive for me to go to the gendarme prosecutor's office with my disclosures. I decided that I should go instead to the Minister of Justice, so that I could hold him accountable to the State Duma. (This was two or three months before the elections to the Second Duma.)[8]

The Minister of Justice was then I. G. Shcheglovitov. I know that this name is despised and that much shame and sorrow is associated with it. I know also that none of the Russian Ministers of Justice abused the judicial system as badly as Shcheglovitov. Nevertheless, I feel obliged to say what I know to be good about him, especially since I am indebted to him for my insignia as a lawyer. I do not intend to use the truth as payment for his services, but I have no right to hide it, if it is in his favor.

I got to know Shcheglovitov when he was still an assistant prosecutor in the Petersburg Circuit Court and I was just beginning as a lawyer-in-training; and I never lost sight of him, especially during the years just before he became Minister. I got to know him even better during that period of his career when he was

[8] [The First Duma was dissolved in July, 1906, and elections to the Second Duma were set for late January, 1907, the new body to convene in February. The Duma had been granted limited powers of interpellation, whereby it could submit to the Emperor a document of censure of any governmental minister. Although such a censure did not require disciplinary action or dismissal, it had some effect by making ministerial behavior public.]

Chief Prosecutor of the Department of Criminal Cassation of the Senate and president of the criminal section of the Petersburg Juridical Society.

I regard him as one of the finest Russian trial lawyers. For a practicing attorney he was well grounded in theory, and he was an expert on court proceedings. He had a hand in writing all the explanatory notes for the work of the Muraviev Commission on the revision of the judicial statutes relating to criminal court organization and procedures. It was exemplary work. Despite his burdensome official duties, he lectured on criminal case procedures at the School of Jurisprudence, and he continued these lectures even after becoming Minister of Justice. He permitted himself only one privilege: in order to economize on time, he gave the lectures at his home.

As Chief Prosecutor, he submitted a succession of excellent legal arguments, at least one of which—in the Semenov case on the rights of the defense—will not be forgotten in the history of the Russian court. His personal qualities also contributed to his reputation. He treated everyone equally, did not ingratiate himself, and pursued his career quite properly. He was extremely cautious about becoming intimate with people, but once having done so he was loyal to them and did not desert them.

I got personally acquainted with Shcheglovitov in the Juridical Society due to a particular incident. Professor S. K. Gogel was presenting a report on religious crimes as dealt with in the draft of the new Criminal Code. During the debate on this report, I indicated that some of the provisions in the draft of the new Code were unnecessarily severe and that even the archaic code of punishment then being used paid special heed to superstition as an extenuating circumstance. I cited the fact that in the annotation to one of the articles in the section on religious crimes, superstition was considered a circumstance that exonerated one of responsibility. Gogel began to argue with me and pointed out that a law so important as this did not exist and that my memory had failed me, since only a few days previously he had taken his magister's examination, for which he had to re-read the entire Code several times. I persisted, but in the fervor of the argument, I could not specify the number of the article, which I had not had occasion to read for many years. When the session was over, Gogel, Shcheglovitov, Professor Borovitinov, and I joined in a heated argument. They all maintained that I was wrong and that there was no such law. I insisted and rashly challenged Gogel, who was known for having an excellent memory, to a wager, the proceeds to go to a farm for juvenile lawbreakers, the governing board of which had Shcheglovitov as its chairman. Upon returning home, I feverishly began to read the Code, article after article, until I found the one I needed. I still remember distinctly that in the annotation there was a reference to some Siberian tribesmen who had performed ritual murder because of their superstitions, but had been exempted from punishment. I immediately wrote to Shcheglovitov, citing the number of the article and the text of the annotation.*

Subsequently, a rather close relationship developed between us, thanks to which I managed to get him to arrange pardons or commutations of sentence for those convicted of political crimes. I often bothered him with these petitions, but he never indicated that I was imposing on him.

It was absolutely incomprehensible to those not connected with the mysteries of making a career in the civil administration that Shcheglovitov left the high post of Chief Prosecutor of the Senate and transferred to a subordinate position as deputy director of a department in the Ministry of Justice. Only the "insiders" smirked and said, "We'll soon be congratulating Shcheglovitov on his appointment as Minister. First as a deputy director and then as a director, he'll accompany the Minister from time to time in making reports to the Emperor; he'll develop connections at Court and begin to render influential services to those who solicit them there; and generally he'll flourish."

The "insiders" were not mistaken. In a year and a half or two, Shcheglovitov was appointed Minister of Justice. However, at the beginning, he steadfastly maintained his independence. In the presence of the Emperor, he spoke out resolutely against the dissolution of the First State Duma and later against the June 3 revision of the election law. During that period, he was even suspected of being secretly in sympathy with the Kadets.

He displayed no less courage in approaching the Emperor about clemency for political criminals. In one case, with which I was well acquainted, since I was the one who urged the clemency, Shcheglovitov's courage bordered on impudence. I have in mind the case of the student Dashevsky, who was convicted of a murder

---

* Incidentally, after our dispute, the annotation in question was deleted from the next edition of the criminal code; however, this was simply a part of the codification procedure and not the result of legislative action.

attempt on Krushevan, the organizer of the Kishenev pogrom.
Notwithstanding the fact that the Emperor sent Krushevan a
telegram of condolence and regularly inquired about the state of
his health, Shcheglovitov, in the very first months after his appointment as Minister, was not afraid to respond to my request
and submit a report to the Sovereign about the commutation of
Dashevsky's sentence, which still amounted to over a year and a
half. The report was approved. I could cite three other such instances in behalf of Shcheglovitov, but there is no need to go
further.

Often I have asked myself whether I would have acted as resolutely as he, if I had been in his position as a minister who still
had not consolidated his power. I must admit that my conscience
has not provided me a complimentary answer.

However, people, like the passing of the day, must be judged
not only according to their rise but also their decline. The moral
decline of Shcheglovitov began very early, and it was rapid and
stormy. There was nothing gradual about it. In fact, Shcheglovitov's
moral transformation was actually not so much a decline as a
roaring avalanche. Here was a man suddenly deprived of his self-
esteem, to say nothing of his dignity—a servant of the Union of
the Russian People.

Having perceived that a prolonged reaction had taken hold of
Russia during the period of the Third State Duma—if it had not
been for the war this great country would have thrashed about
indefinitely in the iron clutches of an insane regime—Shcheglovitov strove to retain his ministerial post as long as possible and at
any cost. It is frightening to recall what all he did. He treated
judges like lackeys. He sent out such insolent bureaucratic terrorists as Glishchinsky, Khabro-Vasilevsky, and Lyadov to review
not the courts as such, but their specific verdicts. These reviewers
shamelessly questioned the older judges as to why they, as presiding
judges of the Special Tribunals of the Chambers of Justice, had
permitted acquittals or lenient sentences (that is, lenient in the
opinion of the reviewers) in certain political or literary cases. Distraught and embarrassed by this humiliation, these older men,
fearful of leaving their families destitute, resigned themselves to
prattling some feeble tale of self-justification. And indeed they
could not help but be intimidated, when Shcheglovitov's ministry
went as far as to make outright forgeries, such as the publication of
Imperial decrees on the dismissal of judges "in compliance with

their requests"—requests that they had not submitted. I doubt that Shcheglovitov would have allowed himself to treat a domestic servant the way he did the prosecutor's office. If some governor showed the slightest dissatisfaction with a prosecutor, the latter was immediately transferred. There were even cases of demotion. The primary task of the Ministry of Justice came to be one of shameful subservience to the lusts and desires of the Ministry of Internal Affairs. In essence, there was no longer a Ministry of Justice, for it turned into one of the sections of the Department of Police. It was like the fulfillment of the Biblical prophecy that the day will come when seven women shall take hold of one man, each vying for him and imploring him, "Enter into my house and be my master."

Everyone gave orders in the Ministry of Justice; everyone among the active members of the rightist parties in the State Duma, especially the lawyer Shubinsky and the former assistant prosecutor Zamyslovsky, influenced judicial appointments.

But to get back to my story. I decided that I must go to the Minister of Justice Shcheglovitov, so that I could hold him accountable to the State Duma. However, I thought that our long-standing personal relationship might hinder the success of my petition, since he could easily pass it off with some confidential reference to his insecure position. Therefore, P. N. Milyukov, I. I. Petrunkevich, my assistant G. F. Weber, and I met and decided that it would be best if the former chairman of the Agrarian Commission in the First Duma, A. A. Mukhanov, went with me, since Herzenstein had been the vice-chairman of that commission.

The next day, Mukhanov visited me. Although I had been warned that he was incurably ill with cancer of the stomach, I was still struck by his exhausted appearance, his ashen face, and the heavy odor of his breath.

Mukhanov was one of the most interesting figures among the Russian liberals. He was a rich landowner and had been an officer of the guards in the same regiment as Nicholas II, with whom he was on familiar terms. After retiring from the military and holding a governmental post in Chernigov province, he became an active member of the Kadet Party as soon as it was formed. Then, following his election to the First Duma, Mukhanov, because of his personal qualities and agrarian experience, quickly assumed a prominent position in the Duma faction of his party.

At the time of our conversation about the forthcoming visit

with Shcheglovitov, I sensed painfully that Mukhanov recognized the hopelessness of his physical condition and was trying somehow to hold onto his ebbing life. I telephoned Shcheglovitov and asked him to arrange a time outside his official reception schedule, so that an hour or so would be allotted to our forthcoming conversation. On the following day we called on Shcheglovitov, who attentively examined the material we had collected. It seemed strange to me that Shcheglovitov claimed not to know that the Union of the Russian People even existed. He declared that the material I presented was very serious and convincing, but that he did not see how he could specifically involve a Russian prosecutor in supervising an investigation, since the murder had occurred in Finland, which operated under complete judicial autonomy. In reply, I pointed out that those responsible for the crime were indeed under the jurisdiction of the Finnish courts, but the question was really one of a *criminal association*, which was organizing political assassinations, and that the governing body of this society was located in Petersburg.

Shcheglovitov replied, "What you are saying is correct. Since it is a question of an association, the matter is indeed within the jurisdiction of the prosecutor's office of the Petersburg Chamber of Justice. However, it will be difficult to initiate proceedings."

I suggested that as a start it would be sufficient to assign someone from the prosecutor's office to conduct an inquiry. Shcheglovitov agreed to this and proposed that I indicate whom from among the ranks of the Petersburg prosecutor's office I would like to see in charge of this inquiry. I replied that I had no right to deal with this question, since such an assignment should originate with the prosecutor of the Chamber of Justice, P. K. Kamyshansky, and that I did not consider it possible to bypass him. Shcheglovitov replied with a smile that he himself held the rank of prosecutor as Prosecutor-General. "Don't you think that the best candidate would be V. Ya. Gvozdanovich?" he asked. I replied that I respected Gvozdanovich, but considered him to be poorly suited for such a rigorous job, since he was extremely weak-willed.

Actually, Gvozdanovich enjoyed a general reputation as a man of irreproachable integrity and goodness, distinguished by complete personal independence. Being very rich and alien to any kind of career ambitions, he became known for his letter to the former Minister of Justice N. V. Muraviev. Gvozdanovich served in Moscow in the prosecutor's office during the time that Muraviev was prosecutor of the Chamber. It was well known that Muraviev was always in extremely difficult financial circumstances. More than once he borrowed money from Gvozdanovich, the result being that he accumulated a large debt. When Muraviev was named Minister of Justice, he sent Gvozdanovich, with whom he had been on familiar terms, an official letter, containing the following message, worded in formal language: "Dear Sir, Vasily Yakovlevich! In view of my appointment as Minister of Justice, I do not consider it possible to be a debtor to my subordinates. Please do me the kindness of indicating how much I owe you."

Gvozdanovich replied to this in an equally official letter: "Dear Sir, Nikolay Valeryanovich! I have always considered that in debts among friends it should not be the creditor who keeps track of the amount, but the debtor; and, therefore, I can be of no help to you on this question." We had to settle for Gvozdanovich, who was not the best man for the job, but one who would suffice, because at least he would not turn traitor nor play to both sides.

Before leaving I asked Shcheglovitov to tell me how to handle a question that had been bothering me. Larichkin, like several others who had exposed the Union of the Russian People, was entirely without means. It was clear that while the defendants were awaiting trial, they needed some kind of material support. However, if we began providing this support, there would be talk of bribing witnesses and even defendants.

Shcheglovitov interrupted me, "For goodness' sake, don't let this question bother you in the least. If you are going to handle this whole business yourself, why should there be any doubt about a misunderstanding? We know you well enough."

My premonition regarding Gvozdanovich was quickly confirmed. He conducted himself quite properly, but passively. However, this did not damage the case, for the little country of Finland demonstrated that, despite its oppression, the integrity of its judiciary still provided considerable strength.[9] The judge in Kivenepa [Kivennapa], which was in the district where the assassination occurred, took the materials we submitted and began to prosecute those members of the Union of the Russian People who were guilty of Herzenstein's assassination. One after another they were brought to trial: Larichkin, Polovnev, Alexandrov, and even the

[9] [Although Finland was part of the Russian empire and was subject to varying degrees of Russian administrative control, it maintained its own judicial system.]

84

menacing head of the Fighting Brotherhood of the Union of the Russian People—Yuskevich-Kraskovsky himself.

When this once seemingly unassailable leader of these legalized assassins was arrested in Petersburg and sent to Finland, the members of the Union of the Russian People were filled with fear and confusion. "If this keeps on," they said, "it may reach all the way to Dr. Dubrovin." [10]

In fact, as the case proceeded, Dubrovin's turn did come. However, shortly before this, the Kivenepa judge (whose name I have unfortunately forgotten) said to my assistant, G. F. Weber, "Speak to your patron about our being released from further participation in this case. You understand that we are bringing upon our country the displeasure and even the wrath of the Imperial Court. All I ask is that we be freed from these proceedings, though if for some reason this presents difficulty, we will certainly fulfill our duty."

Soon a request for Dr. Dubrovin's arrest arrived in Petersburg. The prosecutor of the Chamber of Justice, P. K. Kamyshansky, told me with great irritation, "At this rate, you'll soon be all the way to Tsarskoe Selo!" [11]

I replied in the same tone of voice, "I'll do whatever the law requires."

Although Kamyshansky was a talented speaker and a man of shrewd intellect, he was also noted for his utter unscrupulousness. Naturally this case caused him great anxiety. I said to him, "Of course, you'll honor the request of the Kivenepa judge, won't you?"

He suddenly began to speak as if charged with upholding the dignity of the Russian prosecutor's office. "For goodness' sake, this case is under the jurisdiction of the Russian courts. After all, the criminal association is acting in Russian territory, and its Central Council is located in my district. It is we who should look into this case."

It was not difficult to understand Kamyshansky's game. I answered him, "My own opinion is that you should have looked into this case long ago, but unfortunately you apparently have not shared this opinion, since B. Ya. Gvozdanovich's activity has been

[10] [A. I. Dubrovin, a St. Petersburg physician, was president of the Union of the Russian People.]

[11] [Tsarskoe Selo, or "the Tsar's Village," located fifteen miles south of St. Petersburg, comprised an elaborate Imperial palace, as well as mansions for members of the court. The Emperor spent much of his time there.]

paralyzed from the very start. The question now does not concern the liability of this criminal association, but the liability of individual persons accused of murder, including the liability of Dr. Dubrovin. This case is under the jurisdiction of the Kivenepa judge."

Kamyshansky told me frankly that he had requested the judge to forward all the proceedings of the case to him so he could familiarize himself with them, but the judge proved to be, as Kamyshansky put it, "terribly rude." In reply to the request, the judge sent him a form asking that he indicate which of the records of the proceedings were needed by the Minister of Justice; upon receiving this information, the judge would forward *copies* of these records. Thus, the firmness of the Kivenepa judge foiled the trickery contrived to take the case away from him.

Having received no answer to his request that Dubrovin be arrested, the judge sent two Finnish police officers to Petersburg to pursue the matter. As a result, Kamyshansky forwarded the request for Dubrovin's arrest to the Minister of Justice for his consideration, but Shcheglovitov indicated that the request should not be carried out. Later, after the February Revolution, he gave the childish explanation that he did not have the money at his disposal for having Dubrovin sent to Finland under the protection of the Russian police authorities.

However, the Dubrovinites, having ascertained that nothing could be done with this minor but steadfast Kivenepa judge, hastened to send Dubrovin for "asylum" to General Dumadze in Yalta. One after another, all the participants in the assassination, except Dr. Dubrovin, who was now in hiding, were sentenced by the Kivenepa judge to prison (or, according to the Finnish scale of punishment, a house of detention).

In addition to Weber, two other colleagues of mine, P. N. Pereverzev and later A. S. Zarudny, acted as civil plaintiffs for the Herzenstein family during the hearing of the case in the Kivenepa court. Naturally I told them about my conversation with Shcheglovitov, and during the trial Zarudny rashly made reference to this conversation. It was a regrettable disclosure, since it placed Shcheglovitov in an awkward position. In response to Zarudny's statement, the counsel for the accused, P. F. Bulatsel, acted genuinely bewildered. "That's strange," he said. "The Minister of Justice told me exactly the opposite and indicated that those representing the Herzenstein family would not be permitted to provide material support for the participants in the assassination."

I was struck by such duplicity on the part of Shcheglovitov, especially as I recalled how he calmed my fears about the possibility that we would find ourselves in a fraudulent situation. The further things went, the worse they got. Having returned to Petersburg from a trip to the provinces, I found my assistant, G. F. Weber, greatly disturbed. An examining magistrate from the Petersburg Circuit Court had summoned him for questioning about the alleged bribery of witnesses brought to Finland in the Herzenstein case. Present at this interrogation was even an assistant prosecutor named Kukranov from the Petersburg Chamber of Justice.

I immediately went to see Kamyshansky and asked him to tell Shcheglovitov that if this pressure on Weber was not stopped, I would appear before the examining magistrate with an affidavit to the effect that the payments incriminating Weber had been made with the knowledge and consent of the Minister of Justice Shcheglovitov. As a result of my conversation with Kamyshansky, the investigation was halted and transferred to the Council of the Bar for examination as a case of alleged impropriety on the part of Weber. I wrote a short explanation to the Council, in which I pointed out that the action with which Weber was charged constituted a crime, namely, inducing witnesses to give false testimony; such a charge pertaining to a criminally punishable act was not under the jurisdiction of the Council, but was subject to prosecution by judicial authorities. Consequently, there was nothing for the Council of the Bar to do. Either Weber had committed a crime, in which case he should be tried for instigating false testimony; or, if there was no such instigation, Weber's actions, from the point of view of professional ethics, were quite proper. This is precisely how the Council treated the situation. At its first session, it decided to dismiss the charges.

From then on, I clearly understood that Shcheglovitov was a captive of the Union of the Russian People and that the legal proceedings I had initiated only served to obligate him further to the Central Council of the Union. The investigation entrusted to the assistant prosecutor Gvozdanovich unfortunately turned out just as I supposed it would. Gvozdanovich floundered around helplessly, not knowing how to handle the case. Despite my good relations with him, I did not consider it prudent to offer him advice, lest in the future both he and I would be open to criticism.

All those brought to trial were convicted by the Kivenepa court, at which the principal witness was a junior officer from the Kuokkala police station named Zapolsky. He provided detailed and truthful testimony about some strangers who appeared in Kuokkala and approached him with credentials from the Okhrana, signed by the governor of St. Petersburg, von der Launitz.

Several months passed, when quite unexpectedly for the Finnish authorities an official from Petersburg appeared and presented an Imperial order to release all those convicted, except Larichkin. As the one who had exposed the crime, he was not granted Imperial clemency.

Soon after the Kivenepa court convicted Herzenstein's murderers, Police Captain Dukelsky, dressed in civilian clothes, came to see me. He announced, "On order of the Minister of Internal Affairs, I have come to inform you that bodyguards are being posted for you. According to reliable information the Ministry has received, the Central Council of the Union of the Russian People is planning to kill you. Such bodyguards have already been posted for Milyukov and Hessen."

To this I replied, "I wish to thank the Minister for his concern about my life, but I don't understand why there should be bodyguards for me, when it is your duty to arrest those who, as members of a gang of criminals, are plotting the assassination."

Dukelsky replied, "I can't judge the actions of my superiors. I've come only to tell you that two Okhrana agents will be on duty outside the entrance to your building."

To this I remarked, "From what I have been able to observe, there have already been bodyguards here for some time."

Dukelsky smiled, "Those 'bodyguards' have been here for surveillance. The guards that the Minister is posting for you now have nothing to do with the others."

Indeed, from that day two agents stayed outside the entrance to the building. They were very obliging. Whenever I returned home at night, they quickly unfastened my sleigh robe and brushed the snow off me. And sometimes I sent them for cigarettes.

About three weeks after the "posting of the guard," Captain Dukelsky came to see me again. He said to me, "My agents complain that it is hard for them to do their job properly, since you leave home early in the morning without telling them where you can be found at any particular time."

To this I replied, "You've posted bodyguards for me without my asking, and I don't doubt for a moment that your agents belong

to the Union of the Russian People. Why should I keep them informed about when I'm leaving and where I'll be? I'm certainly
not obligated to assist those I don't trust. Besides, it so happens that
my place is already protected. Just above me lives the head of the
gendarmes Kurlov, who, as I've learned from acquaintances we
have in common, likes to joke that he is guarded by Gruzenberg.
Tell the Minister that I am very touched by his concern, but that
I don't have the slightest doubt that if I am killed, it will be with
the assistance of the agents posted to safeguard me. They run no
risk. Even the Tsars cannot be protected, let alone a private
person."

Two months passed in this manner, and my bodyguards and I,
whenever we encountered one another, turned aside. This entire
comedy was as distasteful to them as it was to me.

After some time, they came to my apartment and awkwardly
announced that, on orders from their superiors, my protection was
being discontinued and they needed my signature. I signed the
proper paper and said to them, "Well, all in all, I'm indebted to
you, and I'm sorry that because of me you had to spend entire
nights standing in the wind and snow. I hope you won't be offended if I give you a small reward for your trouble."

They were not offended.

Chapter 12

The Lieutenant Pirogov Case

Early one Thursday morning in December, 1908, in Petersburg, a young colleague, A. T. Z————, who at that time belonged to the Socialist Revolutionary Party, came to see me.

"Late last night," he said, "I received a telegram from Vladivostok, authorizing me to act as the defense for a Lieutenant Pirogov before the Main Court-Martial. He is a valuable party worker, distinguished by his moral principles. I've heard a great deal about him from comrades here. They tell me that Pirogov has been sentenced to be hanged and that the defense lawyers in Vladivostok consider his appeal for cassation to be hopeless. I don't know what to do. I have neither a copy of the appeal, nor of the verdict, nor of the indictment—in short, not a single paper. My selection by telegraph as counsel for the defense caught me by surprise. I don't consider that I have a right to accept such a difficult case. You take the defense. We'll go to the court, and when the judges arrive, I'll transfer the defense to you. The telegram grants me this right."

With increasing consternation, I replied, "The strength of my defense would depend not simply on oratorical ability but on a careful study of the case and a precisely thought-out argument. Mostly, this would ensure the judges' confidence in me. Otherwise, my defense would be useless, even harmful. It would be fine if a courier would bring us the case records from the reporting judge yet this morning, before the trial begins. Then, we could at least look through them. But what if he doesn't? What if the reporting judge brings the records himself, as often happens in major cases?"

How could I take upon myself the agony of being responsible for someone's life, knowing that I could be of no benefit to his case? How could I be associated with those administering the death penalty?

My colleague hesitated and lapsed into silence. Then, barely holding back his emotions, he remarked quietly, "I know. You pay dearly for every defense entailing the threat of the death penalty. But under the exceptionally difficult circumstances that have arisen, do you really think that it would be safer to place Pirogov's fate in my hands?"

He was right. I had to go. I began to change my clothes, making arrangements as I went. I asked my closest assistant, Vladimir Vasilievich Butkov, to whom I am greatly indebted, to fill in for me where necessary. All of this I did hastily, since I could feel the defense attorney's fighting spirit, so full of suffering and yet of ineffable happiness, bearing down and taking possession of me. When this spirit prevails, everything prosaic and egotistical empties out of a person, and the soul, like the body, as death draws near, is arrayed in clean apparel. At times like this, one feels no vanity nor desire to utter enticing words with ambiguous meanings. Everything inside you, beginning with the heart, contracts, gathers together, becomes as taut as a string, and directs itself toward only one goal, a single point—the forthcoming struggle.

You pray like a schoolboy before an examination; and, like a schoolboy, you mix prayer and speculation. You are ashamed and indignant with yourself, but, all the same, you guess at the future by playing betting games with the numbers you see on houses, streetcars, calendars, everything that catches your eye.

As soon as I was ready, we proceeded to the Moyka, and then on toward the Main Court-Martial. During the twelve years before the March Revolution, I made my way along this joyless path almost every Thursday, the day that the Main Court-Martial was in session.

How did it happen that as a seasoned lawyer with a solid reputation as an expert in cassation procedure I had joined the ranks of the political defense attorneys? What had brought me to this point? Political passions? No. Then, as now, I was not interested in politics. Ambition? Even less of a reason. People with ambition go through politics on the way to fame, but never in the opposite direction. Chance had brought me, though what kept me there were the experiences of my youth. Painful and tormenting, they blazed up with invincible power after many years, burning away the thin film of complacency.

Strange as it may seem at first glance, I always preferred the Main Court-Martial to the Senate in political trials, even though I had dismal memories of the lower courts-martial, which examined the substance of the cases. In the Senate, those judges assigned to the section of the Department of Criminal Cassation that handled political trials were either malevolent or weak-willed senators, who acted according to ministerial orders. They treated the law as a self-righteous person treats a submissive wife—condescendingly and contemptuously. With unconcealed annoyance, they listened as the law was cited and analyzed in court; and any mention of the grounds on which it was based or commentaries on it, any opinions of scholars or references to comparable legislation, they took as a personal offense. This was also the case, for the most part, among the judges appointed to the Special Tribunals of the Chambers of Justice.

If there was no blood on the robes of the civilian judges, it was not because of judicial leniency, but only because the government, filled with hypocrisy and deceit, preferred to stain the military uniform with the blood of fellow citizens. I am sure that if the right to impose the death penalty had been given to the civilian courts, the percentage of execution verdicts would have reached a greater proportion than in the courts-martial. The names of Lagoda, Krasheninikov, Khlodkovsky, and others, who were just as refined in their brutality as General Nikiforov and his kind, attest to this fact. (I am naming only persons who have died or who have kept out of range of those who would take revenge, and not others, because I do not want these executioners to be turned into martyrs.)

Among the military jurists, especially those who had graduated earlier, one could observe at least some respect for the law. I do not know whether a sense of personal worth, nurtured from childhood, expressed itself here; or whether, perhaps, the novelty of the work—that is, the administration of justice in political cases—had not yet let the souls of the judges become deadened. In any event, a serious and energetic defense counsel recognized that his task in court-martial cases was not a pointless one, as long as the judges had not been selected because they were amenable to higher authorities. I was always less apprehensive about the composition of the crime than about the composition of the court.

Nevertheless, in the Main Court-Martial, where, by virtue of the law itself, the leading role belonged to the Chief Military Prosecutor (who also held the post of Director of the Main Court-Martial Administration, that is, Minister of Military Justice), the judges frequently disagreed with the prosecutor's legal arguments.

It might be construed at this point that I am an admirer of the military courts. No, I am not an admirer. I simply remember what Dobrolyubov said in his review of *The Thunderstorm*: "What a fine society it is in which the living envy the dead, even those who have committed suicide." Indeed, civil justice has not spoiled us by being lenient.[1]

And besides, I honor the commandment, "Thou shalt not steal." I honor it, and I believe that it applies not only to someone's purse, but equally to someone's work or to someone's merits.[2]

In prolonged silence, we rounded St. Isaac's Cathedral and turned onto the Moyka, where we passed several private homes and then the Circuit Court-Martial building. I could feel a melancholy creeping into me. For some reason, whenever I thought about this building, in which I could recall every corner and every turn, only one room came to my mind—a tiny room without windows, completely dark, where the defendants were taken during court recesses. With special permission, the defense lawyers could bring relatives of their clients here for a few minutes. They could not see one another, but so much the sweeter was the music of the voices, so much more tender the hand that touched the hair, the face, the fold of clothing. I frequently thought how this room will be visited with vengeance when the days of the great wrath come.

Next stood the Academy of Military Jurisprudence; beyond it the Main Court-Martial building with windows facing the Moyka River; and, looming on the other side of the Moyka, the enormous barracks of the Tsar's Naval Guard. Its cold windows stared at the court as if impudently teasing, "All right, all right, enjoy yourself for a while yet. When the time comes you'll be promptly

[1] [In the last scene of A. N. Ostrovsky's play *The Thunderstorm* (1859), Tikhon cries, as he throws himself across the body of his young wife Katerina, who has just drowned herself, "You're all right now, Katya! But why must I remain alive and go on suffering!" In his review, Dobrolyubov interprets Katerina's and Tikhon's desperation at having to exist under the tyranny of vindictive family members and local society in a small town on the Volga as being representative of the oppressiveness of Russian life and institutions in general. Gruzenberg applies this criticism especially to the administration of justice.]

[2] [The inference here is that Gruzenberg will not deprive the military courts of whatever merits they may possess.]

finished off by machine guns." But the barracks did not boast. They knew what kind of devil's broth had brewed from tears and gall within their walls for many years. They remembered how in the fall of 1906 the combined units of the guards' regiments besieged them and in the dead of the night led out the sailors who had mutinied, one after another.

We entered the Main Court-Martial. Things began badly. As luck would have it, the reporting judge had not sent the records of the case beforehand; he would bring them with him. The hope of becoming acquainted with them, if only superficially, proved in vain. The only hope remaining was to listen intently to the report and at the same time sort out and combine pertinent points from the rapidly passing material.

I paced up and down the corridor, avoiding the members of the chancellery and the prosecutors, as they came along, because I was afraid that if I talked with them I would reveal my complete ignorance of the case I was defending.

The judges began to assemble, and after a few minutes the trial got underway. General Baskov was the reporting judge for the case. Since he possessed an excellent memory, he never looked at the court records or even at notes during a report. He would stare at the wall with unblinking eyes and give the report without any hesitation, no matter how complicated or lengthy it might be. Usually, when I had been able to prepare thoroughly, I liked his reports, which proceeded smoothly and steadily, as if they were riding on patented tires. But this day I was annoyed by his venerable gray beard, his eyes that never focused on anyone, and his voice that never faltered for a second. I wished for another reporting judge, who would glance around after every paragraph, first at his notes, then at the proceedings in the courtroom. This would at least have provided some intervals in which to comprehend the successive parts of the report.

"The case of the Nikolsk-Ussurysky military organization," General Baskov's measured voice rang out, as he read rapidly. "By verdict of the Amur Circuit Court-Martial, former Lieutenant"—why "former" I did not understand—"Vyacheslav Pirogov of the Turkestan Infantry Battalion and also Kastorsky, Tebenkova, and Ivanov are found guilty of forming a secret society in Nikolsk-Ussurysky in 1906, having as its goal the overthrow of the existing regime, the introduction of a republican form of government, and, if necessary, the assassination of the reigning Emperor.

...In order to realize this goal, the lower ranks were drawn into the society, not only in Nikolsk-Ussurysky, but also in other garrisons, with the intent that after becoming sufficiently strong, they would launch an armed uprising. . . . The court has sentenced Pirogov to death by hanging and the rest to various terms of exile at hard labor. All the defendants have filed appeals for cassation. Pirogov's appeal. . . ."

The reporting judge stated the appeal, point by point. He ran through the first point—nonsense; the second—indefensible; the third—the same. Still another point: Pirogov claimed that he had not been allowed a civilian lawyer for his defense. But right here he himself added that naturally it had been impossible to allow him a civilian lawyer, since he was being prosecuted for a purely military offense—mutiny (According to Articles 110 and 112 of Book XXII of the Military Code). But he argued further that since he had already been deprived of his rights by the court—at this point the thought crossed my mind that perhaps he had been on trial before this case—and since, during the present trial, he was no longer in the military, he presumably had obtained the right to have a civilian defense. Childish. In deciding this kind of question, it was important only what the defendant's status was at the time of the offense, not at the time of the trial.

Again I listened attentively to the measured flow of the report, as Baskov's voice resounded, "In assessing the statements of the complainant about being deprived of the right to have a defense lawyer of his choice, it is necessary to refer to the conclusions in the indictment, according to which the defendants have been brought to trial. They are as follows: Ivanov, Kastorsky, and Tebenkova have been indicted according to Part 3 of Article 102 of the Criminal Code, while Pirogov has been indicted also according to Articles 110 and 112 of Book XXII of the Military Code."

At last, General Baskov took his eyes off the wall and turned part way toward the presiding judge. The report was finished.

"The defense has the floor."

I had the floor . . . but I could not begin. Had I heard correctly? Or had I been dreaming? Had not the reporting judge pronounced the conjunction "*i*" before citing the military articles according to which Pirogov had been tried?[3] Or had it been my imagination? Could it really be possible that so many people, who had looked at the case before me, had not noticed the main item?

[3] [The Russian "*i*" is the word translated above as "also."]

"The defense has the floor," repeated the presiding judge, with a note of surprise in his voice.

I made up my mind. "Your Honor, the case involves a human life. Forgive my somewhat unusual request, but could the conclusions in the indictment be read again?"

The presiding judge nodded his head toward the reporting judge, who, having opened the records of the case in deviation from his usual procedure, read, "Ivanov, Kastorsky, and Tebenkova have been indicted according to Part 3 of Article 102 of the Criminal Code, while Pirogov has been indicted *also* according to specifications in Articles 110 and 112 of the Military Code."

A wave of joy began to simmer, to rise, to seethe. The little hall, with its low arches, was filled with dazzling light, despite the lateness of the hour of that December day. Everything within me and around me was singing, "Pirogov is saved, saved!"

"I hardly need to address the court, Your Honors. The strongest argument for the defense consists of one conjunction, more precisely of one letter—"*i*." According to Part 3 of Article 102 of the Criminal Code, that is, on the charge of organizing a criminal society for overthrowing the existing regime, not only were Ivanov, Kastorsky, and Tebenkova brought to trial, but *also* former Lieutenant Pirogov. The fact that military articles were added to this general civil article does not alter the undeniable right of all those on trial to have a *civilian* defense. Pirogov faces the threat of death, and at the same time he is deprived of his legal right to have a defense counsel of his choice. Here, in a court of cassation, the relationship of the criminal toward the law is not so important as the relationship of the law toward the criminal. Do make known by your decision that one cannot take the life of a defenseless man."

The Assistant Chief Military Prosecutor, General Gursky, in addressing the court, explained that the argument just made came to him as a complete surprise, that there was no mention of this in the appeal for cassation—and therefore it was not open to discussion by the Main Court-Martial—and finally that the defendant had had a military defense counsel. Therefore, the verdict of the Amur Court-Martial should stand.

I had to make a rebuttal. "Your Honor, may I speak? I do not wish to engage in a lengthy legal debate. I shall confine myself to only one question. If the spokesman for the Chief Military Prosecutor's Office can raise no objection to the factual points of my argument, then on what basis does he regard such a violation of legal procedure as immaterial? Surely he would agree with me that a criminal trial that bars a lawful defense ceases to be a judicial contest and becomes only an instrument of persecution."[4]

The judges retired to their chambers for deliberation. During the more than two hours that the deliberations lasted, several officers from the cassation department and the prosecutor's office, having finished their day's work, approached me, because, as some of them joked, they had heard about the scandal over the letter "*i*", so small that everyone had overlooked it.

"Do you know against what you were fighting today?" one of them asked me. "Against a comment by the Emperor," he added with a smile and began to tell me what on the face of it seemed an incredible history of the case.

Lieutenant Pirogov was an excellent combat officer who had become incensed by the rout of the Russian army and the needless loss of tens of thousands of Russian officers and men in the dishonorably initiated and carelessly conducted Japanese war. With all the energy of a passionate and active nature, he gave himself completely to the revolutionary struggle. He was soon arrested, tried, and sentenced to be shot.

The Commander-in-Chief of the Amur Military District did not forward the convicted man's appeal for cassation, but in view of Pirogov's distinguished combat record and personal qualities, he spared his life by commuting the death sentence to life imprisonment.

In accordance with the law, the Commander-in-Chief informed the Ministers of War and Internal Affairs about the commutation. On the Minister of War's report to the Emperor, it pleased the Emperor to write: "This won't do."

Once informed of the Emperor's will, the prosecutor of the Amur Court-Martial hastily engaged in some legal maneuvering to have the same case tried as though it were an entirely new case. This time the court again sentenced Pirogov to death. The Commander-in-Chief, having been officially notified about the Emperor's comment, did not venture to exercise his right to commute the sentence, but he did forward the appeal for cassation of the second death sentence to the Main Court-Martial.

"So that's what you were fighting against today!"

---

[4] [A synopsis of the case and Gruzenberg's argument can be found in *Pravo* [*Law*], December 14, 1908, 2795–97.]

I was stunned by the incomprehensible cruelty of the Sovereign. Why had he caused needless pain to someone, when it was in his power to grant mercy? Why had he impinged upon the conscience of the prosecutor's office and the court? And we were taught at the university that the right of clemency is the finest pearl in the monarch's crown.

"This can't be! It's impossible!" I repeated in bewilderment.

"Impossible?" remarked another officer with considerable irritation. "And what about the case of General Kazbich? You know about it, don't you? At an audience with the Emperor, General Kazbich reported to the Sovereign that those serious political disturbances that occurred under his jurisdiction in Vladivostok, which were like those occurring almost everywhere in 1905 and 1906, had been quelled without bloodshed, solely by means of persuasion. The Sovereign suddenly cut short the audience, and when Kazbich, bowing, began to take leave, the Sovereign angrily shouted at him, 'You should have shot them, General, shot them, and not made speeches!' "

We were all beginning to feel rather out of sorts, and after standing there in silence for a few moments, we dispersed. I returned to the hall where the trial was being held and began to gaze into the whitish haze of the twilight, as it closed in upon the Moyka. The judges had not yet come out. My joyful excitement, overwhelmed by the sinister stories I had just heard, flowed fearfully away. Again the black melancholy of recent years began to take possession of me—a melancholy which I usually reduced by forcing myself to work, by struggling obstinately, and by straining my already agitated nerves.

"Impossible!" I had just said to the officer. Why impossible? What about the outrageous instructions on one of the recommendations of the State Council? I remembered how, some two years previously, I had been hunting for the origin of a law in which I was interested. I began to rummage through the reports of the State Council, but somehow the reference evaded me. Standing at the bookcase, I searched through volume after volume, page after page. Suddenly my eyes were pierced by the angry, biting instructions of the Emperor, boldly written on the margin of one of the pages. Many years have passed, but those instructions still burn and sparkle before me with all the colors of a rainbow: "I'll abolish it when I see fit!"

What did this mean? What had evoked such a lack of restraint

—and in connection with the highest legislative body in the state, which at that time consisted entirely of persons named by the Sovereign? It turned out that these instructions pertained to a recommendation on the abolition of corporal punishment among one of the minority nationalities in Siberia. In studying this recommendation and complying with it, the State Council drew up a statement, in which it emphasized a contradiction, so distressing to the national dignity: corporal punishment, while considered humiliating for a subjugated Asian minority nationality, would continue to be applied as normal punishment among the victors. The State Council expressed the hope that millions of Russian peasants would soon be completely freed from the last vestiges of this shameful punishment.

So this is what it was in the opinions of the State Council that incensed the monarch. The old fellows were rebelling. They dared, however meekly, to protect the backsides of the peasants with the folds of their own uniforms. How then could the Main Court-Martial fight against the Emperor's will?

Finally the judges came out. I fixed my attention on their faces. They were tired and at the same time satisfied. They announced the decision, worded rather clumsily, as is often the case when it is necessary to change what has been prepared beforehand. The decision stated that since Lieutenant Pirogov had been denied a civilian defense lawyer, to which he was entitled under the charge brought against him according to Part 3 of Article 102 of the Criminal Code, which fact had removed the necessity of considering other grounds for cassation, the verdict of the Amur Circuit Court-Martial was reversed, and the case was transferred to the original court for a new trial with other judges; the appeals of the other defendants were dismissed.

I shook hands with my colleague, and at the door two or three military lawyers heartily congratulated me on the victory over the Emperor's will. One of them, unable to contain himself, remarked with impetuous candor, "But for how long? Unfortunately, the case will soon be back here."

"Don't spoil the good moments," I replied. "Indeed, 'blest is the day of cares'⁵—but one need not hurry it along. Why not just count up how many months can be added to Pirogov's life because of today?"

⁵ [This is a line from a passage in Pushkin's *Evgeny Onegin*, in which Lensky is pondering the approaching day of his duel with Onegin.]

"Well, both the prosecutor's office and the court will push the case along. All the same, for the case to get from here to Vladivostok, be assigned a new verdict, and make its way back to us—indeed, for it to be heard here again will likely take four months."

"So, there, you see how long Pirogov will be given to live. He will see another springtime—and a springtime by the ocean besides. And what then . . . ? Then, I'll say, like Turgenev's sparrow, we shall fight, we shall fight."[6]

The officer, in his skepticism, erred by only two months. The case was brought back at the end of May to be heard in July. Again it entailed the death penalty.

During these six weeks, while awaiting the trial, I gave every minute that I was free from other cases to Pirogov. He became as close to me as if we were related—this unknown lieutenant, who for the third time was standing beneath the gallows. How many people had a hold on him! Even the Tsar. I felt an anxiety gnawing at me constantly, and I knew that I must devise something, contrive something.

Crucial defenses were for me like a pregnancy is for a woman. You do things every day, both big and small, as if nothing is happening; but until you deliver, there persists in your heart only anxiety and anguish.

Along with feeling pity for a young life, I burned with indignation at the Amur Military Prosecutor, who, out of a subservient willingness to oblige, had brought to life, by means of forgery, a completely finished case. But how to help? What hope was there for a new cassation because of some legal technicality? None whatever. I decided to raise the question of the irregularity of having resurrected the case at all. What of the fact that even according to this "new" charge the case was being tried twice, that it had gone to the Main Court-Martial?

And what of the fact that before delving into the essence of the question, I would be accused of impudence? To be impudent is impudent indeed, but death is even more impudent.

The day of the new hearing of the case by the Main Court-Martial arrived—July 19, 1909. I had to interrupt a vacation in the

---

[6] [In one of his "poems in prose," entitled *The Sparrow*, Turgenev tells about a sparrow that flutters defiantly before the open mouth of a hunter's dog, ready to sacrifice itself in protecting one of its young, which lies helpless on the ground.]

Crimea, but I did not regret doing so, since I was so irritated by the Tsar's meddling in the administration of justice.

This time I did not listen to the report as anxiously as in December. I had studied and checked and considered everything to the smallest detail. I knew beforehand that the legal argument of the Chief Military Prosecutor would be contrary to mine, and from the tone of the report I gathered that the reporting judge was in accord with him.

"So be it," I thought. "So be it. I am right, and not they. The heavens cannot be moved, but people can always change their minds."

At the end of the report, I requested the publication of the interrogation sheets from the first case, as well as from the second. To every thoughtful person it had become clear that the charge, in regard to the period of criminal activity, was absolutely identical, both in form and in substance. The difference was only in the designation of the places where Pirogov made his speeches calling for the overthrow of the regime. In the first trial the Razdolnoe station had been indicated and in the second trial, the Nikolsk-Ussurysky. (I omit here my defense speech. Since it was strictly legal in character, I hardly have the right to include it in a general literary work.)[7]

The Assistant Chief Military Prosecutor limited himself to an expression of bewilderment regarding my determination to have the court consider such a clearly irregular question, particularly after so long a period had elapsed between the time the case was tried in the Court-Martial and its arrival in the highest court of cassation. The appeal, he declared, should be dismissed.

He did not tear me apart, nor for that matter even strike at me, but just offhandedly brushed aside the entire mass of argumentation as if it were a speck of dust. And what had so recently seemed logical and irrefutable to me began to sound banal, like some presumptuous philosophizing.

How often this happens with thoughts that have been nurtured silently in one's mind. You go to the races. You are burning, trembling, straining all over at the start—and suddenly, having looked around, you see that the race is over. The horses have long ago trudged back to their stalls for their next bucket of oats.

[7] [The speech, along with a summary of the proceedings, appeared in *Pravo* [*Law*], July 12, 1909, 1590-94.]

During the several hours of deliberation, I felt numb, and I did not expect anything good. Then, with a firm voice, the presiding judge announced the decision to reverse the verdict of the Amur Circuit Court Martial and to dismiss any further hearing of the case, inasmuch as it had been handled improperly.

Except for the staff of the court, there were only a few military lawyers in the room, along with a newspaper reporter. Deep in my soul, I was glad for the absence of spectators. In the pride and vanity of success, I would not recklessly display my joy.

I went downstairs, then suddenly remembered: Who was going to notify Pirogov? During the previous trial, as was customary, I left this task to my colleague, who had invited me. But this time, he was not there; he had gone somewhere on urgent business. Neither were any of Pirogov's friends and acquaintances there. No one had even inquired when the case was to be heard. After all, it was the middle of July and time for vacation, for personal enjoyment.

I went back upstairs to the chancellery to find out from the prosecutor's notes where Pirogov was being held. The officer in charge of the department showed me, incidently, the excerpt from the report of the Minister of War that contained a copy of the Emperor's comment: "This won't do."

I felt overwhelmed with impetuous joy, like a schoolboy who has successfully beaten off the toughest guy in class; and in a boyish way, to my own surprise, I exclaimed aloud, "Oh, but it did very well, very well indeed!"

I sent a telegram to Pirogov in prison in Vladivostok. At the beginning of August, I received a letter from him. It read: "Permit me in a few words to express to you my profound and sincere gratitude for restoring me to life a second time. I had not dared to count on such a brilliant and conclusive victory from your defense, and therefore my gratitude to my defense counsel is now all the greater. I shall try to fulfill your wish for me to live a long life, so that I in turn might sometime be in a position to be of use to you. Respectfully yours, V. Pirogov.—P.S. I am sorry that I could not thank you immediately upon receiving your telegram, but I had no money for a telegram of my own. And letters can be sent only once a week. I am making use of the first possibility to do so."

There had been no money for a telegram—not even fifty kopeks! It was just the same in Vladivostok as in Petersburg. There was no one, during these terrible days of being suspended between life and death, who could bring warmth and consolation to the condemned prisoner.

And he was thinking of the whole of humanity, the teeming mass, the world. For the sake of their happiness he had given himself completely, had given his young life hardly yet begun.

What anguish! Many such selfless Lieutenant Pirogovs, unknown young men, have perished not so much from bullets or from nooses as from isolation and neglect. They have perished when their dreams, which they would not surrender as they did themselves, were shattered against the stone wall of life.

Several months later, an article by V. G. Korolenko, entitled "The Fantastic Story of Lieutenant Pirogov," appeared in *Russkoe bogatstvo* [*Russian Wealth*]. This article contained several factual inaccuracies, since Korolenko wrote it while in the country with no access to the court report but only to the words of a neighbor, a well-known political defense attorney. However, its range of emotions and beauty of aroused feelings, as well as its masterful creation of sustained suspense, made it, perhaps, Korolenko's best journalistic work. At times, he rose to the level of historical clairvoyance. Surely it was clairvoyance, for instance, in these closing lines: "Let us hope that when the high tribunal of history issues its verdict of liberation, the Russian people will reserve some strength for joyfully organizing their new freedom and not just for wreaking vengeance on the terrible past. And that in the midst of the intoxicating but already poisoned joy of this coming liberation, the old nightmarish specters will not arise out of the blood and tears, only to be turned in the other direction."

Chapter 13

The Beilis Case

I have often heard and even read the reproach that none of the defense counsels for Beilis has yet found time to publish his recollections of the case. Although on the surface this reproach is valid, it is hardly just. Speaking only for myself, I must say that it is agonizing to experience anew those nightmarish days. For many people, the Beilis trial seems long ago: twenty years have already passed. But for me, it ended only yesterday; and the shame of those days is still vivid.

This trial buried the childish hopes of those innocents who looked for a peaceful solution to the historical conflict between the conscience of a nation and the unscrupulous tsarist autocracy. The bearer of supreme power, who had relinquished the entire state apparatus to the gangs of the Union of the Russian People and the Union of the Archangel Michael for the sake of preserving his despotic prerogatives, did not stop even when the interests of justice were at stake. There was not a single person in those circles closest to the monarch who was not convinced of Beilis' innocence. Nevertheless, even the ancient Russian principle, "Do not use the court for vengeance or favors," was sacrificed. There was nowhere to go, for the failure to dispense justice always leads to the abyss. One can say without exaggeration that in the Beilis case the monarchial regime committed moral suicide. The nation saw that it had been stripped to its last thread and that it must either perish or do away with this power, so ruinous to the destiny of the country.

The Beilis trial served as a review for all the public-spirited segments of Russian society, and this review showed that the Russian nation was still alive, that neither the autocracy nor its servitors had managed to smother it.

From the very outset of this case concerning the murder of
Andryusha Yushchinsky, I was convinced that it was not going
to be simply a Jewish trial, but one that was purely Russian. And,
indeed, Russian public figures, Russian scholars, Russian writers
and journalists all began to stir. Hardly had the government's intention become evident than they arose in staunch defense of
Beilis, and the question of his acquittal became a question of national self-respect. Korolenko, Gorky, and Milyukov quickly
organized a movement among Russian scholars, writers, and journalists. Gorky, about whom many foul legends are now circulating,
was the first to respond. He was living in Italy at the time, on
the island of Capri, where he was taking the cure for the acute
consumption that plagued him. He sent me a telegram with instructions to include his name among the protestors, confident that
such a protest would inevitably be organized. P. N. Milyukov, on
his own initiative, assumed the task of organizing a protest among
scholars; and V. G. Korolenko promptly organized a protest
among writers and journalists.

Having grown up in a Russian environment and traveled widely
in Russia as a defense lawyer, I had not the slightest doubt about
the outcome of the trial. I believed, indeed I knew, that the conscience of a Russian would never condone the destruction of an
innocent person, that it would not relinquish the task of administering justice to gangs having imperial sanction, which were accustomed to working with burglar's tools and knives.

In truth, I was most concerned about the Jews doing something
foolish. I considered as the utmost folly any attempt, such as was
made in the trial of the Vilna physician's assistant David Blondes
some eleven years before, to deal *theoretically* with the question
of whether the Jewish religion advocated the use of Christian
blood. I considered it an insult even to pose such a question. Why
should I care what someone on the jury thought or said about the
Jewish religion? Honorable people should not have to swear to
their innocence, even under the threat of being destroyed. There is
a limit beyond which one cannot go and still retain some meager
vestige of human dignity.

I expressed this thought at the time of the Blondes case, eleven
years before the Beilis trial. Those who have come across the
brochure published in Russian by the late Paul Nathan in Berlin,
which deals with the legal pleadings in that case, know that I believed there was no reason to defend the religion itself. In my

summation, an excerpt of which I quote from that brochure, I said:

My noble colleague (the lawyer P. G. Mironov) hopes to prove, on the basis of scholarly argumentation, that such a charge is groundless. I wish him success. However, I do not think that scholarly argumentation can, in the course of two or three hours, prevail over passion. Knowledge can confront only knowledge. Yet, the prosecution continually refers not to what is known but to what is believed about the Jews as a result of superstition. And the prosecution presents what is believed without any argument to support it. One can believe only in that which is unfathomable, unknowable, in the abstract origin of goodness, in justice. Wherever knowledge is possible—precise knowledge—there should be no place for what one merely believes. Whenever a Christian tells me that he believes in the cannibalism of the Jews, I reply, "This belief has prevailed for several centuries, but what have you done to verify it, to substantiate it?"

Billions have been spent during this time on universities and theological seminaries; thousands of people have devoted their energy to the study of the history of religion—and what has come of it? Have they found in the Jewish writings even the slightest indication that would confirm the speculation about the existence of ritual murder among the Jews?

Hundreds of scholarly expeditions from various lands have set off annually—and are still setting off—for every corner of the world. From accidental fragments, from scraps that have survived, they have reconstructed the history of the inhabitants of the earth.

Oh, how much we know! We know how people lived thousands of years before us, how they worshipped, loved, judged, and died. But do you know, gentlemen, those people who live with you and among you now—those whom you meet day after day?

I have always held this point of view. Indeed, is it possible to develop an argument in defense of religion within a period of hours devoted to courtroom examinations and speeches? If over the course of many decades, people have encountered the works of esteemed professors, who confirm this malicious fable by their scholarly authority, what can be done in a courtroom?

It is clear then that the greatest danger in court lies in even raising the question of cannibalism as an alleged ritual of the Jewish religion. Those who are ignorant always distrust the religious teachings of others, especially if these teachings belong to a people deprived of all rights and long ago abandoned to moral denigration. If an expert presents scholarly arguments confirming that such savage teachings are alien to the Jewish religion, the majority of the jurors, especially if they are barely literate peasants, will not believe him. To them the religion of the *Zhids* is deceitful, because it is hostile to the Christians, though it never displays its hostility. If someone defends this religion, it means either that he has been bought with money from the *Zhids* or else he is not acquainted with the Jewish books.

For the prosecution, then, especially an unscrupulous one, digressing from the defendant to chit-chat about his religion will serve as evidence of his guilt. And moving into the maze of centuries-old Jewish writings will serve an even greater advantage, for it is easy to bury an innocent person under these writings. It is clear that the task of the defense consists of raising the attention of the jurors above the surface of pedantic rubbish and concentrating only on the person being tried.

The conscience of a Russian will not tolerate judicial murder— the conviction of a clearly innocent person. It was not in vain that Shmakov and the other attorneys for the civil plaintiff spent so much time in court in raising the question of Jewish beliefs and so little in talking about Beilis. They knew that the jurors would feel sorry for an innocent man, but certainly not for the *Zhids'* religion, which, in the opinion of poorly educated people, would lose nothing if it were slapped on the face.

When I looked through the list of jurors, all of whom were village peasants, I said to myself: Not a word about ritual murder, because this not only would be unworthy of your integrity, but it would lead inevitably to Beilis' destruction. He would be smothered by volumes of books, unintelligible to the jurors, and he would be trampled by discussions of the Talmud, Zohar, rabbinical writings, and the like. If talented and experienced writers have not succeeded over the course of many years in eradicating the malicious legend about the use of Christian blood by the Jews, is it possible to turn ignorant and narrow-minded jurors into judges of scholarly work?

In court there should be only one goal: to prove that the person charged with ritual murder did not commit the murder. It is imperative not to permit even one courtroom verdict convicting a Jew of ritual murder. This is the only thing that is important. To think otherwise is not to understand the essence and significance of courtroom work.

Although it is customary to woo the jurors, I considered it my duty to tell them:

You can destroy Beilis—this is within your authority. But you do not have the power to disgrace the Jewish religion. Forgive me, I do not mean to be impertinent, but what would it matter if you, who are entirely ignorant of Jewish writings and the history of the Jewish religion, should say that this religion condones the use of human blood? You would only add another groundless allegation, having no importance for anyone and coming besides from people who are entirely ignorant in these matters.

The Jewish religion is an ancient anvil, and its enemies have broken many sturdy hammers on it. Here in court Jehovah has been turned into a Kievan Jew, who has been deprived of his right of residency and taken into custody.

In the closing words of my speech, I took the liberty to say:

It is possible, Beilis, that you will innocently perish. But what of it? Hardly two hundred years have passed since your forefathers perished at the stake on the same charges. With a prayer on their lips, they went submissively to an unjust execution. In what way are you better than they? You should go the same way. Terrible is your destruction, but even more terrible is the fact that such charges can appear here under the canopy of reason, conscience, and law.

I told Zarudny, "Since experts have been called in on the question of the Jewish religion, let *them* take care of all this nonsense. We have such world-famous Russian scholars on our side as Professor Kokovtsov of the Academy of Sciences, Professor Troitsky, and Chief Rabbi Mazeh of Moscow. I have no doubt that in court they will expose the ignorance and unscrupulousness of the Catholic priest Pranaitis and cut him to shreds. After all, it's ridiculous for us to get involved in the work of virtuosos, to light a kerosene wick in order to help the brilliant sun of scholarship to shine. Of course, as a matter of ceremony, so as not to arouse criticism on the part of Jewish 'civic leaders,' some of us ought to pretend that we, too, are paying attention to this expertise. But now, just as in the Blondes case, I have no desire to give even a moment's attention to rubbish. The important thing for us is to save the innocent Beilis. Through his acquittal, we shall also be serving the struggle against a brutal legend. It is vital to prove that the mighty *'Zhid-eaters'* could not wrest from the court a verdict of guilty in a single trial, provided it was not conducted in some medieval fashion. If some of the civic leaders cannot understand my position, this is of little concern to me. The common Jewish masses will understand, and they will sense that I am acting correctly. They are the only ones in whom I am interested."

In November, 1911, I received the following telegram from Kiev: "A meeting of all the Kiev Jewish organizations requests you to accept the defense of Beilis. Please come as soon as possible."

A few days later, I arrived in Kiev and visited with several civic leaders and the lawyer A. D. Margolin, who was watching the case closely and gathering information on the course of the preliminary investigation through another lawyer, D. N. Grigorovich-Barsky. The latter, as a former assistant prosecutor of the Kiev Circuit Court, maintained good connections in the legal world and received information on the case from the examining magistrate for special cases, V. I. Fenenko, who was conducting the investigation.

The information communicated to me by Margolin, despite its fragmentary nature, provided a complete picture of the intentions and plans of the Ministry of Justice. No one in the Ministry believed that Beilis was guilty, but it had been decided to turn him over to the Union of the Russian People, the Union of the Archangel Michael, and the Union of the Double-Headed Eagle to torment. Meanwhile, the impartial investigation being conducted by Fenenko soon established that the murderers of Andryusha Yushchinsky belonged to a gang of thieves, who had been using the apartment of a certain Vera Cheberyak as a rendezvous.

The following fact seemed especially important to me: When the leaders of the gang—Rudzinsky, Singaevsky, and Latyshev—were being questioned in Fenenko's office and his skillfully conducted interrogation placed them in a difficult position, one of the suspected members of the gang, Latyshev, threw himself from the office window and fell to his death on the stones below. The remaining members of the gang resorted to a kind of defense usually resorted to only in an emergency. They unanimously testified that on the very day that Andryusha Yushchinsky was killed, they were committing a burglary in a large optical store. Thus, it became clear that they had decided to buy their supposed nonimplication in the murder of Yuschinsky at the cost of accusing themselves of another crime. This kind of defense on the part of experienced thieves strengthened Fenenko's conviction that before him were Yushchinsky's murderers.

However, Fenenko did not dare to bring charges against them,
since he ran up against stubborn resistance from the prosecutor
of the Chamber of Justice Chaplinsky. This, of course, reduced
the extent to which Fenenko was to blame, but it did not alter
his responsibility to his conscience. No prosecutor of the Chamber,
not even the Prosecutor-General, i.e., the Minister of Justice, could
forbid, let alone prevent, an examining magistrate from bringing
charges against someone of whose guilt he was convinced. But let
us make allowances, because in tsarist times even such examining
magistrates as Fenenko were a rarity.

Incidently, in legal circles Chaplinsky was subject to unconcealed
ridicule, and not without reason. He had made his career from
the outset in the anterooms of the Ministry of Justice; and when
he worked his way into the office of the Minister of Justice Shcheglovitov, he quickly became a success as a teller of jokes about
Jewish life. Congenial, obsequious, not only capable, but capable
of absolutely anything, he was just what one would expect in a
prosecutor of the Chamber.

Chaplinsky guessed the will of his superiors, not that this was
difficult, since the Minister of Justice Shcheglovitov sent the deputy
director of one of the departments in the Ministry of Justice,
Lyadov, to Kiev to put things in order. Lyadov was a refined and
outwardly highly proper person, but one who was exceptionally
unscrupulous. He "advised" Chaplinsky to bring charges against
"Mendel" immediately.

Thus, an innocent man was deliberately arrested and thrown
into jail—alone, helpless, denied any defense at the inquest. During the night, a band of Okhrana agents burst into the lowly hovel
of this common laborer, whose day of toil began at four o'clock
in the morning and ended late in the evening, and cast him into
jail, where he spent almost three years before a jury acquitted
him. It is not widely known that along with "Mendel" his nine-
year-old son Pinkhus was apprehended and held for three days
in the damp cellar of the Okhrana. Why was the child tormented?
Let him who wishes to forget this deed do so, but I shall never
forget it.

At an evening meeting of civic leaders, I found that all the distinguished Jewish citizens of Kiev had gathered. They were most
likely respectable people, but this made little difference to me.
That which they could contribute to the case—financial resources
—did not serve as an enticement for me. In order to remain com-

pletely independent, I had made it a rule from the very beginning
of my career as a lawyer not to accept a fee or even reimbursement
for expenses in civic, political, and literary cases.

The meeting quickly concluded since I considered it unnecessary
to acquaint its members with my plan of defense. I limited myself
only to indicating those persons whom I wished to see in court
as associates in the defense.

After this initial visit, I still had to make several trips to Kiev,
so that I could learn first-hand certain details about the course of
the investigation. Each visit left a painful impression. It was clear
that Beilis was destined for a lot of suffering, since the Minister
of Justice Shcheglovitov had committed himself, during a visit by
the Emperor to Kiev, by reporting that Andryusha Yushchinsky
was the victim of a ritual murder and that the perpetrator of this
murder was the Jew Mendel Beilis.

During one of these trips, I learned that the Kiev journalist
Brazul-Brushkovsky was conducting a private investigation of the
case and that the person promoting and directing this investigation was a local colleague, a talented lawyer, who was deeply
devoted to the Beilis case.[1] In view of my close relationship with
this colleague, I told him quite frankly that I did not expect any
good to come from the investigation. It could provide no appre-
ciable benefit, since one could hardly expect that Vera Cheberyak
and the members of her gang would be imbued with such noble
feelings that they would confess to committing the murder and
go to prison in order to keep the Jewish religion from being unjustly defamed and an innocent man from being destroyed. If
indeed it was impossible to count on such a romantic circumstance,
why place our untarnished case in jeopardy? The accusers, who
lacked material for successfully conducting their campaign of
lies and slander, would welcome the opportunity to declare that
the witnesses for the defense could not be trusted, since their testimony had been unduly influenced in advance.

Unfortunately, this advice was not heeded. In his zeal to solve
the case, my colleague accompanied Vera Cheberyak to Kharkov,
in order to get the truth from her there. What he got as a result

[1] [This colleague was A. D. Margolin, who describes his role in the
Beilis case in his book, *The Jews in Eastern Europe* (New York, 1926),
155–247. Margolin presents essentially the same facts as does Gruzenberg,
but he defends his own pre-trial investigation and contends that his
consequent disbarment was to some extent a political reprisal.]

was that at the trial Vera Cheberyak told about this trip and the private investigation, embellishing everything with lies. And my colleague, who was so devoted to the case and guilty only of acting imprudently, was disbarred. Only after the February Revolution was he reinstated to his rights as a member of the legal profession.

Upon entering the courtroom of the Kiev Circuit Court on September 25, 1913, I saw a small group of persons standing by themselves. These included Professors Pavlov, the surgeon; Bekhterev; Karpinsky; Kokovtsev, an expert on the Jewish language and writings and a member of the Academy of Sciences; Troitsky of the St. Petersburg Theological Academy; and Tikhomirov; as well as Chief Rabbi Mazeh of Moscow.

What was it that caused them all to interrupt their scholarly pursuits and teaching activities, to leave their homes, and to spend a month in Kiev hotels? Was it material gain? Except for Professor Bekhterev, who suggested that, in place of a fee, a donation be made to the St. Petersburg Psycho-Neurological Institute, which he had helped found, all the experts not only refused any personal compensation, but also turned down the offer to meet their travel and hotel expenses. Were they carried away by a love of glory? What glory is there in being a hireling of the Jewish *kahal*? [2] What was it that impelled them to accept insult, abuse, pain? Why had they come to court?

How does one answer this question? Why does the sun melt the ice in the spring, flood the fields, water the grain and flowers, and make them grow? It does so because that is why it exists. And that is why the Russian people have been given a great soul, which aches with another's pain, as with its own. That is why they have been given a great conscience, which cares about all the affairs of the world, about every untruth.

Some distance from these men I saw the jurors, the future masters of Beilis' fate, almost all of them peasants. Among the peasants

[2] [The *kahal* was the traditional Jewish community organization for administering religious, educational, social, fiscal, and to some degree judicial affairs. The power of the *kahals* had been severely curtailed in Russia during the nineteenth century, but they continued to function as best they could. Gruzenberg's inference here is that these expert witnesses risked the *accusation* of being paid for their testimony by the *kahal*.]

one could catch sight of a few persons in suit coats—city dwellers. Especially noticeable was a minor official, his pince-nez hanging
on a cord jauntily draped over his ear, who was scurrying from
one little group of jurors to another. I shall never forget this man.
His name was Melnikov, and he had chanced to become foreman
of the jury. For thirty-three days, from morning until late at
night, I saw his ingratiating countenance, gazing deferentially,
with a canine obsequiousness, at the prosecutor, the judges, and
the attorneys for the civil plaintiff, and turning disdainfully away
from the counsels for the defense.

Court convened each morning at nine or no later than nine-
thirty, and, with brief recesses, it ran until late at night, sometimes
until one o'clock.

The hearing of the case began. The judges entered, with F. A.
Boldyrev presiding. Boldyrev was known for his obsequiousness,
adaptability, and skill at playing mean tricks while maintaining
an air of kindness and avoiding unsightly scandals. The Minister
of Justice had good reason to consider him suitable for presiding
over the Beilis case. Therefore, Boldyrev had been transferred from
Uman to Kiev. He had also been promised that, at the conclusion of the trial, he would be appointed to the post of Senior Presiding Judge of the Kiev Chamber of Justice, an unheard-of prize
for baseness. Next to him sat three other judges, who did not dare
utter a word during the entire time of the trial and who slavishly
concurred with the presiding judge in everything.

The prosecutor was a lean, pale-faced, nervous German named
Wipper, a typical representative of the Hitlerism that later gained
the upper hand in Germany. Untalented, insolent, despising the
very people who had given him a splendid position, he strongly
emphasized, as he addressed the court, that he was not a Russian
and did not understand the softness of the Russians.

On the bench of the attorneys for the civil plaintiff sat the
Moscow lawyer Shmakov, who, I might note, was not by nature a
malicious man, as popularly supposed, but rather one who had
become completely possessed by a blind anti-Semitism. Next to
him sat Zamyslovsky, a man of great ability, but exceptionally
vile. His activities in the State Duma are sufficiently known to
everyone, and, therefore, it is not worth dwelling on him.

Sharing the defense bench with me were N. P. Karabchevsky,
V. A. Maklakov, and D. N. Grigorovich-Barsky. All around—

behind the judges' seats, throughout the chamber, in the gallery—were enemies, with the exception of V. G. Korolenko, who looked at me affectionately from the gallery, as well as the calm and stately V. D. Nabokov. One should also include among the friends of the case five or six of the newspaper correspondents.

The case went on, as I have already noted, for thirty-three days. What did I go through during these terrible days and especially during these terrible nights of tossing and turning in bed, as I vainly tried to sleep, unable to free myself from the savage effects of the trial? It is not worth recounting. To the readers, it does not matter; and to me, it is still painful. I shall say only that upon returning home from court at night, I would scrub my face in the bathroom. It seemed to me that my face had been spat upon, and that I could not succeed in washing off the spittle. In my weaker moments, I envied those who were dead. In the darkness I tried to guess whether my wife, who had not wanted to leave me alone during the trial, was asleep at the opposite end of the room.

Let me dwell only on three aspects of these terrible days in court: on the examination of Lieutenant-Colonel Ivanov of the gendarmes; on the examination of the actual murderers of Andryusha Yushchinsky, that is, Rudzinsky and Singaevsky, who had been brought from a Siberian prison at my request; and finally on the expert testimony of Kokovtsev and Troitsky.

Lieutenant-Colonal Ivanov conducted the gendarme investigation, which convinced him, as well as his superior, Colonel Shredel, that Yushchinsky's murder was entirely the work of a gang of thieves, namely Vera Cheberyak, Latyshev, Rudzinsky, and Singaevsky. Ivanov did not conceal his views on the results he had obtained. In a conversation with a member of the State Council, Professor Pikhno, who published *Kievlyanin* [*The Kievan*], a rightist, anti-Semitic, though still decent newspaper in Kiev, Ivanov shared his information. This prompted the defense to call him as a witness. However, in court, to my complete surprise and indignation, Ivanov became the most unceremonious of Beilis' accusers.

The triumphant Zamyslovsky got up and petitioned the presiding judge Boldyrev to ascertain on whose request Ivanov had been called as a witness.

Boldyrev, stroking his sideburns, turned innocently to the secretary, "Somehow, I don't remember. See on whose request Lieutenant-Colonel Ivanov was called."

The secretary proved to be more straightforward than his superior, and without consulting the record of the case he replied, "On the request of Counsellor Gruzenberg."

Then Zamyslovsky turned to the jury. "I ask you to keep in mind that the witness, Lieutenant-Colonel Ivanov, who has given us such valuable testimony, was called on the request of the defense, and not on our request."

I lost my composure at this insolence and replied, "There are neither witnesses for the defense, nor for the prosecution. In court it is necessary only to distinguish between those telling the truth and those telling lies, between honest and dishonest witnesses."

In mock horror, Zamyslovsky asked that my words be entered in the record of the case. The court declared a recess. Upon returning to the courtroom after a prolonged consultation, Boldyrev read the following resolution: "Counsellor Gruzenberg's statements about the witness Ivanov will be entered in the record of the case, a copy of which will be sent to the Prosecutor of the Circuit Court for appropriate action."

I shall never forget the examination of Rudzinsky and Singaevsky. When I began to question Rudzinsky[3] about why he and his comrades Latyshev and Singaevsky were in such a hurry to leave for Moscow on the very next day after Yushchinsky's murder, he replied with a stammer, "We robbed an optical store on the Kreshchatik the night before and went to Moscow to sell the binoculars."

I asked, "Why was it that all *three* of you went? Why, since you did not have much money on those days, did you waste it on three tickets?"

By this time Rudzinsky was so flustered that he was at a loss for words. Then, after some hesitation, he replied, "We wanted to see Moscow, since we'd never been there."

The reply was clearly ridiculous. "It's surprising," I said, "that you got a desire to see Moscow on the next day after Andryusha's murder."

[3] [The questioning that Gruzenberg recounts here was actually that of Singaevsky, not Rudzinsky. Otherwise, Gruzenberg's summarization is essentially correct. *Delo Beilisa: stenograficheskii otchet* [*The Beilis Case: Stenographic Report*] (3 vols.; Kiev, 1913), 2, 70–71.]

At this point the presiding judge Boldyrev came to Rudzinsky's aid. "Did you perhaps not trust one another with selling the binoculars?" he said, interrupting me.

Caught up in the intensity of the examination, I brushed aside this remark and said to the presiding judge, "Don't interfere."

Taking offense, Boldyrev exclaimed, "Counsellor, may I ask you not to forget yourself."

In my agitation, I retorted, "And may I ask that you give me the opportunity to conduct the examination without harassing me."

"Tell me," I said to the witness, "weren't there only one or two dozen of the stolen binoculars, and aren't stolen goods usually sold to a fence for almost nothing? Surely you must have realized that the three of you were making this trip at a loss."

In addition to these two aspects of the trial, let me dwell for a moment on the expert testimony. Professor Kosorotov, who held the chair of forensic medicine in Petersburg, was questioned by Zamyslovsky. "Tell us, Professor, did you and the other expert witnesses called by the civil attorneys for the mother of the martyred Andryusha receive any compensation for your long trip or any reimbursement for expenses?"

Kosorotov contemptuously shrugged his shoulders. "Not a kopek!"

"Incidentally," Zamyslovsky continued his questioning, "have you any knowledge as to whether the experts on the side of the defense are as unselfish in their motives as you are?"

Having cast a contemptuous glance at Professors Pavlov, Bekhterev, Kokovtsev, and Troitsky, Kosorotov loftily declared, "I do not know."

However, the fact was that Professor Kosorotov received four thousand rubles from the Department of Police, for which he gave receipts to the director of the Department, Beletsky. These receipts, which were found in the department's secret safe after the February Revolution, also revealed a characteristic trait of the department. Unwilling to trust Kosorotov, who perhaps would be intimidated in court before the other expert witnesses and under pressure from their arguments would alter the opinions he had given in the preliminary investigation, the Department of Police gave him the four thousand rubles in two installments—two thousand at the time of the trip and the remaining two thousand upon his return from Kiev. Beletsky understood the mercenary nature of those with whom he dealt, and he was extremely wary.

As director of the Department (one of the sections of which was Shcheglovitov's Ministry of Justice),[4] he vigorously supported the false charges by finding the Asian expert Pranaitis and a variety of preposterous "*Zhid*-eating" brochures.

Now, in regard to the experts on questions about the Jewish religion. Professor Kokovtsov, a member of the Academy of Sciences, was, of course, the most profound and comprehensive of all the experts on the question of ritual murder. His replies to the prosecutor, the attorneys for the civil plaintiff, and the presiding judge were scathingly scornful. He did not engage so much in argumentation as in issuing decrees, as if to say: Why bother casting pearls before swine? It is not truth you want but a conviction. However, what matters to me is neither you nor Beilis; to me the most precious thing is scholarly knowledge. Everything about this celebrated scholar—his introspective gaze, his parchment-yellow face, his dispassionate voice—breathed a kind of other-wordliness.

Meanwhile, Professor Troitsky impressed everyone not only with his precise knowledge of the ancient Hebrew language and its rich writings, but also with a unique sense of honor and an unquenchable grief that such a clearly unfounded accusation could find its way into one of the courts of his own homeland—into a Russian court. His voice rang with sorrow for the scholarship flouted by the ignorant Pranaitis and with fear that an innocent man would perish. His openness and sincerity, his conscientiousness, and his unusual modesty and unpretentiousness, which paid no heed to the insolent attacks of the prosecution—all of these won him the sympathy of the overwhelming majority of his listeners.

He was a little, short-legged man, with a high forehead and intelligent eyes, who trustingly and seriously scrutinized those with whom he was conversing. With a quiet dignity, he answered any question, even if it was unrelated to the case or put caustically. And, thus, he completely disarmed his adversaries. At such moments, the most that one could sense in his voice was a mild vexation, like a gentle reprimand: "You're not catching on, my dear fellow. Hold on a bit and I'll try to explain it to you."

When one of the members of the prosecution addressed Troitsky

[4] [Gruzenberg makes this parenthetic remark sarcastically. For his views on Shcheglovitov's subservience to the Department of Police, see p. 82.]

with an insolent sneer, asking him if he could explain why the Jews always supported those who were accused of ritual murders, he did not answer, as Professor Kokovtsov and Professor Tikhomirov had done, with a scornful shrug of the shoulders and a cold, "This question does not concern me."

No, Troitsky affably and intelligibly explained, "This response is perfectly natural. When a Jew is accused of simple murder, the other Jews do not support him in the least. But any accusation of ritual murder is an accusation against all of Jewry. And the Jews know very well that ritual murders do not exist among them. Therefore, when a Jew is accused of ritual murder, the Jews consider, first, that an innocent person has been accused, and, second, that all of Jewry has been accused. How could the Jews help but speak out?"

Troitsky was filled with a profound benevolence, which did not permit him to display his strength to its fullest. He could have replied to the insolence and sarcasm of the prosecution with the devastating words, "How is it that I am an expert for the defense? Was it not the prosecution that questioned me for two months in Petersburg, as an authoritative expert, and turned away from me only when I resolutely refused to support the ignorant fabrications of Pranaitis?"

Although he could have demolished the prosecution, he did not do so, for he always thought not about crushing an adversary, but about exalting the truth. Only after he had returned to Petersburg, where the examining magistrate Mashkevich lived (the one who for two months had tried to persuade him to testify as an expert for the prosecution), and only when he was certain that his reply could not reach the jurors in Kiev and consequently influence their verdict, did Troitsky grant an interview with the press. Among other things, he reported the following fact, unparalleled in legal annals:

Those equivocal allusions and unseemly attacks that have appeared against me in several rightist newspapers have in no way affected my honor. The authors of the articles undoubtedly know that I have not been "bribed by the Jews" and that my expert testimony has been the independent opinion of an impartial specialist. Those who make sordid allusions about me know very well that earlier this year the examining magistrate for special cases Mashkevich requested me to join the Catholic Priest Pranaitis in investigating the

use of Christian blood by the Jews. My work with Pranaitis and
Mashkevich lasted more than two months and took place under the
strictest secrecy. I differed radically with Pranaitis on this question
then, and Mr. Mashkevich was well acquainted with my position.
That which I told Mashkevich concerning this question, I only
repeated later in court.[5]

For Troitsky to have had such a weapon at his disposal in court
and yet to have spared his adversary from it was indeed a mag-
nanimous act.

Korolenko wrote that he heard comments among the young
Russian magistrates, in regard to Troitsky's expert testimony, that
"at last true Russian scholarship has begun to speak."

When the expert testimony had been completed, the court, dissatisfied with the strong impression produced by the experts for
the defense, arranged to give them an insignificant remuneration,
which could not defray even half of their expenses. During one
of the recesses, the presiding judge Boldyrev said cynically, "Not
enough? Then don't come from Petersburg on business for the
Zhids. Anyway, the *kahal* pays well."

But the fact was that poor Troitsky complained to his colleagues
that the high cost of the hotel—an agricultural exhibition was
then in progress in Kiev—had consumed all the money he had
brought with him.

The experts left before the final arguments, as soon as they were
released. The morning after the acquittal, I also left for home.
The intense nervous agitation that I had experienced during the
trial, which had lasted almost five weeks, as well as during the two
months preceding it, had taken its toll. On the third day after
my return to Petersburg, I realized that I could neither take a case
nor see a client. And I knew also that there were all kinds of
celebrations still to come. I rushed to the city governor's offices
and within an hour obtained visas. Returning home, I informed
my wife, who had known nothing of the decision, which even
I had not anticipated, that in four hours we would be going abroad
on the evening train. I began to give out assignments to my assistants and to pack, but suddenly I felt that before leaving I absolutely had to see those two persons who had been closest and
dearest to me during the trial—my old friend A. S. Zarudny and
Professor Troitsky.

[5] [*Rech'* [*Speech*], October 26, 1913, 5.]

I went to Zarudny's home, where I found him in bed, completely prostrate.

"How can you hold up?" he exclaimed. "You must be indestructible."

"That's where you're wrong. I'm not holding up either. Forget about the clients, and the cases, and the fees. I'm leaving in a few hours. By the way, give me Troitsky's address. I have only an old edition of *All Petersburg*."[6] Zarudny, who was not only a prominent defense lawyer but also a precise record keeper, quickly located the address in his notebook.

Troitsky lived near the Alexander Nevsky Monastery, in one of the homes that belonged to it. I climbed the dark, slippery stairs and rang the bell. Troitsky's wife, dressed in a worn cotton jacket and carrying a tin kitchen lamp in her hands, opened the door for me.

"Let us go into the parlor," she said. "Ivan Gavriilovich[7] will be out in a moment. We have just finished dinner."

We entered a poorly furnished room, in which there were a few decrepit chairs with broken seats. Troitsky's wife set the tin lamp on the table and began to inquire about my health. Before I had time to reply, Troitsky came in, dressed in a gray canvas blouse, worn outside his trousers and tied with a sash. I stood up.

"Ivan Gavrilovich, I want to shake your hand and thank you for everything, most of all for being the person that you are."

We embraced. I reached the door and finally ventured to say, "Ivan Gavrilovich, permit me at least now to be of some aid to you. We know you were robbed by both the hotel and the court in Kiev."

"I have everything. Thank you for your warm feelings and tender words."

And now, here, looming before me, is the newspaper report of his death. What was it that Tolstoy's soldier Karataev said? I think it was: "Lay me down, O God, like a stone, and raise me up like a loaf." No, Troitsky will arise no more.

I have looked through all my notes. May the good Ivan Gavriilovich forgive me, if I do not succeed in reflecting as I ought that

[6] [A guide book and street address directory of the capital.]

[7] [Troitsky's wife refers to her husband by the archaic form of the patronymic—"Gavriilovich"—whereas Gruzenberg addresses him shortly afterward by the commonly used "Gavrilovich." Later, Gruzenberg writes "Gavriilovich," as he reflects on the memory of Troitsky (see below).]

reverence which I, together with thousands of others, feel for his majestically simple image.

Then came the revolution of 1917.

During one of the first days of the revolution, I received a telephone call from a colleague, who had been appointed to guard the files of the Department of Police. "Would you like to look through the secret materials from the Beilis case?" he asked me.

Naturally, I accepted the offer gratefully, and by evening I had been furnished with five volumes. I seized the materials greedily and spent the entire night reading them, as a result of which I learned much that had remained unclear to me in court.

I learned, for example, that police agents had been sent to the villages where the jurors on the sessional list lived. According to an official paper, this was in order to prevent the Jews from influencing the jurors in advance. It is not difficult to surmise how these agents prepared the jurors under the pretense of defending them from an imaginary Jewish influence.

I saw in these same files how the Ministry of Justice hunted all over Russia for experts on Jewish ritual from among Russian scholars and clerics. It did not find a single Russian priest with scholarly authority who would agree to meet the wishes of the government. The Ministry could find the expert it needed for its purposes only in the person of the Catholic priest Pranaitis, who had been removed for misbehavior from his post in Petersburg and transferred to Tashkent in Asia. All the prosecutor's offices of the various Russian courts were set to work getting the necessary slanderous brochures about Jewish ritual murders. An assistant prosecutor in Vilna, Karbovsky, turned out to be especially diligent and expeditious in the search for such brochures, as a result of which he was immediately transferred to Kiev and appointed to supervise the investigation of the Beilis case.

In these same secret papers of the director of the Department of Police Beletsky, I found the correspondence about placing under police surveillance those persons who sent us, the defense attorneys, sympathetic telegrams and letters during the trial. Apparently, disbelief in the fanatical ritual attributed to the Jews qualified as political unreliability.

In these same papers I saw the correspondence of Governor Giers, who did not believe that Beilis was guilty and was sure that he would be acquitted. Giers recommended postponing the hearing of the case to a later date, since Beilis' acquittal might have an effect on the government's success in the elections to the State Duma.[8]

I also saw letters addressed to me in Kiev, containing valuable information pertaining to the case. In addition, there were copies of the letters I had written to my daughter and son in Petersburg, after returning late at night from court.

I saw the instructions to detain the murderers Singaevsky and Rudzinsky at the Fastov railway station just outside Kiev, as they were being brought from prison in Siberia. This delay was to allow time for the prosecutor of the Chamber of Justice Chaplinsky, Wipper, Zamyslovsky, and the presiding judge Boldyrev to discuss the question of whether or not they should permit these witnesses to be taken to Kiev for the trial.

Think of it. A man is held in jail, the entire Jewish people is kept in fear of impending disaster, and yet the actual murderers are concealed from the jury. How, then, could any honest person, even among the monarchists, fail to recognize in this fact alone the baseness of the autocratic regime?

If one were to assume that Chaplinsky, Wipper, Zamyslovsky, and Boldyrev considered Beilis to be guilty, why did they conceal from the jury those persons who actually murdered Andryusha Yushchinsky? Apparently, they were afraid that suddenly in court the truth would burst forth, that suddenly one of these convicts, under pressure from the questioning by the defense, would spill the secret. I began to understand why the presiding judge Boldyrev cut me short and hastened to help Rudzinsky, when the latter, having become flustered, could not explain why he and two of his accomplices all went to Moscow to sell one or two dozen binoculars, when such a sale could not cover even the expense of the trip for three persons.

Then, at the very end, I read how the presiding judge had put

[8] [The trial was scheduled for the fall of 1912 and would likely have been completed just before the October elections to the Fourth Duma. Giers suggested that in the event of an acquittal public opinion would be so aroused against the government for having pressed the case that the voters would lack the "requisite peace of mind to act intelligently," that is, to vote for candidates of parties loyal to the government. His letter is reproduced, along with an English translation, in Alexander B. Tager, *The Decay of Czarism: The Beilis Trial* (Philadelphia, 1935), Appendices I and II. The trial was postponed, for various reasons, until September, 1913.]

a disguised gendarme in the jurors' deliberation room under the pretense of his being a guard, posted to attend to their needs.

While reading these papers, I recalled how Boldyrev came over to me during one of the recesses and in a humorously reproachful tone of voice remarked, "Because of you, I have to spend some of the meager funds of the Kiev Circuit Court to hire an extra guard for the jury room. The case has dragged on so long that our guard is completely worn out and cannot keep going."

I replied in the same tone of voice, "That's all right. You'll cover your extra expense by imposing costs and damages on the convicted Beilis."

I read in this secret dossier the reports of two agents of the Department of Police—Lyubimov and the former prosecutor Dyachenko. The latter sent daily telegrams to the Department of Police, in which he reported on the progress of the case. Each of these telegrams invariably noted that there was no evidence against Beilis. One of them expressed the hope that "although there is no evidence, the ignorant members of the jury, guided by a hatred of the Jews, will find the defendant guilty even without evidence." In the last of these reports, Dyachenko wrote, "The partiality of the presiding judge was especially pronounced in his charge to the jury, which bore a clearly accusatory character, in spite of the fact that the evidence against Beilis, in my opinion as a former examining magistrate and prosecutor, was very weak, or, to put it better, did not exist at all. When Boldyrev asked me what I thought of his charge to the jury, after it had gone out for deliberation, I told him frankly that I had expected greater impartiality from him."

And after Beilis' acquittal, Lyubimov wrote in despair to the Department of Police, "It was a legal Tsushima!" (Tsushima was the site of the destruction of the Russian fleet during the Japanese War.)

When I finished reading the secret materials of the Department of Police that had been sent to me, dawn was already breaking. I went to the window, looked at the empty street, then across from my apartment at the barracks of the Volynia Life-Guards Regiment, bedecked with red flags, and I said to myself, "We can thank fate that a people in revolt has swept away the dishonorable tsarist regime like a cobweb."

Am I right? Should not an infected sheepskin be thrown into the furnace? Or has personal resentment blinded my mind and

123

along with it my conscience? As verification of my views, let me quote a statement made a few days after the abdication of the Tsar by M. O. Menshikov, a favorite journalist of the upper bureaucracy and circles at Court. Writing in *Novoe Vremya* [*New Time*], he said, "The autocracy, having betrayed its people for centuries, finally betrayed itself."

Chapter 14

The Delirium of War · Part One

Late in the winter of 1907, I was invited to defend several persons at a court-martial in Vilna [Vilnius]. They were charged under Article 102 of the Criminal Code with belonging to an association that had as its goal the forcible overthrow of the existing regime and having at their disposal explosives and weapons, smuggled in by some of their fellow members. They were also found to have leaflets in their possession.

I arrived in Vilna, got acquainted with the case, and visited the defendants, but I could understand neither the case nor them. They were ignorant, with no conception of the political parties and their aims. Two of them strongly resembled knights of the green custom house;[1] indeed, they fitted the part exactly. When I asked about the weapons and explosives, they claimed to know absolutely nothing and in bewilderment conjectured that someone must have planted them.

The day of the trial arrived with the court convening behind closed doors. The indictment was read, and the examination began. Although the chief witnesses for the prosecution, some insignificant Okhrana agents, did not appear, this failure to report was lawful, since they resided in another judicial district. Those who did appear were of little consequence.

There were several defense counsels, among whom I recall a talented and amiable lawyer from Kovno [Kaunas], V. P. Shipilin. We put questions to the witnesses as a matter of form and did not listen to their answers, because we knew in advance that the answers would be as empty as our questions. Both were like a

[1] [A current jocular name for contrabandists.]

slight splash in an abandoned well, hardly drawing anyone's attention.

The court directed that the reports from the searches and inspections of the confiscated goods be read intermittently with the examination of the witnesses. It also asked that the testimonies of the absent witnesses be read. This was all very boring, which was dangerous to the proceedings, because boredom carries with it indifference, toward both the defendants and the truth.

"Now the interesting part begins," whispered my colleague, as he glanced at the list of witnesses. "It's time for the gendarme officer Myasoedov, who's a witness to the 'good name' of my client, since he's well acquainted with him from Verzhbolovo [Virbalis]."

Myasoedov entered. He gave an excellent testimonial for the defendant who had called him. The defense began to see a glimmer of hope. Maybe it would be possible to get something from the witness that would be of benefit to the whole case. We began carefully, as though treading with bare feet on broken glass. Before coming to the important questions, we needed to comprehend the character of the witness. Our questions moved from the general to the particular, from the indifferent to the important, gradually becoming narrower, with the intent that should something go wrong, the interests of the defense would suffer only on insignificant points. On the basis of Myasoedov's answers, we formed the following impression: He was more cunning than intelligent; he would aim diligently, but just as he was about to pull the trigger, he would lose his aim; he was easily excitable, in spite of being rather flaccid; he would say more than he intended, particularly things that he had intended not to say; and, finally, he had been offended by something. Thus, we were able to narrow the circle of questions and proceed to the main ones with a good chance of success. The defense posed them quickly and decisively.

"Have the defendants present here appeared on your lists?"

Myasoedov replied with pride, "I serve in the railroad police, not in the Okhrana."

"It is precisely because you are in charge of a gendarme *border station* that you surely have lists of political suspects. So, I repeat, have these persons appeared on your lists; and, if so, what was said about them?"

Myasoedov responded, "But, you must know, such information is a matter of official secrecy, and I have no right to disclose it."

The defense cited the Senate's decision in the case of the Moscow newspaper editor Kazetsky and asked the presiding judge to order the witness to answer.

I should note that in the Kazetsky case the Senate had handed down an amazing decision, which came at a most reactionary time, not only for us but for the whole of Europe. It occurred during the controversy over the Dreyfus affair with its sad performance in court, when the generals refused to answer the most important questions posed by the court, hiding behind "official secrecy," and in some instances even behind "a veiled woman."[2] At exactly the same time, a decision of historical significance was handed down here in Russia. The editor Kazetsky, who had been charged with slander, called as witnesses the officers who were members of the arbitration tribunal handling the plaintiff's case.[3] Referring to a disciplinary statute, the witnesses refused to testify about what had taken place in the closed session of the tribunal. Thus deprived of witnesses, the defendant was convicted of slander. The case proceeded to the Senate. The report was entrusted to A. F. Koni, who applied to it not only talent but also a noble persistence and a large measure of professional tact. Under his influence the Chief Prosecutor requested the opinion of the Minister of War. The legal counsel for the Ministry, Lokhvitsky, wrote a brilliant argument, in which he admitted that in the interests of justice all other considerations must give way. The Minister of War Kuropatkin concurred in this reasoning. The Senate instructed that the famous term "official secret" must not interfere with the court in its quest for truth. However, with the assigning of political cases to the courts in 1906, this interpretation was soon turned into empty words. The civilian judges rarely paid any attention to it, and neither did the Senate. Only in the courts-martial did one still find strict adherents to the law, who considered the Senate's interpretation still binding.

Our presiding judge turned out to be one of these adherents to the law. He recognized that the citation to the Kazetsky case was

[2] [In the Dreyfus treason case, which took place in France during the 1890s, it was alleged that an anonymous "veiled woman" had supplied a copy of a secret document from the Ministry of War, proving Dreyfus' guilt, but that for reasons of official secrecy this and other incriminating documents could not be made public, because they might provoke a war against France.]

[3] [An arbitration tribunal, or court of honor, attempted to resolve personal conflicts among officers; it was not actually a judicial body.]

relevant, and he told the witness, "Since I did not rule out of order the question put by the defense, then it is both legitimate and pertinent to the case. Be so kind as to answer it. The counsel for the defense wants to know whether the defendants present here appeared on your lists."

Myasoedov hesitated for a moment. Then, as though a dam had broken inside him, disclosures, each more surprising than the last, flowed forth in a raging torrent. I posed the questions more emphatically.

"No, they did not appear on my lists. Some of them were suspected of smuggling, but not one of them of political activities."

"You say not one. However, bundles of leaflets, weapons, and explosives were found in their possession."

Myasoedov replied with a smirk, "Of course, they were found. They could have been found in my possession, too."

"I don't understand. Please explain."

"The game is a simple one. Okhrana agents gave some of the defendants packages to be smuggled, without saying anything about their contents; and they planted weapons and explosives on others during the search."

"Who did this? Your people?"

"My people don't so such things. Some of Captain Ponomarev's people were working here under his direction. He would come here. . . ."

"You said that explosives and leaflets could have been found in your possession. How should these words be taken—as a manner of speaking or as a fact?"

"Those of us at Verzhbolovo often go to Eidkunen [Eydtkuh-nen] out of boredom. I do so myself. I've made a lot of friends there during my long years of service in Verzhbolovo. Once when I was returning from Eidkunen late in the evening, I discovered explosives and literature in my automobile. This coincided with the period when Captain Ponomarev was working here. If I hadn't noticed what was happening in time, even I would have been publicly disgraced."

"Who would be interested in bringing a false charge against you, the head of a gendarme section?"

"Someone who wished to have me replaced would be greatly interested."

"But who do you think would have wished to do this?"

"Why, Captain Ponomarev, of course."

"Now, which Ponomarev do you mean—the one who used to be a student at the Petersburg Mining Institute?"

"That's the one."

I recalled the story told by Professors L. I. Lutugin and V. I. Bauman about the triumphant diligence with which a former student named Ponomarev had conducted a search of their dwellings.

The prosecutor submitted two or three questions for verification, but soon, having given up the task as hopeless, he broke off the questioning. The presiding judge gave orders to enter into the court record Myasoedov's testimony in its entirety. The judges sat there, confounded and offended.

The trial lay in filth, and a palpable feeling of repugnance hung heavy over everyone. If only it were possible to leave sooner and wash oneself thoroughly.

Somehow, the rest of the examination passed quickly. The prosecutor gloomily upheld the charge without looking at the judges. The defense sensed that the judges had reached that high state of inner tension after which a rapid descent begins. It limited itself to a careful observation that in the amusing comedy disclosed by the gendarme captain, the judges and the defendants had been assigned equally tragic roles: the former to impose punishment without guilt, the latter in their innocence to endure the torment of this punishment.

The judges remained in the conference chamber for a long time, but not because they were discussing the fate of the defendants. There was, of course, no question as to acquittal. Rather, the judges were preparing a special ruling, which not only acquitted all of the defendants but also directed that the Ministry of Internal Affairs be notified about the activities of the gendarmerie that had been disclosed.

The fact that the case had been heard behind closed doors did not prevent the press from devoting considerable attention to the verdict and the special ruling of the court, as did also the State Duma.

Two or three months passed. One evening, as I was receiving clients, a portly man in civilian clothes walked into my office. Automatically I pointed to a chair and asked the stereotyped question: "How can I be of service?"

"You didn't recognize me. I am Myasoedov . . . the witness."

I took a closer look. His face was sunken, his eyes frightened.

"Forgive me for not recognizing you. Civilian clothing changes military people so much. And besides, there was no chance to get acquainted with you. I saw you only from a distance."

"It's not only the clothing that has changed me. Grief has changed me even more. You said, and the presiding judge supported you, that before the court there can be no official secrecy. All the same, my Minister considered that in answering your questions I violated an official obligation. I am being dismissed as chief of the Verzhbolovo gendarme section and offered a transfer to the Northeast. I am going to quit altogether and retire. They'll get rid of me in a few months anyway. You don't know what the Okhrana is like. It's a hornets' nest. I've stepped on it, and I shall never be forgiven. If I had gone over to the revolutionaries or committed a major crime, they would have forgiven me more easily than for the testimony I gave in court. No, I cannot even think of serving any longer. Help me find a position in a bank or in some business."

"I'm sorry that I unintentionally caused you harm. I'm ready to do anything for you, but I'm not in a position to do very much. I have few connections in the financial and business world."

Myasoedov looked dejected; and, apparently offended, he abruptly changed his plea to a reproach.

"Of course, for you I am not a human being—only a hated gendarme. You must remember, however, that if it had not been for your questions, I would not have to be pleading with you."

I answered that I did not feel any guilt. I had fulfilled my duties as a defense counsel, and he as a witness. I was not refusing to intercede for him, but was merely warning him of probable failure. I asked him to stop again in a few days.

I began to work diligently on his behalf, but unfortunately without any success. It was not so much his previous service that was a hindrance, as his lack of training for a position of responsibility. People were ashamed to offer him something petty.

Myasoedov came to see me again. My news of failures only saddened him, and we parted with the agreement that if I were to find anything I would write. I did not need to do so, since I found nothing for him.

More than four years passed. Then, one day I read in the newspapers that Myasoedov was again serving in the gendarme corps and had been assigned to the Minister of War. A few months later, a note appeared in one of the evening papers, unequivocally attributing Myasoedov with espionage. In revenge against the paper, Myasoedov rudely assaulted the editor. Two or three days later, A. I. Guchkov, the chairman of the Commission on State Defense and a member of the State Duma, repeated the same accusation in a newspaper interview. And a few days after that, he fought a duel with Myasoedov, who had challenged him. Thus, Guchkov as much as admitted that his accusation was unfounded, for one must assume that spies are not the kind of men with whom one would care to fight a duel.

This purely logical deduction of mine unexpectedly found factual confirmation from a person whose competence was beyond dispute. Toward the end of May, General A. A. Polivanov, who was then Assistant Minister of War, entrusted me with a case involving a certain respected military family. One of the persons who met with us to discuss the case was the Chief Military Prosecutor, A. S. Makarenko, who had recommended me. After we completed the business arrangements and began to talk about other things, Polivanov turned to General Makarenko. "By the way, Alexander Sergeevich, how is your investigation? Have you questioned Alexander Ivanovich (Guchkov)?"

Makarenko answered gloomily, "Indeed we have. He gave us nothing—not a single fact."

After Polivanov had gone, Makarenko, somewhat annoyed, explained to me, "We were talking about Myasoedov. Prior to my present assignment, General Belyaev sent an inquiry to staff headquarters, requesting all their secret information, but there was nothing that could substantiate or even explain to some extent the campaign against Myasoedov. Then inquiries were sent to the Department of Police, but again not a thing. After this the Minister of War put me in charge of the investigation, and I appointed M. N. Palibin* to conduct it under my supervision. We impatiently awaited Guchkov's testimony. And what came of it? A complete disappointment. Nothing concrete, nothing factual. All he would tell us was that he was convinced and that he had some kind of information. From whom was he concealing facts and names? Whom was he afraid to trust with them? The Chief Military Prosecutor's office? Staff headquarters? And finally, if one were to assume that Guchkov had carelessly promised not to reveal

* M. N. Palibin was head of the legislative section of the Main Court-Martial Administration. His wide juridical knowledge and strict fairness gained him general recognition in the military judicial community. In 1917, on the recommendation of his colleagues, he was appointed as a member of the Main Court-Martial by the Provisional Government.

his source of information, he could and should have been com-pelled, in the name of important interests of state, to say who was concealing himself by extracting such a promise, as well as con-cealing evidence for exposing the traitor. The same with the jour-nalists. Apparently, they were drawing their information either from Guchkov or from the same source he was using."

When I raised the point of why Guchkov would unjustly im-pute guilt to a person whom he did not know, Makarenko replied, "It must be that someone cleverly made up stories for him. After Myasoedov gave his testimony in court, he gained many enemies in military circles. It was easy for Guchkov to believe what he heard, and in his political struggle with Sukhomlinov he hastily made the most of it."

A little over two years later, the war broke out. Everyone tried somehow to ease the suffering of those at the front. I, too, helped supply a train with gifts from the Petersburg Jewish community. One day I stopped at a store for officers on Bolshaya Konyushennaya Street. In the crowd, lined up in all directions. I came across Colonel Myasoedov. He bowed and stopped me. In spite of the six and a half years that had passed since the day he appeared in my office, he had changed very little. He had only gotten flabby and looked more haggard. With an unpleasant smile he muttered, as he put out his hand, "There can be no secrets before the court, isn't that the way it goes? How much grief that damned trial has brought me."

"What can be done?" I answered. "At present you should feel gratified, since both newspapers that made statements against you retracted their accusations." And using the crowd to my advan-tage, I bowed and moved on.

A few months later, I became aware that Myasoedov was intri-cately linked with the needless destruction of two persons. The episode to which I refer took place during the second half of Feb-ruary, 1915. One evening, during office hours, the assistant pros-ecutor of the Kovno Circuit Court, A. H. Freinat, came to see me. He had visited me several times before, during his trips to Petersburg, about a case involving a close acquaintance of his. Though he had always been calm and reserved, that day he was very excited.

"I am in great trouble," he began. "Three days ago my brother, Otto Heinrichovich, was arrested. Only today I managed to learn from one of his former colleagues in the Ministry that he is being charged with state treason. Colonel Myasoedov was arrested at the front on a charge of espionage, and my brother is being drawn into this affair. He asks you to take his defense."

I vividly recalled Kishinev: the Jewish pogrom trial, the Special Tribunal of the Odessa Chamber of Justice, the members of the court, and among them the cheerful, energetic figure of the examining magistrate for special cases, Otto Heinrichovich Freinat. Russian liberals and the Jewish population were dissatisfied with him, for he conducted the case prejudicially, trying to cover up the guilt of the officials in the pogrom. However, everyone recognized his diligence and remarkable capacity for work. After the trial he was appointed as an assistant prosecutor, and a few years later he was transferred to Petersburg to the Ministry of Internal Affairs, where he served on special assignments under the Minister.

A. H. Freinat continued, "I managed to learn that the main evidence against my brother is that not long before the war, while representing his ministry at an exhibition of police and military dogs in Petersburg, he gave explanations to some foreign delegates in German. The fact is also being cited that upon his retirement at the beginning of the war, he became a member of the board of directors of several stockholding companies, which, though they were Russian, had Germans as major stockholders." I expressed the hope that everything would be cleared up and that his brother would not require a defense.

Two days later, another man came to see me. His name was Boris Freiberg. I doubt that I shall ever forget him. He was a tall, stately, handsome man, thirty to thirty-five years of age, with sad eyes and a voice that touched the heart. After an hour's conversation, I understood, or rather sensed, that this was one of those clients whom a criminal defense lawyer is afraid to encounter. They rapidly tear down the thin but sturdy wall that distinguishes a client from a friend, and without which a lawyer may change easily and imperceptibly from a legal adviser to a concealer of crime.

There are many books dealing with legal ethics. They are mostly devoted to simple questions, which any decent person could adequately answer. But they are powerless in instructing you how to conduct a conversation face to face with a person whom the law has entrusted you with helping, how to resist his melancholy plea for advice and assistance. No one will hear, no one will ever find out, so why not lighten his suffering and give him directions? A book cannot insulate you nor rescue you from the compassion that entangles you like a web.

Over the years every defense counsel subjectively and uniquely works out his own manner of rescuing himself from the crossfire of compassion and duty. One of them, with whose experiences I am intimately acquainted, would conjure up the following vision during the hours of conversation with criminal clients: He would imagine his personal foes standing on both sides of him, and as soon as he felt himself wanting to lower his voice or glance at them during the answer to one of his client's questions, he would stop short and get hold of himself. But this struggle to keep from being overcome by another's grief, this struggle with oneself for the right to self-esteem, consumes so much inner strength that frequently a criminal defense lawyer feels more fatigued after half an hour of private conversation with a client than after a courtroom battle that has lasted many days.

Freiberg told me that he lived in Libava [Liepaja], where together with his brothers, he had owned an emigration office for about ten years, which had been converted into the Northwest Steamship Company. For dealing with the ministries and administrative officials, they had selected as president of the company, in 1911, a retired Colonel Myasoedov, whom they had known from Verzhbolovo. Around Christmastime, one of the directors of the company, Robert Falk, was forbidden residency in the Baltic area. When local attempts to have this regulation revoked failed, they decided to call on Myasoedov, who, according to their information, was on friendly terms with the Deputy Commander of the Military District, Governor-General Kurlov. Recently Freiberg had telegraphed Myasoedov several times, summoning Myasoedov to meet him in various towns, but there had been no answer. Meanwhile, the gendarme captain in Libava, who fully trusted Freiberg's loyalty, informed him that instructions had been received by telegraph from the front to search Freiberg's home and make an arrest. Freiberg thereupon left for Vilna, where he had earlier summoned Myasoedov to meet him. Here he learned that Myasoedov had been arrested on a charge of espionage. He immediately left for Petrograd to consult with me. What should he do? Go home to Libava or into hiding? The latter would be very distressful for him, since he was not guilty of anything.

I replied that one does not consult a lawyer about such questions, but rather one's pillow—that one resolves these questions with his own mind and conscience, and at his own risk.

"You are answering me as a jurist, and I am asking you as a human being."

"I can answer you only as a jurist."

"All right. But what would you do if you were in my place?"

"It is not easy to answer this question either. One way is an assumed danger, and the other is a real one. As for myself, I would not run away. I would seek justice in order to cut the throats of my accusers. To the devil with them—it's one or the other of us."

Freiberg rose quickly, and, shaking my hand, he said happily, "Now I know what to do. I am going home!"

"Here now, you've decided too quickly. Think about it! You surely know the saying: 'I can easily unravel another's troubles, but I have no idea how to solve my own.'"

But Freiberg was not listening any longer, and, retreating toward the door, he persistently repeated only one thing, "I must go home. May I count on your defense?"

"Perhaps a defense won't even be allowed, and you'll be handed over immediately to a field court."

"I understand this. But if a defense is allowed, will you come to defend me?"

"Absolutely, no matter how busy I am. But once more, don't go by what someone else would do. Take good counsel with your pillow."

At the door he turned and glanced at me with a good-natured smile. A handsome man, tall, broad shouldered.

About two weeks later, one of his relatives came to see me. He told me that on the day after visiting me, Freiberg left for Libava and went to the gendarme captain. The latter arrested him and handed him over to the military authorities in Warsaw. He was followed immediately by his wife and a lawyer-in-training from Libava by the name of Livshitz.

It seemed that everything was going legally and properly. He was taken to Warsaw, where Colonel Myasoedov was to be tried. This was necessary according to basic legal procedure, which required that all participants in a crime be tried in the same court, specifically in the one to which the main defendant was assigned.

Two or three days later, I was surprised to read in the newspapers that Myasoedov's trial had been held on March 18. He was the only one tried and by a *field court* at that—and just a month after his arrest! He was hanged the same night that he was convicted. This haste aroused some extremely serious doubts. Myasoedov's accomplices had been brought to Warsaw, and the material for the accusations against them was the same as against Myasoedov, and vice versa. The forthcoming general trial should have and could have revealed major clues to an espionage organization, but suddenly, with incomprehensible haste, they exterminated the culprit, the central figure of the criminal organization. It looked as though it was not the co-defendants who were afraid to meet their leader at court, but rather the prosecution.[4]

The further things went, the worse they got. From one of Freiberg's relatives, who came to see me about a month later, I learned a new, incomprehensible fact. Freiberg's brother David had gone to Warsaw to see him and was granted permission to do so. A few days later, the lawyer-in-training Livshitz visited the prison in order to give some money to the prison administration for improving Boris Freiberg's food, a customary procedure for him, though on that day he brought seventy-five rubles instead of the usual fifty. Upon leaving, he joined David Freiberg, who had been waiting for him in the street. They had barely started on their way when they heard someone running behind them, shouting "Stop!" It turned out to be officials of the prison administration as well as some others.

Both men were arrested and charged, David Freiberg with belonging to an espionage organization and Livshitz with preparing an escape for members of a criminal organization. Together with Boris Freiberg, O. H. Freinat, and some others, they were tried in the summer of 1915. Freinat and Livshitz were acquitted, but David Freiberg was sentenced to several years of hard labor, and Boris Freiberg—the one who had gone of his own free will—was sentenced to be hanged. They were tried without defense counsels, since a defense was not permitted.

The sentence was carried out, but even at that the Supreme Commander-in-Chief, Grand Prince Nikolay Nikolaevich, scheduled a new trial, this time in Dvinsk [Daugavpils], for Freinat

---

[4] [Doubts about Myasoedov's guilt have persisted over the years. A recent study, utilizing extensive archival materials, has concluded that Myasoedov was falsely convicted of espionage in an effort to help explain Russian war losses in the sector where he served. K. F. Shatsillo, " 'Delo' polkovnika Miasoedova" [The Colonel Myasoedov 'Case'], *Voprosy istorii* [*Problems of History*], No. 4 (April, 1967), 103–16.]

and Livshitz, who had been acquitted, and David Freiberg, who had been sentenced to hard labor. The directive for this trial included a clause prohibiting a defense, an unprecedented action in the history of the court. The law for these defendants was revoked by the will of the Grand Prince, though only recently it had been confirmed by the Chief Military Prosecutor, A. S. Makarenko, as applicable in a case pertaining to a client of mine, the miller Chekhovsky. (I shall return to this case later, when I discuss A. S. Makarenko, a sympathetic man, who was a steadfast guardian of the law, even in the lawless time of war.)

I rushed to Makarenko. In answer to my plea he said, "I cannot help you. The theater of military operations is outside my jurisdiction. The will of the Supreme Commander-in-Chief is the law there. Unfortunately, our military affairs are going badly and it's necessary to find excuses. They are looking for guilty parties, and, of course, they lay the blame first of all on the ethnic minorities, since that is the simplest thing to do. But they accuse others, too. I received a copy of the interrogation sheet from the Myasoedov case. It was outrageous, even if he was a disgusting fellow. They found him guilty on the basis of the first question: espionage before the war. But in this question there was not a single factual indication, even a remote one, as to what evidential material the judges were supposed to examine. The text of the law on espionage had simply been copied down—and that was the extent of it. That way it was possible to charge anyone with anything. Then there was the question of whether Myasoedov was guilty of espionage *during the war*. They broke this question into three parts. In the first, they concluded that, for the purpose of gathering information for the Germans, Myasoedov had obtained addresses and gone to the front. Of course, they failed to acknowledge that in regard to the addresses and his trip to the front he had been acting on orders from his superiors! But in the second and third parts of the question, which dealt with charges of passing on this information to the Germans, they came up with nothing. Twice they had to answer: No! This is how the charges of espionage turned out. However, they did find him guilty of pillaging, that is, of pillaging the Germans. You see, they discovered several figurines and engravings in his possession."

After this conversation, it became clear to me how it had been possible to convict Boris Freiberg without any facts and to schedule a double trial for his brother by crudely violating the laws of ju-

dicial procedure. An "obviously malicious person"[5] had been convicted, so those close to him, because of their posts as directors of
the steamship company, had to be convicted, too.

It should be added that the solicitation of the Supreme Commander-in-Chief ended in success. David Freiberg was also sentenced to death, and O. H. Freinat paid for his conversation
in German at the "dog exhibition" with hard labor. Only the lawyer-in-training Livshitz was acquitted for the second time.

Soon afterwards, David Freiberg's wife visited me while returning home through Petersburg. A small, tormented woman,
dressed entirely in black, she told me about the last hours of her
husband and his brother, and asked me what she should do about
the family and the tiny remains of the property.

I listened to her story, which was as meek, quiet, and sorrowful
as she herself. I looked at her, but in the place where she was
seated at the desk I saw someone else, someone who half a year
before had anxiously sought an answer from me: Should he trust
himself to the court?

The force of prejudice.

Soon after General A. A. Polivanov was appointed Minister of
War, I had occasion to talk with him on a serious matter. The
Jewish community was disturbed about the blatant unfairness of
one of General Yanushkevich's plans. In proposing to call up
ahead of schedule a new quota of students from the institutions
of higher learning, in order to replenish the enormous losses among
the officers, he recommended that Christians be sent to accelerated
officer courses, and Jews to the lower ranks at the front.

I called Polivanov. He confirmed the rumor and invited me to
stop and see him during the evening. He ended our lengthy conversation on the question by admitting the validity of my arguments that this abusive inequality among those giving their blood
in the line of duty was inadmissible; and he declared categorically,
"The Ministry of War will not propose nor approve the draft
of such a law. Either the new quota of Jewish students will go
through the officer courses on the same basis as their Christian
classmates, or they will not be called up at all. That is, unless
headquarters issues this law without consulting me."

---

[5] [This was a popular expression at the time and a typical judgment by
lay persons, which Gruzenberg apparently used in this instance to
emphasize the unprofessional attitude of the judges.]

Then, as he walked around the huge study of the ministerial apartments, he remarked with a smile, "Myasoedov used to stroll around these apartments, and, taking advantage of the carelessness of Sukhomlinov, who would leave secret documents on the desk and in unlocked drawers, he made the necessary excerpts from the documents for getting information to the Germans."

Surprised by such certainty and so precise an account, I replied, "Why then did the investigation by Alexander Sergeevich not yield the slightest confirmation? Why did neither headquarters nor the Department of Police provide anything in support of the accusation?"

Polivanov's injured neck twitched nervously, but his uncommonly affable smile remained unchanged, as he proceeded softly, "Do you think that such cases are easily discovered? However, I do recall a document from the Department of Police. It indicated that Myasoedov, while a member of the Ministry of War, was at the same time engaged in private business for pay, that he headed some steamship line for transporting emigrants. In fact, it was because of this document that my relationship with Sukhomlinov was irreparably spoiled. It arrived during one of his official trips"— Polivanov indicated either Turkestan or some other region beyond the Caspian Sea—"while I was performing the duties of Minister of War. Since the envelope was addressed to Sukhomlinov as Minister and not as a private person, I was obligated to open it, despite the fact that it was marked secret. I don't know how, but the contents of the document became known to certain members of the State Duma. Sukhomlinov depicted me to the top authorities as an intriguer. There was nothing left for me to do but resign."

Chapter 15

The Delirium of War · Part Two

The press indicated, with reference to *War and Peace*, that Myasoedov's fate was analogous to that of the merchant's son Vereshchagin in the Patriotic War. This comparison was hardly correct. The governor of Moscow, Rastopchin, abandoned Vereshchagin to the incensed crowd just as deliberately as travelers, in order to save themselves, throw some game to the wolves pursuing them. In the case of Myasoedov and the brothers Freiberg, the reason lay much deeper. And if we need a literary reference to understand it, then the following lines, at the beginning of the third volume of *War and Peace*, seem most appropriate: "Millions of people were inflicting countless acts of evil on one another: frauds, treasons, thefts, forgeries, issuance of false currency, robberies, arsons, and murders, which for centuries would not be collected in the annals of all the courts in the world, but which during this period were not regarded as crimes by the people who were committing them."

In this list of crimes accompanying war, crimes not concealed because they are only a pale shadow of the main shadow, Tolstoy missed the most characteristic one. It is the one born amid the curses and groans of the wounded and dying, which creeps along with the bloody fog from the fields of battle, meandering, drifting afar, at times covering the entire land. At first it rustles in a whisper, then begins to rumble more loudly, until it ends with the erratic cry: Treason! Treason! Treason!

In thousands of localities in the war zone or only adjacent to it, this cry awakens and ignites a slumbering hatred toward individuals—"obviously malicious persons"—and toward groups, ethnic

140

ones in particular. One hears the reproach: "What is our homeland to them? They dream about how to ruin it, how to make it
worthless." Whoever is branded with this scorching mark—"treason"—will rarely be saved. Rarely, even by the crown.

During the last war, which required such superhuman effort
and produced such inhuman cruelty, the country began the delirium early, as soon as the reverses began on the Polish front. As
a bear bitten by a swarm of gnats rolls bellowing on the ground,
clawing at its body, so millions of people, having become panicky
from the losses and injuries, began to confuse the innocent with
the guilty. There would have been some excuse, if it had been
only the crowd. But it was not. It was even those who ought to
have been sensible, not only in their heads but in their hearts and
in their very blood. It was even the *judges*! They were inflamed,
shaken by the feverish, almost inconquerable delirium of war.

My personal observations dated from the following incident.
Five or six months after the beginning of the war, two distinguished Polish lawyers requested me to defend a client of theirs
before the Main Court-Martial. He was a German engineer, who
had been sentenced to death. For many years he had lived in
Warsaw, where he owned a technical business. On what evidence
had he been brought to trial and convicted? First of all he had
hung on his wall a map of military operations with little flags
pinned to it—something that could be found in every home at that
time. Second, an anecdote in the form of a livestock dealer's letter
to his family had been discovered among the accused man's diaries
and papers. The gist of this "Witz"[1] lay in the interchanging of
family endearments with the names of various kinds of livestock.
The authorities bringing the charges had decided that this was a
code used for espionage, and that by pigs it meant infantry, by
calves—cavalry, and by bulls—artillery. In vain the man assured
them that he had heard this anecdote from a lady he knew at a
resort and that he had idly written it down because it was amusing.
They did not believe him and sentenced him to death.

Grounds for cassation proceedings were weak, or, to be exact,
imaginary. From a technical point of view, the case was moving
along smoothly, and I had nothing to get hold of in writing an
appeal. I felt that if anything could save the accused man, it cer-

[1] [German for "joke."]

tainly was not cassation procedures. Only some striking fact, which would explain the ill-fated anecdote, could dispel the delirium. It occurred to me that I had either read or heard this anecdote some two years before the war. My assistants began to rummage through the "weeklies," and one of them managed to locate it. Word for word it was the same as that found in the possession of the accused.

A major technical difficulty remained to be overcome. How could we acquaint the Main Court-Martial with the material we had obtained, when the law forbade not only the introduction of new evidence into cassation proceedings, but anything touching on the substance of the case? We were fortunate that the presiding judge, S. A. Bykov, was a man of insatiable intellect. Attracted by the uniqueness of the case, he did not prevent the truth from breaking through the cordon of legal technicalities. He allowed me to use the new material to illustrate a particular technical argument and to point out that the fundamental fault of the verdict and of the indictment was the lack of analysis, for if the anecdote indeed were written in a figurative language, it should have been deciphered in order to reveal whether it carried any secret message.

The Main Court-Martial reversed the verdict and directed that the case be examined anew. About two months later, it was heard by the same Warsaw Court-Martial, and this time the ill-fated lover of anecdotes was acquitted.

For a long time I could not divorce myself from the distressing question of which was more absurd—the clumsy German "Witz" or the casual formulation of a court case entailing the death penalty.

Let me recount another incident I experienced involving the delirious visions that are a consequence of war. On September 26, 1914, during a raging artillery battle near Druskeniki [Druskininkai], a whistle blew for work to begin at the steam mill belonging to the merchant Chekhovsky, a well-known resident of the town. But the riff-raff decided that there was more to the whistle than this, that it was a signal for correcting the enemy gunfire; and their conjectures infected even those who were more stable. A crowd rushed to the mill. Since the worker who had blown the whistle fled to safety, and the miller Chekhovsky took refuge with a respected Christian family, the crowd vented its enraged fear by killing an innocent deaf-mute German, who had long been

known to everyone and who had no connection whatsoever with
the mill. They threw his corpse into the woods outside the town,
barely covering it with fallen leaves. Later, the dogs dug it out and
mutilated it badly.

After a few days, when the excitement had died down, Chekhovsky returned home; and there he was arrested. The investigation
that was conducted yielded nothing. Nevertheless, an indictment was drawn up, and Chekhovsky was handed over to the
Vilna Court-Martial. Some civic leaders in Vilna requested me to
take the defense and filed the appropriate application. However,
I received a telegram that the presiding judge had handed down a
decision not to allow a defense. What was there to do? Sit back
with folded arms and await the verdict on a defenseless man, so
that afterwards on behalf of the condemned prisoner we could
make an appeal for cassation, which might not get past the military
administration? I considered such passivity to be inadmissible;
and being convinced that there was a judicial error in the court's
decision, I went to the Chief Military Prosecutor, who was also
head of the Main Court-Martial Administration.

I have already mentioned A. S. Makarenko, and I shall need
to refer to him subsequently as well, for I am one of those indebted
to him. Neither time, nor the anguish of emigration, nor a re-
assessment of my former relations with people can weaken my
gratitude and affection toward him for all the good he did. He
enchanted me with his intellect and his marvelous gift for understanding people, as well as the most tangled situations. I knew
that he was a staunch monarchist, inclined toward the right, but
I was also certain that he would use the court neither for vengeance
nor for favors. Nothing could have moved him to seek personal
or professional success at the expense of another's fate or by acting
with servility or deceit. At the same time, he knew and trusted that
I would not misuse his clemency and that my frequent interces-
sions on behalf of those involved in political cases were not connected with any kind of personal gain.

When the espionage scare began, I was overwhelmed by the grief
of many of the families, and I found myself unexpectedly interceding for "the spies"—the imaginary spies. Makarenko did not
waver in his relationship toward me, and with his previous trust
he responded to each of my requests. It was touching to see not
only what he did, but how he did it. Only Russians, and then only

very good ones, are able to give joy in such a way that the receiver sometimes cannot discern whether he is receiving it or is himself giving it.

Makarenko withstood the impact of the delirious wave and tirelessly fought for the preservation of legality, even in time of war. The battlefront, as it grew wider and wider, was at the same time narrowing his jurisdiction; but even in the war zone, he contrived to get his way by recommending his associates for positions there. His recommendations, however, were at times rejected, for his associates were not always to the taste of those at Court. For example, the Petrograd military prosecutor Manteuffel* was soon compelled to leave his post at the front, where he was working with General Ruzsky, because his personal adherence to the law and his demand of the same from others annoyed the Chief of Staff, General Bonch-Bruevich.

Makarenko did even more good by administering mercy and easing the fate of those convicted. As head of the Main Court-Martial Administration, he had jurisdiction, as before, over those who had been convicted by the courts-martial, except for those sentenced to death; and this allowed him to correct errors and to soften the cruelty. He was not well liked in "higher circles." However, he was still so greatly respected that when the government made a feverish attempt to make peace with society during the first days of the February Revolution, Makarenko was appointed—not only without his consent but without his knowledge—to be Minister of Internal Affairs. But as we know, this new government was not destined to fulfill its obligations.

On February 23, Makarenko was arrested by the revolutionary crowd and taken to the Peter and Paul Fortress. On the way he became so exasperated at the revolvers placed to his head that he shouted sternly, "Either pull the trigger or take them away." After a few days, a small group of us lawyers managed to free him from the fortress. Two months later, as soon as I was appointed chairman of the Commission on Corruption in the Navy Department, I asked for his collaboration. However, we were not able to work together very long, for when October came, the commission was disbanded. I kept track of his subsequent fate only from hear-

*After the October Revolution, Manteuffel, being in desperate need, became a freight hauler, but soon overexerted himself and died in great suffering.

say. Apparently, he was Minister of Justice under Denikin, and then transferred to the Main Court-Martial.*

But to return to the case of the miller Chekhovsky. When I pointed out to Makarenko, as Chief Military Prosecutor, the attempt by the Court-Martial Administration to close the doors to a defense, he did not hide behind technicalities nor refer me to cassation proceedings, but sent a directive to Vilna that a defense was to be permitted. This legal interpretation was extremely important. I hastened to have it officially confirmed in writing, and I sent copies to prominent lawyers in the war zone, as well as to the press.

Chekhovsky's case had been proceeding behind closed doors for two days. The presiding judge, who made the ruling against permitting a defense, was a rather unfeeling, proper German. The other members of the court were an infantry lieutenant-colonel and a cavalry officer, a former adjutant of General Rennenkampf. On the first day the infantry lieutenant-colonel followed the intricacies of the examination with great concentration. It appeared that he was soon convinced of the innocence of the defendant, since he later ceased to be interested in the aimless fussing. He only looked sympathetically at the defendant and the defense. The third judge, the former adjutant of Rennenkampf, who strongly resembled his patron both in his face and in his huge, threatening moustache, cast menacing glances at the defendant. But his fierceness did not alarm me, and looking at him I remembered the pun I had heard from one of the officers, who referred to the adjutant's superior not as "von Rennenkampf" but as "Rennen von Kampf" (flight from the field of battle).

The examination was going nicely. The only serious question in the case was clarified quickly and entirely to the benefit of the defendant. The prosecution wanted to know why the mill, which had been stopped for several days, was started again on that particular day. The witnesses replied that for a long time there had been no delivery of grain, and on that day the peasants had brought some.

From then on the examination floundered in a jumble of naive

---

* Recently I was able to learn of Makarenko's whereabouts. He was serving as a clerk in a state grievance office (a prosecutor's office) in a small town in Yugoslavia, content to have an opportunity to participate in juridical work.

assumptions and absurd analogies, which did not yield anything that even someone filled with suspicion and hatred could use. And yet, in the hall, overcrowded with members of the judiciary, one did not sense the previous serious and thoughtful mood. During the recesses there were loud exchanges of opinions about Jewish treachery and the ingenuity of Jewish spies in covering up the tracks of their crimes. One of the most furious of those expressing their views was a barely sober captain with a caved-in nose, who I was told served as an assistant military prosecutor for minor cases.

In spite of the obvious failure on the part of the prosecution, the prosecutor made accusations vehemently in that irritated—and ir-ritating—tone that is typical for a person trying to convince himself more than someone else. The defendant was acquitted.

As some of the participants related later, it was Rennenkampf's gallant adjutant who kept the judges so long in the conference chamber. He stood behind the charges.*

Neither joy for Chekhovsky and his family nor the satisfaction of success could dispel the oppressive feeling that had taken hold of me in court. I could scarcely sit through a half-hour of the cel-ebration arranged by the civic leaders in Vilna, and I hardly listened to the welcoming speech. Then, pretending to be ill, I spent several hours in solitude in an untidy hotel room, waiting impatiently for the time to come when I could leave.

I could sense that the front with its cruelty and unavenged in-jury, as well as a madness that shone through its outward ration-ality, had moved all the way to Vilna.

During the retreat of the army from Warsaw, crowds of "hos-tages" under guard, consisting of our own citizens, were loaded chaotically into railroad cars. To these were added a great number of prisoners, who had been charged with treason and even more who were suspected. Some of them were dropped off at military posts along the way: Vilna, Dvinsk, Pskov, and other places. The rest were taken to Petrograd. All of them—old men, women, and children—were thrown into jails. Most were not only without doc-

---

*Four years later, when we met in Odessa, this did not prevent him from greeting me with a lot of fanfare and telling me, while foaming over with poorly pretended enthusiasm, how difficult it had been for him to persuade the lieutenant-colonel, who was of the old regime.

uments, but even without any indication of why they were being kept under guard. The prosecutor's office, afraid of being held responsible for exceeding its authority and illegally depriving citizens of their freedom, refused to keep them in prison. Therefore, the Petrograd military authorities had to assume responsibility for them. As a result, their custody became lawful only outwardly, while in essence it remained senseless and arbitrary.

Several cases from this living cargo, delivered to Petrograd after the evacuation of Warsaw, were brought to trial by the military prosecutor's office.

The most difficult of these cases was considered to be that of the tailor Holzmann, because the testimonies of the Cossacks serving as witnesses were categorical, while the fact to which they were testifying seemed very improbable. Such cases are frightening because of the responsibility one has in the destruction of an innocent person. Therefore, the defense counsels to whom the civic organizations turned refused, one after another, to take the case. Finally a bold spirit was found—a young, talented lawyer. However, two days before the case was to be heard, this colleague came to me, asking me to relieve him of the defense.

"I have studied not only the case but also the attitude of the court," he said. "Ever since the front got close to us and the Petrograd Court-Martial became the court for the theater of military operations, the judges have become unrecognizable. Distrust and bitterness have taken hold of the most lenient of them. I have no doubt that Holzmann will perish. He should be defended by one of the senior colleagues."

Within a couple of hours, I was already familiarizing myself with the case at the Court-Martial. The records were scanty, about twenty half-pages, containing absolutely identical testimony from the two Cossacks. They had been walking through the little town and had seen smoke rising from the chimney of a certain shanty. It was not locked, so they went inside. No one was in the room. They climbed upstairs to the attic, and there, pressed against the chimney, was Holzmann. He stood there, trembling. They said to him, "What are you doing, you so-and-so?" But he just kept trembling and muttering something. So they took him to their cornet[2] and told him what had happened.

Then came the record of the inspection of the attic and the roof.

[2] [A junior officer in the Cossack cavalry.]

Nothing of importance was found. On the roof, on one shingle near the chimney, there was a burned place the size of a copper five-kopek piece.

I felt a sense of dread. I already recognized the psychology of war and its judicial trials. I understood that no matter where and when a war might be taking place its trials were no better than the one in which the French tried Pierre Bezukhov. "This trial," wrote Tolstoy, "as every trial, had only one purpose: to form a channel through which the questions of the prosecution would flow, in order to lead to the desired result—a conviction."

Could there be any choice between the two Cossacks and an unknown Polish *Zhid*, one of the tribe that allegedly was settling its satanically evil account with the Russian people, their army, and their government during this difficult time? "I must flee!" I thought. "I cannot save this unfortunate man. His execution will crush me. It may be desertion, dishonor, but I must flee without a backward glance."

Still, I felt my conscience taking hold of me. "It is not difficult to leave, but who then will defend this unfortunate man? The trial is the day after tomorrow. No one will agree to take him. I cannot push him back onto my younger colleague, whom I've just relieved of the burden." My conscience held me firmly. "Let fate decide. I shall go at once to request a postponement of the case. If I can manage it, I shall ask one of my associates, who are more cool-headed and composed than I, to take my place. They know that inside me it is not nervousness nor sentimentality, but a fundamental terror before the death penalty. I am always ready, no matter how slim the chances, to fight for a life; but when I know my efforts are useless, I am not disposed to assist in murder. Fate has been merciful to me thus far. Not once have I had to listen to a death verdict. Perhaps it will also be merciful now, and the case will be postponed. If not, then I shall have to go through this unknown and terrifying ordeal."

"Who is presiding in the Holzmann case?"

"General so-and-so." I had become acquainted with the general several years before, while defending a case in which he was presiding, the difficult and apparently hopeless case of the students Yanovitsky and Shishkin and the worker Sukhleev. He had been able to sort subtly through the tangled, bloody material. He remained calm in spite of the horrors that were piled up. He himself became convinced of the innocence of the defendants, and he convinced his colleagues. A noble elegance of thought, self-respect, and respect for others—this was the impression he left with me.

"What a stroke of luck," I thought. "Tell the general that I need to speak with him."

I had not seen him in about a year, and when I entered his study I was amazed, for before me stood a stooped old man, with dull, sunken eyes.* After we sat down, I said to him, "I have a request to make in connection with a defense that is scheduled for the day after tomorrow."

"The day after tomorrow? But those are nothing but espionage cases. Who is it that you are defending?"

I told him. The general looked at me with surprise, and a hostile flicker crossed his eyes. "Only yesterday," he said, "the chancellery gave me the name of another defense counsel."

I understood and accepted the challenge.

"Yes, I am defending Holzmann. He is *charged* with espionage but has grounds for acquittal, and I want to ask you, Your Excellency, to postpone the case. Certain circumstances of a purely personal nature make it very difficult for me to conduct the defense the day after tomorrow. You could very easily comply with my request, since there are no witnesses or experts in the case. It consists entirely of a few records and should take no more than an hour and a half or two."

The general, having reverted to his usual proper manner, answered courteously, "This time I cannot comply with your request. This evacuation case has been in our court for quite some time. Don't forget that we are now the court for the theater of military operations. Speed is of the essence for us." I bade him good-by. Now, I thought, I *must* take the defense.

I registered to defend the case, got permission for a visit, and left for the Vyborg prison. They brought in a worn-out old man, with graying hair. His mournful eyes were accompanied by a bitter smile. Talking with him was difficult, since he did not speak a word of Russian, but only Polish or Yiddish.

"Tell me what happened," I said.

He responded with his bitter smile and a hopeless gesture. "What's there to tell? They've been tormenting me for the last six months. They know very well that I'm innocent. Otherwise, they'd have hanged me long ago. If they can find anything at all,

---

* His only son had been killed in the first months of the war.

you hear right away. And in twenty-four hours you're finished. They've hanged a lot of us already."

And again there was an agonized smile, filled with suffering. "I had a cold and was lying on a bench, shaking. My family'd gone to the apothecary. The Cossacks came and right away said to me, '*Zhid*, give us your money.' I told them, 'I don't have any.' '*Zhid*, give it to us.' 'I don't have any.' They kept on at me, and I kept telling them. Then they began to beat me. I screamed, 'I'm going to the general!' They started to curse. They kept poking around, but there was nothing to take. So they went upstairs. Then back to me. 'So, *Zhid*, you want to go to the general. Let's go.' And they took me."

His face was constantly distorted by his bitter smile, which at times became contemptuous.

"I beg you, don't smile in court. The judges may not understand. They'll consider you insolent. Don't be offended, but you'd better get rid of that smile."

"My God! How could I be smiling? Some smile!"

Two days later, the trial took place. I do not remember the reason, but it was held in a small room. Most likely the usual hall for these cases was being used. A large desk and three chairs with straw seats were arranged for the judges and two small tables for the prosecutor and defense counsel. The defendant, with a guard on either side, was placed on a chair behind me. This setting, so simple and domestic, made the situation even more frightening.

Then the judges came in—the general and two temporary judges. Everyone took his place. There were nine of us in the room without the usual space between us. Everything was cramped and crowded together. There was no room for death, but it was imminent.

The questioning of the defendant began. It was discovered that he did not speak Russian, so a chancellery clerk who spoke Polish was summoned. The technicalities of the questioning were completed. There were no witnesses. In accordance with the laws in time of war, none had been called because of the distance involved. After a few minutes the indictment was read.

"Interpreter, tell the defendant that the charge against him is that at a certain time and place he sent prearranged smoke signals to the enemy for the purpose of aiding it in its hostile acts against Russia."

The defendant started to answer. Suddenly there was an enraged shout from the presiding judge. "Don't you dare smile! Interpreter, tell the defendant that he is not to forget himself. He is before the court. If this insolence happens again, he will be removed, and the trial will take place in his absence." Sobbing convulsively, the defendant wavered and then quickly finished his explanation.

"Are you done? Read the testimony of the witnesses."

The secretary read it, taking less than half an hour. The prosecutor asked permission to refer to the inspection reports, and he briefly addressed the court on the subject of denial when guilt is obvious.

Now it was the defense's turn. I did not make a formal address. I wanted to convince the judges simply by discussing the circumstances with them. I pointed out that it is impossible to send signals to a distant enemy from the chimney of a tiny house that does not stand on a hill but is crowded among other houses of the same kind, and that it is impossible to send signals in the wintertime, when all the houses are being heated and smoke is rising above all of them.

I was standing so near the judges that I had to restrain my gestures and movements. I looked into their faces, trying to get them to meet my gaze, but they would not. Their eyes were dead. They were not letting me through. There was no way in. A curtain of steel had been lowered. In despair I repeated my meager arguments. With clumsy, leaden words, I pounded against the stone within their hearts, against the steel of the lowered curtain. But it was in vain. They were set, immovable.

"Defendant, have you anything else to say?"

"I've already told you everything."

The interpreter sat down, and the judges left for the conference chamber. After about ten minutes they returned. All three of them stood at attention.

What I had always feared was happening. I heard distinctly the words: "On the basis of the articles . . . the accused shall be deprived of all rights and subjected to the death penalty by hanging."

"Interpreter, tell him!"

Whistling and hissing, the Polish words about death flew over me and burst above the defendant. I turned around. Having opened his eyes widely, he was smiling his sad smile and shaking his head reproachfully, like an older person acts toward presumptuous children.

The judges turned and left, and after them the prosecutor. On the way out, the presiding judge snapped at the secretary, "Get the next case ready." The secretary rushed out into the hall.

Holzmann was led out. I followed him and looked into his eyes, the eyes of a mature man. I saw reproach in them, not only toward the court, but toward me as well. To be sure, it was meant for me, too, as if to say, "If you are powerless to break the noose, don't meddle, don't interfere with death. Don't insult these last, these most important hours by making a fuss."

And yet, I grabbed his arm and shouted, "You will live, Holzmann! Trust me for another two or three days. You will live!"

At the end of the corridor, I ran into a military judge, General Speshnev. Whether because his brother was one of our colleagues or because he had a responsive soul, those in the legal profession felt that he was sympathetic towards them.

"Tell me, what now?" I said to him. "What happens next?"

Speshnev turned his eyes away from me. "If the announcement of the verdict in its final form is set for today, the case will be sent tomorrow evening to Pskov to the Commander-in-Chief of the northwestern front."

I rushed along the Moyka, past two houses to the Main Court-Martial.

"Announce me to the Chief Military Prosecutor."

"The Chief Military Prosecutor isn't here. He's been ill for five days now."

I hurried to his home. His orderly unlocked the door. "You can't come in. The general is very ill."

I pushed the orderly aside, quickly advancing into the study and from there into the bedroom.

"Alexander Sergeevich, do not be angry with me. A great misfortune has occurred. An innocent man has been sentenced to death. Help me."

I looked around. On the bed, dressed only in a nightshirt, lay Makarenko, red from fever, his eyes inflamed. He was covered with a blanket, as well as with his overcoat. I began to waver. But a moment later his fearless bass voice was rumbling, "Well, let's take a look. Let me get myself together. I'll be right with you."

In a few minutes, with his overcoat thrown over his bedclothes, he came into the study, ready for me with a bit of humor. "So, you say they condemned an innocent man. Well, of course. That's how it always is with you. Either no one is guilty, or no crime has been committed. You never settle for anything else."

But, having glanced at me, he cut the joke short. "All right. What is the problem?" I told him.

"Yes, a dubious case. But how can I be of help?"

"Most likely the case will go to the front tomorrow. Give me a chance to think it through, to figure out what to do. I was so taken aback. I've never experienced such horror. Even in cassation trials, things have gone well for me. But this burden is too much. Help me to get out from under it. Insist that the case be forwarded to you. I'll gain a day or two, and you'll be convinced that I am right. Could you give me a letter to the front? I'll deliver it and plead with them, and maybe I'll succeed. Are there any of your magistrates at the front?"

"Yes, General Shavrov."

"So, there! General Shavrov, I believe, is himself a responsive person, and he will take your wish to heart."

Makarenko thought for a moment and then called his orderly. "Ask General Lykoshin to come in."

Lykoshin entered.* Nodding in my direction, Makarenko said, "Alexander Sergeevich, we need to help. Get me the Holzmann case, which was just decided, from the presiding judge."

I went along with Lykoshin. I wanted to make sure personally that Holzmann's death was postponed for at least a few days, that the case was indeed taken up. Without this assurance, I was afraid to go back home.

In the corridor of the court building, I met a colleague. From his pale, distressed countenance, I gathered that his client had also been sentenced to death. Nearby, at the door to the chancellery, stood an enormous, wide-shouldered, bear-like prisoner between two guards, who were waiting for forwarding papers. Like an engine that must let off steam upon arriving at a station, my colleague began to tell me about the case of his client, a Latvian cabby by the name of Lucis. He had been in a hurry with some passengers. Lashing his horses with a long whip, he had caught and broken a telegraph wire. It was decided that he had done it on

---

*A talented, superbly educated jurist, Lykoshin was at one time a professor at the Military Law Academy. His ill health, due to a serious nervous disorder, which sometimes prevented him from working for months, did not allow his remarkable potential to develop. Family ties with Professor V. I. Semevsky brought him into contact with scholarly and literary circles.

purpose, in order to aid the enemy. While my colleague was telling me about this, a public defense counsel, an officer, rushed out of the door of the courtroom. With unsure step and his whole body quivering, he made his way past us, exclaiming as he went, "The slaughterhouse is running in top form!"

At last Lykoshin emerged with the case in his hands. We agreed that I would call on him towards the end of the next day to see whether there was a letter for me to Shavrov. As we were parting, Lykoshin advised me to procure a letter to General Bonch-Bruevich, chief of staff to the Commander-in-Chief, General Ruzsky. I went to the writer Bonch-Bruevich, whom I had known since Kiev at the time of the Beilis trial. He gave me a cordial letter to his brother, pleading for Holzmann and for Lucis.

On the next day, I dashed off an appeal for cassation, took it to the court, stopped at headquarters for a pass to Pskov, and went to see Holzmann. I anxiously awaited his appearance. I saw the same bitter smile and the same bewildered, shrugging shoulders, but the expression of reproach was gone. In its place was a sort of humble resignation. With exaggerated cheerfulness, I told him about my "achievements." He remarked softly, "Why bother? You ought to help those who can still be helped. As for me, I figured out during the night why I'm so scared. There are so many doors for death to come through, and this is the one it chose. Where I never expected it. That's why I'm scared. But does it really matter which door it comes through?"

Then, with a smile, no longer bitter but childishly shy, he added, "We have a saying that if the Sanhedrin decrees even one death verdict, it has to be dissolved. If such a law went into practice now, would there be enough judges?"

I began to bid him good-by. At the door he stopped me. "I have a favor to ask you. When 'it' happens, let my family know." He told me their names and addresses.

From the jail I went to the Main Court-Martial. There Lykoshin gave me, together with his best wishes, a letter to General Shavrov, prepared according to instructions from the Chief Military Prosecutor. I left on the night train. Just before my departure, my colleague stopped in to tell me good-by and to remind me about his client.

That night I dreamt about Holzmann, who now was no longer of this world, and beside him the huge Latvian with a whip in his hands. The train reached Pskov at dawn. The crowded station was bedlam. In the waiting room one could hardly see because of the tobacco smoke. Officers dressed in overcoats were gulping down boiling water. I tried to make myself comfortable but could not. I left the station only to find that all the cabbies had been taken. It was better this way, I reasoned. It was some distance into town, and by walking in the cold I would chase away the drowsiness that was stubbornly clinging to me after a sleepless night.

I knew Pskov well from previous defenses. The house in which General Shavrov had his quarters was far from the railroad station. By the time I got there, it was close to eight o'clock. The house stood on a corner, with the front door on one street and the gate on the other. I hesitated to awaken anyone by ringing, and so I walked in through the gate. The orderly was brushing some clothing.

"The general's still asleep. Come back later. Maybe in thirty minutes or an hour."

"But won't I miss the general?"

"I don't know. He takes his meals and has tea at the officers' club. He'll be leaving as soon as he gets dressed. He might stop off somewhere along the way."

"Couldn't I wait inside?"

"There's no place to wait. Too many official papers. I'm not supposed to let anyone in."

I had to walk back and forth between the gate and front entrance so that I would not miss Shavrov. A light snow was falling. I would sit down for a moment on the little bench by the gate and then jump up in fear that he had gone out through the front door. During this joyless walking, I did a lot of thinking: "What if this same Holzmann, who only four days ago was completely unknown to you, had been dying from an illness and had called to you? Would you have gone to him?" "I doubt it." "No doubt about it. You would certainly not have gone. Many people die. And yet, here you are, fifty years old and in poor health, rushing into a strange town and knocking about its dreary streets at daybreak on a frosty morning. Holzmann was telling the truth yesterday. Does it really matter through which door death chooses to come?" "Perhaps not, but if I don't succeed in defending Holzmann, than I, too, am responsible for his destruction."

At this point I understood something I had always felt unconsciously, which was that regardless of what people say or write about "bleeding heart humaneness," the human conscience will never reconcile itself to a door for death that man himself has hewn out. And anyone who wishes, even in a single instance, to shut that door will not cease to tug at it with all his meager strength, as long as he sees even a glimmer of hope.

At close to nine o'clock, I inquired again. This time I was let in; and in a few minutes, General Shavrov appeared, a tall, well-built, affable man, with a light, youthful gait. We exchanged a few conventional phrases, and Shavrov opened the letter from Lykoshin.

"You got here ahead of the case. It hasn't arrived yet. Why are you so upset?" I explained to him why I considered Holzmann innocent beyond doubt. I added that on the previous day I had submitted an appeal for cassation. It was weak, but still there was something to get hold of, if need be.

"I doubt whether cassation will do you any good. Most likely even a new trial will result in the same verdict. Wouldn't it be better to try to get the sentence commuted, to get the death penalty changed to a short term at hard labor?"

"I'm deeply grateful. But for an innocent person, even hard labor is not palatable."

"You are forgetting that subsequently the fate of a convicted person depends entirely on the Chief Military Prosecutor. Through further commutation, it would not be difficult for him to do away with the hard labor."

"Again I thank you. But, now, I have another favor to ask. As they say, misfortune loves company. This favor is for my colleague's client, a Latvian by the name of Lucis."

I told him all I knew about the case.

"All right, we can intercede for him, too. But right now, I'm concerned about *you*. You ought to go back on the first train." And he told me when the next one left.

"I have with me a letter to General Bonch-Bruevich from his brother. I'd like to deliver it and explain it to him in person."

"Don't you trust me with petitioning the Commander-in-Chief? Of course, the stronger, the better; but you have a false image of Bonch-Bruevich. He is cruel and rude, and worst of all for your client, he hates Jews. I'll try to carry out what I've promised by going around him. You're hesitating? You'd like to utilize all the possibilities? Very well. Let me have the letter. If it should become necessary, I'll give it to him. Don't wear yourself out unnecessarily."

I followed Shavrov's good advice. I stopped at the home of a local colleague, where I warmed myself and rested. He was attentive and gracious, but could not conceal his gloominess. In reply to my questions, he sighed, "We're exhausted here."

In a few hours, I was sitting in a railroad car on my way home. I felt at peace, and yet the horror of what I had gone through could easily be stirred up again.

After a few days, Lykoshin came to me with joyful news. General Shavrov had arrived in Petrograd the previous day and had told him that he had been able to get both Holzmann's and Lucis' sentences commuted.

"Let me gossip a bit," Lykoshin added, laughing. "Shavrov said that Bonch-Bruevich was furious. 'Just think!' he kept screaming. 'Every day people are sentenced to death, and nothing happens, no one stirs! But here, no matter when a *Zhid* is caught, some *Zhidish* "father" comes tearing to the front. *Zhidish* solidarity, of course. And we're a fine bunch. Just let ourselves get soft, and don't even stand our ground.' "

Hatred also began to penetrate the ranks of the military. Brother rose against brother, forgetting their common sufferings and torments. A half-starved old woman from the Poltava region by the name of Hermann came seeking justice in Petrograd. She knocked on every door, including mine.

From the very beginning of the war, the regiment in which her son served as a soldier was stationed at the front. Fate kept him safe from the enemy, but during the last attack it did not protect him from his own comrades. The Germans stormed the trenches. After a heated battle with bayonets, they were beaten back. Hermann lay down on the ground to rest. One of his fellow soldiers, a corporal of the guard, came walking by. "Just look at him, the bloody *Zhid*. Wallowing in the mud, getting his overcoat all dirty. Get up!" And he kicked Hermann in the chest with his boot. Hermann swore at him and threatened him with his rifle butt. The corporal of the guard stepped back, pointed his rifle at Hermann, and shot. The bullet hit his right shoulder. It was necessary to remove his arm and to cut his shoulder to pieces.

He was kept in the hospital for a long time. Then he had to appear
before a commission, which discharged him with full disability.
He was only half alive when he was delivered to his mother in
the Poltava region. She took care of him and tried to heal him.
Toward the end of the third week, the police appeared with a summons for Hermann to be returned for a court-martial. He was
accused of raising a weapon against a superior. As soon as he became well, he was arrested and taken away. The court-martial
sentenced him, an armless invalid, to hard labor with deprivation
of rights.

I did not so much listen to the tale of the mother as watch her
eyes. They were suffering and pleading, but at the same time
they were filled with a stubbornness like flint. They were saying,
"Help if you can, but without all of this 'law,' 'time of war,'
'patience'—I have no patience!"

One needs to delve into eyes like these only once or twice in
one's lifetime and reach into the depths of the soul, in order to re-
nounce forever the unfathomable male pride about our imagined
superiority over mothers, wives, and sisters. I looked into the eyes
of this old woman, and I saw in them the eternally worried eyes
of my mother, of all mothers. Such eyes cannot be refused; at
least, they *should not* be refused.

Without waiting for her to finish her story, which I understood
even without her pleading words, I interrupted. "Excuse me, I
must go now or I might miss a good man whom we'll need in
dealing with your misfortune. Stop by to see me this evening."

I went to the Chief Military Prosecutor. As warmly and simply
as ever, Makarenko went out of his way for someone in trouble.
Immediately he said that if the mother's words could be substantiated, he would prepare a report to the Emperor about changing
the hard labor to a short term in prison.

"And then we'll see what to do next," he said, as he bade me
good-by.

That evening, as I glanced from the door of my office into the
reception room, I was seized with joy. There among the others sat
the old woman. Without bothering to find out who was first in
line, I invited her to come in, for joy is always egotistical. I told
her about the promise of the Chief Military Prosecutor.

The flint-like stubborness left the mother's happy eyes, but in a
few moments it was burning again with new vigor. It was clear
to me that in a month or two I would be seeing the old woman

again, that she would not rest until she had freed her son completely.

There was another incident of the same variety, a fantastic
incident, but unfortunately an authentic one. A few months before
the February Revolution, I was informed that a soldier by the
name of Medvedovsky wanted to see me. He was being treated for
his wounds in one of the Petrograd military hospitals. We met
and this is what he told me:

Recently he and another member of his faith by the name of
Datskovsky were serving together in a reconnaissance detachment.
For their distinguished military service, both were awarded St.
George's Crosses, Datskovsky four of them, and Medvedovsky
three. Their regimental and company commanders were fair and
kind people, who always treated them with warmth and consideration. The company commander frequently invited them to his
quarters, and they used to get together there with the officers.
The chaplain also treated them very cordially.

A new regimental commander was appointed, a man by the
name of Yakhontov. Soon after his arrival, there was a ceremony
for distributing medals that had been awarded under the previous
commander. Among those being decorated were Medvedovsky
with his third St. George's Cross and Datskovsky with his fourth.
When Yakhontov began distributing the medals and realized that
they were to be given even to Jews, he became angry and shouted,
"What is this? Crosses for the *Zhids*? Aren't there enough of
our own people?" He handed over the distribution to a senior
officer and left.

A few days later, a reconnaissance group, which included Datskovsky, was sent on a nighttime mission with a fellow soldier
by the name of Mishkin in charge. They returned at dawn without
Datskovsky. Medvedovsky asked Mishkin where Datskovsky was.
Mishkin muttered something indistinctly. When after some time
Medvedovsky repeated the question, Mishkin growled, "He ran
away."

That same evening another group was picked to go on patrol
with the same Mishkin in charge. Medvedovsky was included
in this one. They left late in the evening. After about an hour,
Mishkin ordered a rest. He began to weep and said, "I can't do it.
I don't care what happens. I can't do it!"

Medvedovsky looked at him, wondering what was the matter.

Mishkin wept a bit, groaned, and then confided, "Oh, what's the use, I'll tell you the truth. We killed Datskovsky yesterday. Those were the lieutenant's orders."*

"What for?"

"I don't know what for. I've told you, those were the lieutenant's orders. Yesterday as we were leaving on the patrol, the lieutenant called me over and said, 'Datskovsky is going to run away to-night.' I looked at the lieutenant, and he said it again, 'Datskovsky is going to run away tonight. He won't return. Do you under-stand?' 'Yes, Sir, I understand.'

"So, we walked around for awhile and then finished off Dat-skovsky. He had to be buried, but we hadn't brought a shovel. We began to dig with our bare hands. We dug a shallow grave, laid him in it, and covered him with earth.

"In the morning the lieutenant asked me, 'Did Datskovsky run away?' 'Yes, Sir, he did,' I answered.

"This evening, when it was time to leave, the lieutenant said, 'Tonight Medvedovsky is going to run away. Do you understand?' 'Yes, Sir, I understand.' So I promised him, but I see that I can't do it. You and I have always been friends."

Medvedovsky said that he also began to weep and told Mishkin, "Why should you perish for my sake. Do as you promised."

But Mishkin replied, "I can't." And the others supported him. "Why should we kill you?" they said. "Because our superiors don't like you? Let them do their own killing."

"So we sat there another whole hour," Medvedovsky continued. "Then we went on the patrol and got back at dawn. During the morning, after reporting to the head of our reconnaissance unit, Mishkin whispered that the lieutenant asked, 'And did Medvedov-sky run away?' When Mishkin replied, 'No, Sir,' the lieutenant became angry, but didn't say anything."

Medvedovsky told me this story vividly, with fervor, and in great detail, as though he were again reliving those terrifying hours. His account gripped me with a double fear, one arising from the event itself, incomprehensible in its enormity, and the other from the thought that this might be a madman sitting here before me. I put a series of repeated questions to Medvedovsky, carefully quizzed him about his earlier life, and kept him close to to two hours. Toward the end, he apparently guessed what I

* If my memory is correct, the name of the lieutenant who commanded the reconnaissance group was Yakovlev.

was doing and remarked with a laugh, "You're checking to see if I'm delirious, aren't you? I'd be happy if it were delirium."

We agreed on a new appointment in a few days. Meanwhile, I sent my assistant to the hospital physicians to see if they had noticed anything about Medvedovsky. The physicians who had been treating him over a prolonged period of time assured us categorically that there was no doubt about his emotional health.

At the next meeting Medvedovsky showed me letters addressed to him at the hospital from the company commander and the chaplain. Both of them mentioned the "horrible incident" (without being specific), and both implored him to take care of himself.

I no longer had any doubt that Medvedovsky was telling the truth. My temperament and deep conviction that one should not plead with evil but should scald it with boiling water, as one scalds bedbugs in a wooden bed, dictated the only possible thing to do: file an immediate accusation of murder not only against those who committed it but also against those who instigated it.

I went to see Makarenko. He listened attentively, thought awhile, and then announced decisively, "No, it's impossible to initiate a case. First of all, I don't have the right to do so. You know without my telling you that crimes are prosecuted and judged at the place in which they were committed. If an appeal is submitted to me, I am obligated to forward it to the front. Now, as to the substance of the case. Even if Medvedovsky's story is correct, it probably could not be verified. Wartime, with its conventions and circumstances, is no time for disclosing such unparalleled crimes. Instead of revealing the truth, you could reach the point where the witnesses making the disclosures end up as false witnesses, and Medvedovsky as a false informer. Then watch out or even you will be implicated as an instigator and leader. Add to this the right of the military authorities at the front to impose the death penalty for any kind of crime. No, you ought to wait until the end of the war. What you are venturing to do now is insane."

"All this is true," I replied, "but it's not the whole truth. Let's begin with the danger. I'm well aware of it, but I don't let it bother me. Anyway, they'll have a hard time swallowing me—I'm too bristly. And if they do swallow me, so be it. As for Medvedovsky, he has three St. George's Crosses, which are not awarded without reason. People like him have a high regard for human life. I tried to scare him, but I couldn't. In respect to your legal arguments, I admit that they are irrefutable. However, they do not infringe on your right, as supreme spokesman for the military prosecutor's office, to arrange an investigation. Of course, it would have to be conducted at the front under the conditions that you just stipulated. Still, I don't think that the truth could be trampled underfoot. The investigation probably would not immediately yield material in respect to the instigators, but there's reason to hope that it would present the basic framework and confirm the main facts. Should this be so, then it would not be difficult to get to those who inspired the crime as well. In a crime committed by several persons, some of them intellectuals and the rest simpletons, these persons themselves will invariably, and even against their will, help the judicial authorities. The intellectuals will philosophize too much, and the simpletons will philosophize too little, and the truth will stick out like a hump on someone's back."

"What you say is all theoretical, but I am thinking about reality," said Makarenko.

In a little while, with only brief pauses, I pleadingly repeated my attacks. Finally Makarenko decided to submit the question to the Minister for him to settle. When I stopped back the following day, after Makarenko had made his report, he told me that the Minister, A. A. Polivanov, had said, "You know his temperament. He won't calm down, and all that will come of it is some embarrassing publicity. You had better conduct an investigation."

Makarenko appointed General Lykoshin to carry out the investigation.

This time, my inclination to theorize proved victorious—the hump began to stick out. After about a month and a half, Lykoshin told me that the general features of the crime had been determined and now all that needed to be shown was the identity of the instigators.

In a few weeks the February Revolution began, and out of necessity any further investigation was suspended. But even what had been obtained was enough. One must hope that one of the Russian historical commissions is preserving this material.

I would like to end this sad portion of my memoirs with a joyful episode—a gift of fate, which V. G. Korolenko so aptly called "a black pearl in a spectacular setting."* Let me refer to a passage from the muddled indictment.

* From his article, "On the Mariampol Treason," which was published in *Russkiya vedomosti* [*The Russian Gazette*] immediately after the case

On September 2, 1914, the military investigator of the Third Army Corps was asked to conduct a preliminary investigation concerning a case which dealt with lending aid to the German forces by the residents of the town of Mariampol. According to the indictment, the circumstances of the case were as follows: The Russian forces, while withdrawing to a fortified line of defense, evacuated Mariampol, when almost on their heels the advanced guard of the German forces entered the town. With the appearance of the German forces, the Jewish population quickly changed its attitude toward the Russians. The Russian soldiers could not buy anything from the Jews, who simply locked their doors to them. The Jews denied them even a piece of bread, which the soldiers were not begging, but were willing to pay for. Meanwhile they treated the incoming German soldiers to dinner. As the Germans approached, the Jews who had been serving in the Russian forces began breaking their rifles and hiding themselves among their fellow countrymen. The Russian soldiers, however, defended themselves as they left the town. A crowd of Jews, carrying a white flag, gathered on the square to welcome the Germans with bread and salt.[3] On the day after the entry of the German forces, the Germans selected Herschanovich as mayor. He held a meeting of the townspeople, at which he announced that he was now the mayor and everyone had to obey him. Then he appointed a Pole by the name of Bartling to be his assistant. As mayor, Herschanovich eagerly carried out all the wishes of the Germans. He made arrangements for procuring food for their forces and for delivering horses for transport. The residents gave up the food and horses reluctantly and only because of Herschanovich's persistent demands.

The entire accusation was based on the testimony of a Moslem *imam* by the name of Ibrahim Bayrashevsky. A month later, on

---

was heard before the Main Court-Martial. Later, considerably expanded, it was reproduced by Vladimir Galaktionovich for the Moscow-based Society for the Dissemination of Correct Information about the Jews. It also appeared, together with my speech and an introductory article by Professor Michael Hernet, in a brochure entitled, "The Herschanovich Case." Vladimir Galaktionovich's widow, Avdotia Semyonovna, sent the brochure to me. He had obviously made several additions and corrections in it shortly before his death. It is now available in his *Collected Posthumous Works*. I find it difficult to quote the valuable points he makes in this article, because they are so intertwined with his kind comments about me.

[3] [A traditional symbol of hospitality.]

October 2, the trial took place. Two witnesses, Bayrashevsky and Pendrilo, were called to testify. The latter did not disclose anything of substance, but Bayrashevsky insistently accused both Herschanovich and the Jewish residents of Mariampol. Herschanovich's defense counsel, who was one of the best provincial lawyers, fought in vain. Herschanovich was found guilty of aiding the enemy and was sentenced to deprivation of rights and hard labor for eight years. Bartling was acquitted. The verdict was carried out, and Herschanovich began to serve his term in the Yaroslavl labor prison.

After several months the defense counsel and Herschanovich's family asked me to submit a petition to reopen the case in view of newly disclosed circumstances. My efforts continued for over a year. I had to work with care, a piece at a time, like picking out a splinter. Suffice it to say that since the Main Court-Martial did not wish to ruin the case and did not find it technically possible to comply with my petition, it did not schedule a hearing of the case for almost six months.

The trouble was that the newly disclosed circumstances in the Herschanovich case, despite their impressiveness, did not fully accord with the rigid and restrictive definitions of the law. The reopening of cases that had been decided was a rare occurrence in the annals of the court. There were hundreds of thousands of cases during the fifty-five years that the Judicial Statutes existed in Russia, and not even a hundred of these were reopened.

It was this way not only in Russia but all over the world. Even in France, at the time of the Baras case in 1890, when the defendant was sentenced to death on a murder charge, the laws of judicial procedure were insufficient to correct an obvious judicial error. There was no other way of settling the case than by granting a pardon. It seems that everywhere, instead of seeking truth, people prefer to pay off with mercy.

It would have been possible to obtain such mercy for the sixty-two-year-old Herschanovich as well. However, judgment had been passed not only on him but on the entire Jewish population of Mariampol, and only the truth could give him satisfaction.

When the case was finally heard on July 28, 1916, I frankly told the Main Court-Martial, "If you demand that we present a strictly technical rationale for reopening the case, we must admit defeat from the outset. We do not have a court verdict pertaining either to the conviction of another person for the same crime or to the admission of false testimony from a witness. Our weapons have no official stamp on them. But they are strong and sure. They consist of an extraordinary and highly improbable chain of facts, which no one could ever have invented."

And, indeed, this was true. Only a few weeks after Herschanovich's conviction, this same Bayrashevsky sat on the defendants' bench before the same Third Army Corps court, charged with treason against the state for working with the Germans. He faced the very prosecutor who so recently and so trustingly had drawn material from his testimony—and from it alone—for the charges against Herschanovich. The evidence was so overwhelming that Bayrashevsky bent under its weight and admitted his guilt. It was he who had driven out in an automobile to meet the Germans as they were arriving and who had directed their activities in the town. It was he who at night had posted those very leaflets that, just a few weeks before, in this same courtroom, he had accused Jewish youths of posting. The court found him guilty of treason and sentenced him to hard labor. Only his death, two months after the conviction, prevented the judicial authorities from bringing him to account for his false testimony in the Herschanovich case. Of course, he had had a shrewd reason for testifying against Herschanovich in court, for by his fiery accusation he had hoped to divert any suspicion from himself and other agents.

One would think that no other material would have been needed to exonerate Herschanovich. But fate, which had so cruelly abused his old age, was now pleased to shower the convicted man with juridical generosities. An article by M. Bernatsky, entitled, "Prussians in Mariampol," appeared in *Russky Invalid* [*The Russian Invalid*], the official military organ. The author of the article, a general and a military judge, attested to the fact that two weeks after the withdrawal of the Germans, he visited Mariampol and questioned eyewitnesses, while their memories of the affair were still fresh. The most important of these witnesses was a noncommissioned gendarme officer by the name of Gordey. When the Germans began to enter the town, his superiors ordered him to stay behind, in order to watch the enemy and to observe the behavior of the residents. Gordey became so engrossed in his observations that he did not take time to remove his uniform and came to his senses only when he heard the clatter of horses' hoofs behind him. When he looked around, he saw enemy cavalrymen with lowered lances, galloping toward him. He ducked into an alley nearby and ran into the house of a Jew named Freiberg. The latter took him to the attic, disguised him in some dirty old painter's clothes and shaved off his mustache. After a few minutes a "painter" left Freiberg's house, carrying a bucket in one hand and a brush in the other; and humming light-heartedly, he walked past the Prussian cavalrymen, as they continued their search for the gendarme, who had disappeared somewhere.

So this was the notorious Jewish treachery. The first random Jew, into whose house Gordey unexpectedly ran, risked his own life to save him. According to the laws of war, this Jew deserved to be hanged.

Still another point should be made. Gordey, as a local gendarme, must have been known by a sizable portion of the Jewish population of this tiny Jewish town; and yet he was allowed to live there peacefully, without a single Jew giving him away to the Germans. Moreover, he was a non-commissioned officer from one of the Hussar regiments, who had been ordered by his superiors to remain behind. It is not surprising that Gordey, who was questioned upon my request, gave a warm testimonial not only for Herschanovich but for the entire Jewish population of Mariampol. He certified that when the townspeople were choosing a mayor, as demanded by the German commandant, and had decided on Herschanovich, the latter began to weep and told those who had chosen him, "You want to make a sacrifice of me. I'm a sick man."

According to information gathered by Gordey, the Germans coerced Herschanovich, under the threat of death, to supply them with horses, but he stubbornly refused and never did so.

I shall cite only a few concluding words from my speech before the Main Court-Martial: "It is with pain and sorrow that I leave this case. Many Polish towns and villages are mired in blood and blanketed in smoke from the fires. But out of the blood, out of the ashes, the old Poland is rising, resplendent in purple and gold. The impossible dreams of noble visionaries and poets are being realized. Alongside the Polish people, on the same soil, lives another people, related to me by blood. This people also gave the blood of its youth and its possessions to the great Russian cause. And now it stands in the smoldering ashes, drained of its vitality, impoverished, slandered, branded with the name of traitor. But then, to each his lot. One of the sons of this people, suffering unbearably because of a judicial error, asks through my lips: 'Why am

I being crushed?' And I do not know the answer. I only believe
that the hand that inflicted the wound will heal it. And if in addition to reopening Herschanovich's case you also entrust him with
his freedom while he awaits a new verdict, you will be performing not an act of mercy but of justice."

General Koreyvo, the Assistant Chief Military Prosecutor, supported my argument and indicated that there was little doubt
but had this new information been available to the court that sentenced Herschanovich, he would have been acquitted.

The Main Court-Martial handed down its decision: to reverse
the verdict that had been pronounced against Herschanovich and
reopen his case, as well as inform the Commander-in-Chief of
the northern front that this was being done and recommend to the
Chief Military Prosecutor that Herschanovich be released immediately from the sentence he was serving and allowed to remain
free under police surveillance.

A few days later, a tall, distinguished-looking old man came to
see me. He vividly described how a prosecutor from the court
came to the labor prison on July 28 and awakened him with con-
gratulations that a judicial error had been cleared up. He was
immediately taken to be unshackled, and the fetters that had bound
his hands and feet for almost two years were removed. I was
touched by the old man's lack of malice, his submissiveness, and
his gentle attitude toward those who had caused him this unnecessary suffering.

The Commander-in-Chief of the northern front forwarded the
Herschanovich case to the joint court of the various corps of the
Fifth Army. Trial was set for September 28 in Dvinsk. I decided
to go there, since I feared the obstinacy existing at the front and
the solidarity among the judicial officers, so accentuated by the war.

At that time the Dvinsk fortress was under siege by the Germans, and to enter it one needed a pass from the military authorities. Herschanovich and I arrived at headquarters, where we
were met by a blond-headed counter-intelligence officer, with
watery, bulging eyes and a voice that was overly gruff and guttural.
I showed him the summons of the Fifth Army Court.

"We have nothing to do with all these courts," he said. "I'll see
if it's possible to let Herschanovich through to the front." And
he told us to come back in three days. When we did, he said, "We
haven't gathered the information yet. Come back tomorrow."

I pointed out to him that tomorrow would be just a day before the trial; that the summons, as one could see from the date marked on it, was already very late; and that if we did not leave until tomorrow we would be forcing the court to wait for us.

"This is no concern of mine. I said tomorrow, and that's that."

We came again on the following day, only to be told that permission to enter Dvinsk would not be granted.

"Give me a certificate that the defendant was denied permission to appear before the court," I said. "Otherwise he will be arrested for failing to do so."

The officer retorted, "Excellent! Such gentlemen ought not be left at large."

I rushed to Makarenko. He was outraged by such an insolent attitude toward a request by the court. He sent Colonel Ivanov to General Tyazhelnikov with a categorical request to issue the passes immediately. General Tyazhelnikov expressed regret about what had happened and gave orders for the passes.

We left that same evening and arrived late in Dvinsk. As we rode along the deserted streets, from which all signs of life had disappeared, we could hear the constant thunder of German artillery.

The judges had already been gathered for some time. I explained what had happened, and the court convened with General Rudakov presiding. The charges were brought by the same prosecutor as before. He proved to be obstinate, and even in light of the new circumstances he persistently maintained the old accusation. In a little over three hours, the case was completed. The court pronounced a verdict of acquittal.

When I stopped in the judges' chamber to say good-by, the presiding judge showed me the interrogation sheet.* I was overjoyed. The first question read: Has it been proven that in September, 1914, after the German forces entered Mariampol, the residents of the town supplied provisions and horses? The answer of the court was negative; and the remaining two questions, devoted to Herschanovich, were left unanswered due to the fact that the event itself had not occurred.

Not only Herschanovich but the entire population had been acquitted.

* The court-martial statutes did not allow the questions to be formulated publicly but only during the deliberation itself.

Chapter 16

V. G. Korolenko

Korolenko's family sent me copies of his *Complete Posthumous Collected Works*, issued by the State Publishing House of the Ukraine. The cover, the paper, the print, all were thrifty and modest, befitting a person who possessed such inner wealth that he never adorned himself with pretentious or luxurious clothing.

Nor was the editorial committee the conventional "All-Russian" type, composed of "well-known figures." Instead it consisted of persons who had lived and worked with Korolenko closely and shared his emotional intensity, namely, his widow, Avdotia Semyonovna, and his daughters, Sofia Vladimirovna Korolenko and Natalia Vladimirovna Lyakhovich. In addition, two friends, T. A. Bogdanovich and M. L. Krivinskaya, assisted in the work.

According to its preliminary publication plan, the editorial committee intended to issue forty volumes, twenty-two devoted to artistic works, eleven to journalistic works, six to diaries, and one to biography. But as the work progressed, this plan grew considerably, and the intended number of volumes proved hardly sufficient. Moreover, the books seem to have been issued at random. Volume 5 is followed by 7 and volume 8 by 13; and then after a low number suddenly comes volume 50. Thus far, the editorial committee has issued a total of thirty-one volumes, the last of these being volume 18.[1]

Avdotia Semyonovna explained this apparent randomness to me in one of her letters. "Having read our plan of work, you may wonder why the books are not published in sequence. The

---

[1] [These figures were for 1925, the year that Gruzenberg first published this chapter of his memoirs as an article in an émigré Russian journal in Prague, *Na chuzhoi storone* [*In Foreign Parts*] *13*, 70–85.]

reason depends in part on the committee and in part on the publishing house. Certain things cannot be done quickly; they must be put aside and worked over gradually. And while working them over, one needs some source of livelihood. Therefore, we are starting with those volumes that will yield royalties, thus enabling us to work on the difficult ones. But there are also times when we must work through all the material before we are able to proceed to the next volume."

It is significant that in the publication plan, twenty-two volumes are fiction, and eleven are journalistic works, indicating that half [a third] of Korolenko's creative powers were given to public affairs. Herein lay the essence of his creativity. He was endowed by fate not only with artistic talent but also with a generous and sympathetic heart, and these two qualities competed within him with an intensity that often caused him pain. His heart was restless and active, urging him from one great deed to another, taking possession of his whole being, encroaching on the creative process itself.

Consider the years 1891–1892. Crop failure gripped the Volga region. It was necessary to feed the famine stricken and to appeal to those who had their fill. This was no time for writing stories. The terrible truth was eminent, more terrible than any fiction. Korolenko and his entire family immersed themselves in the tears of others. As a result, several artistic works were ruined, but this did not matter to Korolenko, for in return hundreds of human beings were saved.

Broken in health and having barely finished the last line of *The Year of Famine* (his report to the public about what he had experienced), Korolenko went to America. Inquisitively, he observed and examined life there, carefully taking notes. He brought back with him a great deal of material and a number of sketches, which he began to assemble and refine; and he wrote several excellent chapters, now published for the first time under the title *To America*. Then, suddenly a new misfortune befell him. The newspapers reported an outrageous event: the Votyaks[2] were being

2 [The Votyaks (also called Udmurts) are a Finno-Ugrian people, who at that time inhabited a small area between the Kama and Vyatka Rivers about one hundred eighty miles northeast of Kazan. They had been colonized by the Russians in the sixteenth century and later had been forcibly converted to Christianity. The case in which Korolenko participated involved a group of ten Votyaks, accused of murdering a local resident

accused of practicing human sacrifice. He immediately rushed to
Elabuga, and again there was a long break in his artistic creativity.

If one were to follow Korolenko's life carefully, it would be
apparent that this was almost always the case. Impulses of the
heart stole from his artistic talent. They took not only his time and
energy, but, as I have already noted, they intruded upon the very
process of his creativity.

I have seen how gold used to be transported in the Urals. It
was not carried in silk cloths but in coarse leather bags. Similarly
the gold of artistic creativity needs to be wrapped in coarse fabric,
because a person cannot describe the horrors of life while quaking
with fear or depict someone's grief while viewing it through eyes
filled with tears. I know that there are speakers and writers whose
feelings are so passionate and intense that any word they choose
seems trivial, constrained, and fragile. Finally they use a word that
only faintly conveys the meaning they intended. And even though
they are applauded, they remain sad, for they know that they
have fallen short of expressing themselves adequately.

A poet, at least a Russian poet, such as Korolenko, must let
himself melt into the millions who speak his language. He must
let himself flow across the entire face of the boundless Russian land
with its hills and dales and forests. And then he must draw himself together again, so he can sing of the bondage and dreary existence, as well as the fleeting joy of a dream, that he has felt.

Everything that Korolenko wrote deals with his own perceptions. His stories, whether they tell of noble deeds and selfishness,
heroes and cowards, or animals, birds, forests, and blades of grass,
all express Korolenko's feelings. And this is as it should be. It is
more important that he revealed a poet's heart and dreams than
that he reflected the external world. When a poet such as Korolenko
reveals his feelings, he is not being monotonous and redundant,
because a poet of his magnitude cannot have an impoverished,

---

in 1892, as a sacrifice to pagan gods. At the first trial, held in the village
of Malmuzh in 1894, seven of the defendants were convicted. The case
was appealed for cassation to the Senate, which reversed the verdict on the
grounds of improper use of evidence and returned the case for a second
trial in Elabuga in 1895. Again the defendants were found guilty, but
this verdict was also reversed by the Senate. At the third trial in Mamadysh
in 1896, the defendants were finally acquitted.

Korolenko wrote several articles about the proceedings. They are included
in Korolenko, *Sobranie sochinenii* [*Collected Works*] (10 vols.;
Moscow, 1953–56), 9, 337–92.]

mundane soul. A sparrow may be limited to singing a single note
or two, but not a poet.

Korolenko got to know the depths of Russian life: the prisons,
the way stations for transported convicts, the exile settlements.
He trod those corners of Siberia where even a raven is accepted as
a bird of song. Yet he emerged from this as a cheerful, loving,
and joyful person. He neither harbored resentment toward life
nor became bitter toward people. In the gloom of the prisons and
the way stations, he lit the bright sun of imagination and painted
the silence of captivity with an exhilarating song. One need only
look at the Siberian notes in the first volume of his *Diary*:* they
are cheerful, almost joyful notes.

His love of people, for all living things, was like the sun. It shone
on both the good and the evil, on those who were his own and
those who were strangers. An enthusiasm for life, which nothing
could destroy or even diminish, radiated from him until the very
end. In one of his letters to me, he mentioned the question of
pessimism and the craving for suicide. He wrote sternly, "Why
do people think that life is at fault and not the soul that perceives
life? Is it really always the sound that is at fault in a cacophony
and not the distorted ear that catches the sound?"

It seemed as though he swaddled his readers in soft silks, and
they joyfully submitted themselves, rising with him without a
hint of protest to heights they could not attain by themselves.

Even Alexander III, the stern ruler of the destinies of one hundred and sixty million people, did not escape the bewitching power
of Korolenko's song. Upon looking through several of his works
in 1889, the Emperor was so attracted by Korolenko's talent that
he inquired about him. Too bad that the person he chose to ask
was Durnovo, the head of the gendarmes and Minister of Internal
Affairs. On the report that Durnovo submitted, which consisted
entirely of information he had gotten from the Department of
Police, Alexander inscribed, "All this indicates that Korolenko is
a highly unreliable person." And yet, not being able to overcome
his fascination with this "unreliable person," he added sadly, "But
not devoid of talent."

I recall another incident that illustrates Korolenko's appeal. The
hall of the Special Tribunal of the St. Petersburg Chamber of
Justice was overflowing with people. Korolenko was on the defendants' bench, charged with publishing a certain article (Tol-

* Volume 18 of *Complete Collected Works.*

stoy's "Fyodor Kuzmich") in *Russkoe bogatstvo* [*Russian Wealth*], the journal that he edited. According to the charge, the article was insulting to the memory of the ancestors of the ruling monarch. The prosecutor rose to address the court. I listened carefully, so as not to miss a single accusatory argument. A moment passed, then another, wearisome and long. The prosecutor was silent and rather pale. At last, in a barely audible voice, he began, "Your Honors, I shall not conceal, nor can I conceal, from you the fact that it is difficult for me to bring an accusation against someone to whom I am indebted for many wonderful moments." And, speaking hoarsely, scarcely able to control his emotions, he continued, "I have kept *The Rustling Forest* and *The Blind Musician* under my pillow, and upon awakening during the night or in the morning, I have devoured the fragrance and the music of these poems. It goes without saying that some of you, if not all, have probably shared my experience." Then, of course, he had to proceed with the accusation, but it was timid and confused.

Technically, there was direct evidence that a crime had been committed, but the judges, who also had read Korolenko's stories, were gripped by the confession of their associate and embarrassed about condemning a man who had given them joy.

Much has been written about Korolenko's works and their significance in regard to literature and the growth of Russian public awareness; and critics and historians will write much more when Russian life, which has been so battered by war and revolution, finally settles down.

Those who were close to Korolenko have the added responsibility of collecting the unrecorded memories of his deeds, which have been passed along by word of mouth and are themselves examples of unsurpassed poetry. And poetry they are, for everything that Korolenko did was born in creative ecstasy, like a song, like a prayer.

Korolenko never realized that he was "Korolenko" the writer and public figure whose name was uttered with love and pride by thousands of people. He was what is called a celebrity, that is, someone who has a right to creative leisure, to repose, to the jealous guarding of every moment.

It is interesting how some people organize their lives, not only those who are truly great but also those who even temporarily assume such a role—the vicarious priests of fame. The home is a fortress, the wife a permanent commander of the guard, responsible for everything and everyone. All the members of the household are sentries, armed with rapid-firing weapons of lies and excuses. They are concerned only with utilizing every means available to protect the time of this great man from the demands of life. The phone rings. Before an answer is given as to whether or not the great man is at home, an investigation is begun about who is calling, and why. The answer given depends on who is asking and frequently on how useful the caller may be.

But not so in Korolenko's family. No matter who called, whether his voice was known or not, never would he be asked, "Who is it?" If Avdotia Semyonovna or Sofia Vladimirovna answered the phone, the caller would immediately hear the low, throaty voice of one or the other saying, "Volodya (or Papa), come to the phone." Even the servants were schooled in such a way that it did not occur to them to act like diplomats. The doors of Vladimir Galaktionovich's flat were always open to everyone.

His wife and both his daughters loved him with devotion, cared for his health, and rejoiced at each new chapter of his literary work. But they knew very well that Vladimir Galaktionovich could not be separated into Korolenko the writer, Korolenko the public figure, and Korolenko the man. These blended completely, and there was only one Korolenko, whole and indivisible. The slightest cleavage within himself would not simply have served as a theme for a new literary work but would have been a painful blow to the very meaning of his life.

Korolenko did not care whether his works comprised five or a hundred volumes. His concerns lay elsewhere. He labored tirelessly and ceaselessly over his most important work—his life. In spite of the scope of this work, the host of characters active in it, and the countless events it encompassed, there was not one concocted line. He was always true to himself. It was as if he were protecting himself from the temptations of life with a ring of fire, and even such a common social phenomenon as compromise could not step over that ring.

In 1879, Korolenko had innocently been sent into administrative exile, and subsequently he refused to take the loyalty oath to Alexander III, when he ascended the throne. The Department of Police described his protest as follows: "Blaming the order of the administrative authorities for his exile to Vyatka and Perm provinces, Korolenko has announced that 'a dangerous right has

been given to the lawful authorities—the right of arbitrariness—
and life has demonstrated by a mass of terrifying facts how this
right has been abused, for arbitrariness begets dissension between
lawful demands and demands of conscience.' Thus guided by the
dictates of conscience, he refuses to take the oath in its existing
form."

This was in 1881. But even some thirty-two years later, the old
man still acted with the same proud obstinacy. As editor of
Russkoe bogatstvo, he was brought to trial for publishing an article, "People of Our Circle," by S. Ya. Elpatievsky. He was charged
in the St. Petersburg Chamber of Justice with inciting class enmity, as specified in Article 129. In accordance with current judicial practice, there was sufficient evidence that a crime had been
committed. However, I knew that Korolenko had been living
that entire year in Poltava and had not seen Elpatievsky's article
before it appeared in print. I secured the pertinent information
from the address bureau and calmly awaited the trial.

A few days before it was to begin, I invited Vladimir Galaktionovich to confer with me. Showing him the information, I said,
"This time I'm not going to worry about how to defend you. In
fact, I'll be rather bored with even having to go through the mo-
tions. I'll simply base the defense on the old saying, 'They married me while I was away at the mill.' You don't even have to be
present at the examination, which is purely a technicality, since
you're being charged according to a point in Article 129 that does
not require a personal appearance."

Korolenko replied, "But I don't consider that I have the right
to avoid responsibility on technical grounds. After all, I'm the
editor, and I'm answerable for everything that's printed in my
journal."

"You'll be responsible as the editor, but only for allowing an
article to be printed because of an oversight. And for this a person
usually has to pay a small fine. Otherwise, as the indictment stands,
you face the threat of being sentenced to imprisonment in a fortress for up to three years. I understand your feelings, Vladimir
Galaktionovich, but you're acting solely on principle, whereas I
have the truth on my side."

"It's true that I didn't read the article that Sergey Yakovlevich
wrote, but it's also true that it was my duty to read it. So that
must mean I did read it."

The trial began. Korolenko and I addressed the court in defense of Elpatievsky's article. The judges of the Chamber of Justice were conscientious, and they deliberated for a long time. Finally, they brought in the verdict: two weeks confinement in a fortress.

I carried the case to the Senate. As an appeals case it was subject to total review. Before the hearing, I visited with the Assistant Chief Prosecutor and showed him the information from the address bureau. He agreed that the information altered the case, but unless it was presented to the Senate nothing could be done, because otherwise there was not a sound basis for the appeal.

In his opening statement, the Assistant Chief Prosecutor casually remarked that if there was evidence that the editor of the journal had not become acquainted with the incriminating article until after it was printed, he would be responsible only for an oversight.

With a sense of futility, I addressed the court. Then, Korolenko stood up. I do not know whether he sensed a hint of justification in the prosecutor's opening statement, but he devoted most of his final words to assuring the court that he had read Elpatievsky's article and was in total agreement with it. He spoke with great enthusiasm and with some irritation, tapping on the table with his small, graceful hand.

The Senate did not deliberate long. It upheld the verdict.

We left the hall, I with my head hanging and Korolenko with an air of triumph as he looked at me. His eyes sparkled with sly, good-natured laughter, as if to say, "Well, what do you think? Who won this one?"

I was doubly distraught. I thought, as I still do, that the counsel for the defense is at fault whenever a case is lost. Somewhere he has fallen short, either in conducting the case or in accepting it. But even more than this, I was tormented by the vivid vision of Korolenko, a sick old man, whom I considered to be a saint, flailing about and gasping for air in the stony pouch of the Vyborg prison. A saint. Yes, this is what he was to me, and this is what he has remained. He towered above all the others, no matter how remarkable they might be.

As I opened the heavy front doors of the Senate and let Korolenko through, I noticed how stooped his shoulders were and how frail he seemed despite his stocky figure. I was seized with pain for him, but also with annoyance. Why had he allowed himself to be sentenced to prison?

I knew my temperament, which served well for combat but not for everyday affairs. And so I hastily bade Korolenko good-by, even though we were going the same way. He took my hand, and looking earnestly into my eyes, into my very soul, he asked compassionately, "You seem to be upset. Are you unhappy?"

"Certainly not. I'm glad."

"For what?"

"I'm glad that literature kept you from going into law, as you used to dream of doing. I'm glad for those who might have ended up as your clients."

I promised myself that Korolenko would not be imprisoned. Through various stratagems, solicitations, and at times outright begging, I delayed his serving the sentence. However, it was not easy to fool Korolenko. Seeing that the sentence was not being carried out for a disproportionately long time, he began to fret and construct all kinds of surmises.

Then one day he asked my help in regard to applying the 1905 Manifesto to one of the most deserving women activists in the political struggle.[3] In this connection I received a letter from him, dated February 6, 1913. It read: "Dear and Deeply Respected Oskar Osipovich."

This was a bad beginning. If it was necessary for Vladimir Galaktionovich to add the cumbersome "deeply respected" to the epithet that he usually used in addressing me, he was going to restrict himself solely to business. And indeed he did.

I wrote to you a few days ago to ask a favor regarding the fate of a certain person in connection with amnesty. Forgive me, but as I was reflecting on this, I found myself recalling your customary concern about my mishaps. I am thinking expressly that if the opportunity should present itself for you to render some influence on my fate (which, however, seems altogether unlikely), you would probably not refuse to do so. Am I right? And so, just in case, I

---

[3] [The person to whom Gruzenberg refers was Praskovia Semyonovna Ivanovskaya-Voloshenko, a sister of Korolenko's wife. This sister had been sentenced to hard labor in 1883 because of her involvement in revolutionary activities. Her sentence was reduced to exile under police supervision in 1898, from which she escaped in 1903 and made her way to St. Petersburg, where she again joined the revolutionary movement. At the time of Korolenko's intercession on her behalf in 1913, she was living abroad. Apparently Korolenko hoped she would be permitted to return to Russia under terms of the partial amnesty granted by the Imperial manifesto of October 21, 1905. V. G. Korolenko, *Sobranie sochinenii* [*Collected Works*] (10 vols.; Moscow, 1953–56), 6, 314; *10*, 490, 645.]

want to ask you most earnestly not to do this on any account. Any commutation that would not be purely automatic, that is, not as a matter of course in the general application of the manifesto, would grieve me deeply; and I can tell you frankly that in my circumstances it would even insult me. This is not just because there would need to be solicitations and petitions, but simply because some kind of personal exception would be made for me as compared with others. Perhaps all these forewarnings are unnecessary. In that case, forgive me and consider this missive as never having existed.

Not only would he refuse to ask a favor, but he would not even allow an exception to be made for him. This was Korolenko through and through.

I reassured him, but all the same I delayed the carrying out of the sentence, because at this time in 1913 there was hope in legal circles that a partial political amnesty would come at the end of February or the beginning of March.[4]

During the interim Korolenko came close to being subjected to new and even more serious prosecution. I had been lucky enough to get the Chamber of Justice to review and reverse its own decisions in regard to several charges bearing on Korolenko for articles by Myakotin, Peshekhonov, and Muizhel, but there was still one charge on which a trial at that time seemed inevitable.

As I cautiously felt out Korolenko, I could see that a new misfortune was approaching, because he would behave himself in the same implacable manner as he did in the case pertaining to Elpatievsky's article. I decided to try a bit of craftiness. I told him that the Senate had changed its practice and that it was no longer holding the nominal editors responsible, but rather those who actually edited the publications, which for the incriminating issue of *Russkoe bogatstvo* was either Professor V. I. Semevsky or N. F. Annensky (who died not long before the beginning of the case). I asked Korolenko to help me get this matter straightened out, and I invited him and Semevsky to come and see me.

During the years of defending *Russkoe bogatstvo* from the attacks of the Main Administration for Affairs of the Press and the prosecutor's office, it was much harder for me to cope with the editorial staff than with its adversaries, for it seemed impossible for anyone to reach a compromise with N. F. Annensky, A. V.

---

[4] [The amnesty was announced on February 21, 1913, marking the three hundredth anniversary of Romanov rule in Russia.]

Peshekhonov, V. A. Myakotin, P. F. Yakubovich (Melshin), and the others. However, it was comforting to feel that their integrity and steadfastness in the struggle for their beliefs were combined with a very feminine tenderness toward their friends and a touching appreciation for the smallest kindness. When I read in the anniversary (and, alas, the last) issue of *Russkoe bogatstvo*[5] the kind lines dedicated to me by the editorial staff—"from us and from the readers"—I wanted to reply, but there was no longer any place to do so. I wanted to say, "The thanks should go to you and not to me for the unforgettable joy of our association over the years."

But to continue. Semevsky and Korolenko arrived. In a letter to me, dated February 10, 1913, Vladimir Galaktionovich described the meeting that had forced him to acknowledge the truth of the matter. He wrote:

I have tried to recall our conversation as exactly as possible, and here are the exact, and yet rather vague, results of my recollections. You had begun the conversation before I arrived. When you led me into your study, Vasily Ivanovich (Semevsky) was already there, and you informed me of a plan for the defense that had already been prepared as a result of your previous conversation. In answer to my observation that it would appear as though we were "laying the blame on the dead," Vasily Ivanovich objected that actually the situation was as follows: He had presented the censor's corrections to Nikolay Fyodorovich (Annensky), the only member of the editorial staff available at the time, and they had even conferred about several passages, I believe, by telephone. You added that Vasily Ivanovich should not be asked to make up and say things that actually had not happened. I attempted to say that the editorial staff, which officially meant me, was in fact taking care of the censorship; but I did not particularly insist, since I understood that this would place Vasily Ivanovich in an impossible situation. This was the entire conversation, as I remember it. Why has a question arisen about it?

A few days ago, I sent a note about "ritualistic murders" to *Russkiia vedomosti* [*Russian Gazette*]. I think you subscribe to it, don't you?

In regard to Mrs. V.'s case, I completely agree with you. All I needed was your professional opinion in order to calm down the sisters. One of them in particular longed for a competent opinion,

[5] [The issue of September, 1914, marked the thirty-fifth anniversary of the journal.]

because she felt that there were some prospects in this situation. And, of course, she knew that all I had to offer were general observations. Thank you for your convincing reply. This should put an end to the hopes for amnesty.[6]

This time Korolenko was wrong. A few days after his letter, the amnesty decree of February 21 was published. The decree made me happy for many persons but particularly for Korolenko. The "two weeks" which had so terribly burdened me, fell at last from my shoulders.

Whether because he realized how concerned I had been or because he recalled my harsh appraisal of the oratorical talent he displayed in court, Vladimir Galaktionovich congratulated me on the "monarchial mercy" in his letter of March 16, 1917:[7]

And so, my heinous and unrepented crimes, as specified in Articles 128, 129, 1304, and others, have now been buried in oblivion by monarchial mercy. Among those that have been blotted out are my "two weeks," which I honestly earned with my own oratorical efforts. For these two weeks I congratulate myself, and for the rest I congratulate you. Monarchial mercy has spared you the thankless task of defending such a criminal as me. But for how long? God only knows. At least for the time being. And that's good. Thank you, dear Oskar Osipovich. Avdotia Semyonovna is also grateful to you for her husband, whom you have so long defended. We wish you equal success in other cases that are even more difficult.

A German poet said that his heart was the center of the world, a place where contending sides collided, and that every blow they inflicted on one another caused him pain. Korolenko neither wrote nor uttered such words, but he always felt responsible for the cruelty, slovenliness, and disorder of Russian life. For instance, in 1895 he broke off in the middle of a word while working on the material he had brought back from America and threw himself

[6] [Mrs. V. was Praskovia Semyonovna Ivanovskaya-Voloshenko, the sister of Korolenko's wife, for whom Korolenko had asked Gruzenberg's assistance in securing amnesty (see p. 177). The sisters apparently were Korolenko's wife, Avdotia Semyonovna, and her older sister, Alexandra Semyonovna Malysheva. Again, Korolenko is alluding to the possibility of Praskovia Semyonovna being granted amnesty under the terms of the manifesto of October 21, 1905.]
[7] [The date of this letter should read 1913. The letter is included in O. O. Gruzenberg, *Ocherki i rechi* [*Essays and Speeches*] (New York, 1944), 235–36.]

into defending the Multan Votyaks,[8] who were quite foreign to him, because he considered this to be just as important as his literary endeavors. He expended as much creative energy and endured as many torments in converting his ideas and feelings into words on this case as on any of his best literary compositions.

Although he had not yet seen the Multan Votyaks, his strong artistic perception enabled him already to know them intimately, and he experienced their helplessness along with them. He could not put out of his mind the words of one of the defendants, as reported widely in the press. When the jury announced the first verdict of guilt, the old man turned to the spectators and cried out in despair, "Go down to the market place and ask the people there. Maybe they'll help!"

It was necessary to ward off unjust suffering from these helpless people; and it was necessary to protect the Russian social conscience from one of the gravest of superstitions—those in the area of justice. Korolenko made a careful study of the religious and moral concepts of the Votyak people and their living conditions. He mastered the evidence in the case to the smallest detail. And he brought to the trial his acute sensitivity and vigilant concern. He would spend the entire day in the stuffy hall where the trial was being held and the night thrashing about his room, unable to sleep.

One of his defense associates told me, "There was only a thin wall between our rooms. I would just get to sleep when Korolenko would start flailing about, his boots thumping on the floor. I would yell at him, 'Vladimir Galaktionovich, it's time to sleep.' He would mumble an apology in embarrassment and go to bed. And then, before even half an hour had passed, I would hear his bare feet smacking along the floor. And that's how it was every night until the very end of the trial." I doubt that many people know how much this defense cost Korolenko, both physically and spiritually.

I remember how in 1913, when I asked Korolenko to share the defense of the Beilis case with me, he immediately shrank away. "I'll give you an answer in a couple of days," he said.

He was serious, almost sad, when he came to see me. He began thoughtfully to explain. "I can't. In these two days I've worn myself out. I've felt as though I were already making the defense.

[8] [See p. 170. The Votyaks who had been accused were from the village of Multan.]

Just like with the Multans. After that case I was ill for more than a year. There was no way that I could overcome my insomnia. So many years have passed since that time, but when I remember the courtroom, the defendants standing there bewildered, the struggle I experienced. . . ."

Then he added, "I'm ashamed to say that I simply cannot open the drawer containing the paper and notes from that case."

In Korolenko's story *The Painter Alymov*,* which is strewn with autobiographical features, Alymov complains that three years have already gone by since he abandoned his brush because of getting caught up in an urgent court case.

In January, 1897, Korolenko wrote to his brother Illarion Galaktionovich, "I spent the fall of '95 in a nervous state of excitement, composing reports and writing articles. The only vacation I took that year was another trip to Mamadysh for a seven-and-a-half-day conference at the end of which I began to suffer from acute insomnia." And further on in the same letter he wrote, "The insomnia has lasted for a long time. I have lost so much weight that people who know me hardly recognize me. However, I have felt all along that there would be no use in taking medicine."

I recall that many people were puzzled about how this one case could have such a shattering effect on him. One case! But then, even a sturdy stevedore sometimes breaks down under an excessive load. Similarly, it is possible for a person to break down under a spiritual burden and remain that way forever.

Korolenko told me many times that he used to dream of becoming a professional defense counsel, and since he had not gotten a university diploma, he wanted to register as a private attorney. He concluded one of his conversations with me by saying, "Inside me lives a judicial soul. My father's heritage is showing.[9] But being so sensitive and impressionable, how could I participate in courtroom battles?"

And yet Korolenko did not protect himself altogether, for he became a defender outside the courtroom. Far away from the glamour and beauty of courtroom competition, without the joys of combat, he bore the most difficult part of a defense by becoming an inter-

---

* Now published for the first time in volume 15 of *Complete Posthumous Collected Works*. [The article is more readily available in Korolenko, *Sobranie sochinenii* (*Collected Works*), 3, 273–329]

[9] [Korolenko's father, Galaktion Afanasevich Korolenko, had long been a judge in the Rovno circuit court.]

cessor and mediator for those who could not be saved except through solicitations and personal influence. The only ones who can understand and appreciate the full extent of Korolenko's sacrifice are those who themselves have traveled this same road, who have known how insulting it is to stand in waiting rooms, to make solicitations that have no legal basis, and to submit petitions that carry with them the constant apprehension of running up against individuals who are rude and irritable from fatigue.

If one considers the constancy with which he responded to the misfortunes of others and the number of persons he saved from execution, he matched any of the political defense counsels of his time. Moreover, he surpassed us all by his instinctive horror of the death penalty. We agonized only over those cases which we had occasion to defend; he agonized over cases about which he had only heard. In his mind he sat on the defendants' bench with all those condemned to death; he experienced with them the agony of awaiting the death verdict, and frequently he rushed from the defense lawyers to the authorities in order to save those for whom all the others had lost hope. In one of his articles, which was devoted to the court-martial cases I had conducted, he casually gave his regards to "the Kuznetsovs, and Krasnovs, and Tokarevs, and Akimovs, and the old Jew Koziol (provided he has not died of happiness), and to the sixteen-year-old gymnasium student Petrov." But very few remembered and even fewer knew that in the happiness of most of these defendants were drops of Korolenko's own blood and sweat.

No socially conscious European writer has ever expressed such intense pain, anger, and love in dealing with the death penalty as did Korolenko in his marvelous book *An Everyday Occurrence*. And surely no country could be so remiss as our own when it failed even to remember Korolenko on the day that the Provisional Government performed a most wonderful act of human trust by abolishing the death penalty.

It is hardly necessary to add that most of Korolenko's defense petitions ended in success, not so much because of his name as because of the intensity of his love, which was stronger than the persistence of the avenger. Indeed, he could not help but succeed, for in every case he encountered he would suffer, as if from a dread disease, and he would infect those to whom he appealed.

Having come in contact with the Beilis case, he stuck to it with his whole heart and became my co-worker, or rather my inspirer.

It was he who organized the powerful protest of Russian public opinion. It was his appeal, after it had assembled and united the Russian writers, scholars, and public figures around the Beilis trial, that then spread abroad. Thanks to his influence, scholars in France, Germany, and England rendered unselfish assistance to the defense through their articles and brochures.

As long as the investigation was in process—over a year—he was consumed by the case. He was living at the time in St. Petersburg, across from me on the corner of Kirochnaya and Preobrazhenskaya Streets. Seldom did a day go by without his telephone call to me. "Is there anything new?" "Have you seen this or that book or brochure?" "I received a letter with some curious information. Are you free? I'll be right over."

Whenever any of my colleagues from Kiev who were working on the defense came to see me, or whenever some civic-minded person brought news about the progress of the case, Korolenko came, too, so as not to miss a single conference. And when he went to the Poltava region for the summer, his letters seldom failed to contain an inquiry about the case, some information or advice, or just simply a bit of encouragement.

When the time came for the defense, Korolenko wanted to "hear" the case, but the doctors forbade him such prolonged excitement. I wrote to him that I was leaving and asked him to send me the report on the Multan case. His return letter arrived after I was already in Kiev. He wrote:

I am writing to you from deep in the Poltava countryside and do not know whether this letter will reach you in time. You write that you will be gone after the 20th and will not return until the 15th or 20th of October. Does this mean that you are on your way to the Beilis trial? There are rumors here (including those in the local papers) that after the opening of the session the trial will be postponed again. Is this true? By the way, there is no report on the Multan case. That is, there is no report about the last trial, unless one wants to consider the newspaper reports, which are far from complete. My friends and I compiled a report only about the second trial: I have this booklet in Poltava but have no way of sending it now, because I am in a remote village, twenty-seven *versts* from the nearest railroad station. If you'll give me your address, I'll send it to you later. Generally speaking, is it possible to write to you in Kiev? Are you going there directly from St. Petersburg? I have great faith in your success, and from the bottom of my heart I wish you well.

There are Black Hundred brochures, published by the Pochaev

Monastery, about "the lad Gavriil, who was tortured by the *Zhids.*"
They are also showing his relics in Slutsk. I have a few remarks in
case these brochures were to be introduced in court as evidence
of ritual murders.

Thus, it was clear that the doctors had won, and Korolenko was
not coming to Kiev.

However, on the third or fourth day of the trial, his distinctive
curly head was gaily nodding to me from the gallery of the courtroom. As soon as there was a recess, we got together. It turned
out that he was not alone. He had mobilized the entire family,
and Avdotia Semyonovna and Sofia Vladimirovna had accompanied him. Only Natalia Vladimirovna had stayed at home because of some ailment.

None of the spectators or journalists, in fact not even all the
defense counsels, could match Korolenko's punctuality in attending the trial and his intensity in following its course. I would meet
him in court in the morning, since both of us came very early,
and during the recesses I would get a dose of encouragement from
him, as well as valuable pointers resulting from his keen observation. In particularly difficult moments of struggle, my eyes
would meet his intense, affable gaze.

Suddenly Vladimir Galaktionovich disappeared for three days.
Then he appeared again. What was he up to? I discovered that
he was busy with an investigation as to why Beilis was being tried
by such an unenlightened group of jurors, which was unusual for
Kiev. He studied the current jury lists for other sections of the
court, and with the aid of some trustworthy people he managed
to examine lists for the previous two years, coming to the conclusion that the composition of the jury had been determined arti-
ficially.

Consequently, he wrote an accusatory article, which appeared
a few days later in the newspaper. About three days after its appearance, the newspaper printed a semi-official communication
about bringing charges against Korolenko for disseminating false
information, which was arousing hostility against the government.
"As I said, you'll have to defend me a few more times yet," Korolenko laughed.

At last the final day of the trial arrived. Looking gaunt and
haggard, Korolenko told me with alarm that on the previous day
he and Avdotia Semyonovna had spent some time wandering
around the market places. They had heard conversations about

needing to get bags ready, because as soon as Beilis was convicted it would be possible to break into Jewish shops.

He awaited the verdict with no less anguish than I. What we did not know was something that I learned only after the February Revolution, when I had opportunity to inspect the secret volumes of materials on the Beilis case in the files of the Department of Police. The gendarme authorities, in agreement with the court, had placed a gendarme disguised as a guard in the jury room. At the time of the trial, we did not suspect that the prosecutor of the Chamber of Justice Chaplinsky and the presiding judge Boldyrev could lower themselves to such baseness. But with his sharp perceptiveness Korolenko sensed that the authorities knew from their secret information that Beilis was doomed. When the jurors left for the jury room to make their decision, Korolenko said to me, "I smell a corpse."

He gazed in anguish at the demonstration being staged by the impatient victors. They had begun a requiem for the "tortured" Andrey Yushchinsky in the cathedral that stood on the same square as the court. Government officials arrived in uniform with swords, and after praying they hurried to the court in order not to miss the triumphant moment when the verdict was announced.

However, it turned out that "the *muzhiks*[10] stood up for themselves," and they spoiled the celebration for those in charge.

Indeed a miracle happened. The preliminary vote in favor of convicting Beilis was seven to five, but when the foreman began taking the final vote, one peasant rose to his feet, prayed to the icon, and said resolutely, "I don't want to have this sin on my soul —he's not guilty."

I got together with Korolenko that evening. He was as happy as a child, partly because of Beilis but also for other reasons. Although the old populist had threatened more than once "to take issue with a younger brother," he was happy that his faith in the people had once again been justified.*

Then came the war and with it the revolution. Korolenko feared the one as well as the other. He knew that so much resentment

[10] [The term "muzhiks" generally meant simple villagers or country folk.]

* In the sketch already cited, *The Painter Alymov*, and also in one of its fifteen variants, entitled *Taking Issue With a Younger Brother*, all the faults of this "brother" are listed, but they are all of such nature that they are readily forgiven.

and anger had accumulated in the populace that no government could contain or even assuage the cruel outbursts.

I remember how once, still long before the revolution, I showed Korolenko one of Blok's poems, *Is Everything at Peace Among the People?* At that time both of us were gripped by the hopeless horror of the last line: "Lord! We are fleeing from judgment."

"Will we escape it?" said Korolenko, his voice filled with emotion.

We did not. Judgment came and with it condemnation. In a letter to me after the February revolution, Korolenko wrote with alarm that everything was unclear and uncertain, but he took courage in the observation that this is the way it happens in early spring. The morning breaks in mist and fog but then gradually clears and turns into a fine day.

I saw Korolenko for the last time in the summer of 1918 in Kiev, where he came to intercede before the hetman authorities[11] for his son-in-law, K. I. Lykhovich, who had been arrested in Poltava.

Korolenko loved him with a special kind of love, apprehensive and tender. This love reflected not only his feeling toward his daughter and granddaughter ("the French lady," as Korolenko called her because she was born in France), but also a maternal tenderness toward the doomed man.

Lykhovich was suffering from a severe form of heart disease. With a mournful smile Korolenko frequently repeated that the physicians called his son-in-law "a disgrace to medicine," because they did not understand how he kept on living.

I met Vladimir Galaktionovich on the day that he had secured a categorical promise from the highest hetman authorities to free his son-in-law. Now he was leaving, satisfied with his trip. Nevertheless, our meeting was sad. Korolenko was depressed by the civil war. We began to talk about the yearning to go abroad that was beginning at that time.

"It will be a bitter life for them abroad," he said. "I know this

[11] [When the German armies occupied the Ukraine in 1918, they established a puppet government under P. P. Skoropadsky, a Ukrainian nationalist and ex-officer in the Imperial Russian Army, who commanded Cossack detachments loyal to the Ukrainian movement. Skoropadsky adopted the title of hetman, which had been used in past centuries to designate Cossack leaders. His hetmanate lasted from April 29 until December 14, shortly after the defeat of the Central Powers, when it fell to other Ukrainian nationalists, temporarily aided by the Red Army.]

for myself from my trip to America. How many times without having completed my mission did I long to flee homeward, away from the melancholy that was choking me. Even during my exile in the remote regions of Siberia, I felt much happier than in America, because everything in exile was at least our own. Even the melancholy was somewhat different. It was not as angry as it had been over there, but instead it was as though it had been tamed."

"So, what are you doing now in the Ukraine under the hetman administration?"

"The same thing I was doing in tsarist Russia—coming to someone's rescue, helping someone out, and if someone is particularly malicious blocking his way."

"And how is the literary work? Are you writing a novel at last?"

Korolenko smiled and waved his hand. "My novels don't have women in them," he said. "And without women what kind of novel can there be? I have other things on my mind. More important work always seems to come along." This "more important" work consumed an immense artistic talent and turned it to ashes without permitting it to reveal all the potential pent up in it.

"What a pity!" say the faithful friends of the arts.

"That's how it had to be!" reply others by the tens of thousands, those who over the years have become accustomed to seeking the answer to questions of their conscience not only in Korolenko's books but also in his deeds and personal qualities, those who have become accustomed to relying on his heartbeat as a measure of their own.

Chapter 17

Maxim Gorky

"Yes, I'm dying!"
replied the falcon, sighing deeply.
"I've lived a life of glory.
I've fought with valor.
I've seen the sky.
You'll never see it from so close."

MAXIM GORKY, *Song of the Falcon*

I got to know Gorky during the period of his incredible fame, that kind of fame in which a hero becomes a legend in his own lifetime. It is remarkable how rapidly this fame came, without anyone promoting him, and certainly without Gorky promoting himself.

Gorky was one of the few Russian writers who truly understood the common people and who in turn was understood by them. He was their own, and, as is always the case, "one's beloved is always lovely."

During the latter half of 1904, Gorky asked me to help him organize the defense of a certain provincial group of revolutionaries, and a few months later he himself became my client. Subsequently our acquaintance deepened into a friendship that continued for many years. My first-hand impressions of him do not extend beyond 1917. After this date, we met only once abroad, when together we looked through his letters to me, and he gave me permission to publish them. I am publishing them here for the first time, though even so I am not quoting them in their entirety.[1]

I am sure that I understand Gorky correctly as a man of complete integrity, without pretense or guile. I was always touched by the way he appreciated the smallest favor, a trait so rare among us.

[1] [These letters have not been published elsewhere, nor have I been able to find the originals.]

He believed firmly that the commandment, "Thou shalt not steal," pertains not only to someone's purse but also to someone's merits.

I do not know whether many people have noticed the fact, typical of Gorky, that he did not dedicate his collected works to someone famous or influential, but rather to a humble lawyer from Nizhny Novgorod. Why? Simply because this man treated Gorky with thoughtfulness and human kindness during the time that Gorky worked as a clerk for him. I have before me the first volume of the *sixth* edition of Gorky's works, but the special dedicatory page remains unchanged: "To Alexander Ivanovich Lanin from M. Gorky."

What a naive romantic! Who has ever heard of a patient publicly acknowledging a doctor who treats "secret illnesses!"[2]

I have already noted Gorky's incredible fame. How else can one describe it? I remember a story that I heard in the summer of 1905 from a magistrate, an elderly bachelor, M. P. Shramchenko. He was an intelligent, kindly "khokhol,"[3] who preferred hunting to jurisprudence and his official career, and therefore left frequently for his estate in Nizhny Novgorod.

"Well, Oskar Osipovich," he said to me, "soon we'll be congratulating you on your appointment as Minister of Justice."

"I've not received an offer yet," I replied.

"Just wait awhile, you'll get it. A few days ago I was roaming the woods with some peasant friends. The hunting wasn't going very well, and so we were chatting more than shooting. Suddenly one of them says, 'I hear we'll soon be called to Pieter to set up a Tsar.' 'Is that so? And whom do you want for a Tsar?' 'For sure not a *barin*, but one of our own—Gorky.' Your client will certainly show his gratitude to you with a ministerial post. 'Then, Ophelia, do not forget me in your prayers.' "[4]

I also remember how deeply I was touched by the naive anxiety expressed in a letter from a simple woman in the provinces. It arrived shortly after Gorky was released from the Peter and Paul

---

[2] [Venereal diseases.]

[3] [A Russian nickname for a Ukrainian. The basic meaning of this term is a crest or tuft of hair. In the seventeenth century, many of the Ukrainian cossacks (the *zaporozhtsi*) shaved their heads, leaving only a tuft of hair on top. The Russians identified this characteristic with the Ukrainians in general, hence the nickname "khokhol."]

[4] [A character in Gorky's play *The Lower Depths* recites this line in reference to Ophelia in Shakespeare's *Hamlet*.]

Fortress, because his lung condition had worsened. This kind soul inquired of me how it was with Gorky's phlegm—whether it sank in water or floated on top, because if it sank, then Gorky was a goner, but if it floated, then he would live. I hastened to reassure her that the phlegm did not sink but floated.

Then, too, the railway station authorities had a name for the suburban trains that carried minor civil servants and workers. They called these trains "Maximkas." You could hear them yell, "Hey, there, is the Maximka ready?"

Moreover, the other world, so distant and forever foreign to Gorky, with Grand Prince Konstantin Konstantinovich at its head, rushed to reward him with a membership in the Academy. Of course, Gorky did not remain a member for long. He was expelled in 1902, upon incurring an administrative penalty for "unreliability."[5] Incidentally, this involvement of police action with literature produced widespread indignation. In fact, Korolenko and Chekhov immediately served notice that they were resigning their titles as members of the Academy.

I remember the first performance of the play, *The Lower Depths*, in St. Petersburg. At the end of the performance, a letter of appreciation to Gorky was put out for people to sign. The pilgrimage that took place was remarkable, as people from all walks of life hurried to put down their names.

Gorky's play *Summer Folk* went through twenty-four performances in a month and a half, a figure that was established precisely at a trial in the Senate, in which the marvelous actress, V. G. Kommisarzhevskaya, with my assistance, brought action against the acting governor of St. Petersburg, Wendorf. On January 18, 1905, the governor banned the performance, which had been permitted the night before, because he was afraid that Gorky's arrest the previous week might cause demonstrations by the audience.[6]

I remember the endless flow of telegrams sent by scholars, writers, and lawyers from abroad to the St. Petersburg Council

[5] [Gorky was elected to the Imperial Academy of Sciences (of which Grand Prince Konstantin Konstantinovich was president) as an honorary member in *belles lettres* in February, 1902. His election was invalidated two weeks later, when it was discovered that he had been arrested in April, 1901, on the charge of printing subversive pamphlets, and that he was still under police supervision pending further investigation.]

[6] [Gorky had been arrested for drafting an appeal following the events of Bloody Sunday, January 9, 1905. See p. 201.]

of the Bar. They all expressed the same concern that in the forthcoming trial Gorky be protected from the malicious vindictiveness
of the authorities and provided with a reliable defense counsel.
A telegram from the lawyers of the small Italian town of Trani is
especially etched into my memory due to its unique wording. It
read: "To the Chairman of the Bar in St. Petersburg. Our council of the bar wishes to convey its desire, in the name of the uni-
versal guarantee of the rights of the defense, that these rights shall
not be violated with regard to the thinker Maxim Gorky. President
Dascanno."

A *thinker*. Tolstoy once expressed much the same idea, when he
said to Gorky, "You have a wise heart." *

Did this general infatuation with Gorky bring him joy? Not
really. Whatever joy it brought was infinitesimal. Moreover,
while this joy may have come early in Gorky's life, it came only
after he had already been through a great deal.

Why had he roamed across most of the Russian land, his tattered
pants pulled tightly about his constantly hungry belly? Why had
he taken the groans, the servile fear, the submissive hopelessness
he found and made them part of himself? Was it only because
he wanted personal success? No, this was not his motivation.

If from early youth someone's heart has been repeatedly pierced
and cannot be healed, the only thing that can save that person
is constant and intense work or an overwhelming idea, what
Schiller called tying one's frail bark to a ship that sails the ocean.
Nothing else will do.

Gorky's faith was *Man* and his church was the *Collective*. However, man was not his first love. For a short time Gorky had a
romance with God. This romance did not succeed, but I have no
doubt that it did exist. Like others who have had their love shattered, he buried it, as if to say: I've been an atheist since birth,
and that's all there is to it. I don't care to discuss the subject with
anyone.

Of course, Gorky sought God, but not through the investigative

---

* Incidentally, the expression "a wise heart" was an exceptionally fortuitous
one. Tolstoy made use of it, as did Merezhkovsky in a play. However,
both of them forgot to mention that the expression, now so famous,
belongs to Dostoevsky. In a letter to A. P. Filosofova, he remarked, "You
have a wise heart, Anna Pavlovna." This letter was published after
Dostoevsky's death.

bureaus of "religious-philosophical societies,"[7] nor by means of newspaper publications,[8] nor in the lectures of fashionable wind-bags (the kind who publicly confess the sins of others, while sinning on the sly themselves). He was desperate in his search for God, and he felt he had nowhere to turn. In his younger years he attempted suicide, and the bullet remained in his body to the end. Why suicide? Was he afraid of life? Not at all. Fate tormented him with all kinds of fears, but it did not intimidate him. His only fear was that he could not give meaning to life, not justify his terrible loneliness in the midst of humanity. Like other highly gifted individuals, he always felt alone. This is the horrible price that must be paid for being one of the chosen few.

It was interesting to observe Gorky when he was sitting by himself, certain that no one was looking. He seemed to be listening to a voice sounding ceaselessly within him. It may have been different later, but in my time he did not know how to laugh. He laughed not with his eyes, nor with the wrinkles of his face, but only with his voice, as though he had climbed onto the highest shelf of a bathhouse and there was striking himself incessantly with switches and letting out an occasional cry, whether from pleasure or pain one could not tell.[9]

Gorky was not a drinker, as Tolstoy for some reason used to say. Why should he need wine when his blood was already intoxicated? Gorky had been to the very depths of life and had experienced many difficult and painful ordeals, which would have made anyone else not only a realist but a crude materialist. Yet, contrary to any kind of logic, Gorky was a romantic—an incorrigible romantic. But how else could it have been? One cannot seek faith and social justice if one is not a romantic.

[7] [Gorky was familiar with the *Bogoiskateli*, or God-seekers—Dmitry Merezhkovsky, Zinaida Hippius, Dmitry Filosofov, and other mystical intellectuals—and the Religious-Philosophical Society they formed for exploring the union between God and human beings. Gorky saw himself as a *Bogostroitel*, or God-builder, his God being the perfection of human capabilities.]

[8] [The Russian word *publikatsii* in this case means short articles that individuals or religious or philosophical groups paid to have published in the newspapers in order to disseminate their particular points of view.]

[9] [In Russian bathhouses, the bathers would lie on shelves arranged along the walls, the highest shelves providing the greatest effect from the steam. The bathers would strike themselves with switches as an aid to circulation.]

Gorky read much and knew much. And he knew things thoroughly, not like someone who reads uncritically or superficially. He wrote to me from Capri, "I have over three thousand books, and I read eight newspapers and all the journals."

This was no exaggeration, but the exact truth. In his letters to K. P. Pyatnitsky, who was in charge of the "Znanie" ["Knowledge"] Publishing House,[10] there were more requests about sending various books, collections of folk literature, journals, and newspapers, than instructions pertaining to business affairs.

Gorky treated scholarship with a romantic respect. As a typical example, while speaking of Tolstoy's crude, nihilistic regard of scholarly knowledge, he exclaimed with genuine horror, "And he said all of this after Jenner, Bering, Pasteur—what a scoundrel!"

Some people accuse Gorky of pretending to be a Bolshevik without ever actually being one. This charge is not true, for he was a Bolshevik from the early years of the formation of the party. This affiliation was known not only to people who were closely associated with literature but to the authorities as well. I can personally cite as evidence the fact that he asked me to assume the defense of Burenin, the secretary of the Petersburg committee of the Bolshevik party. This case, which took place in the St. Petersburg Chamber of Justice with participation of class representatives, ended with an acquittal. One can find a reference to the case in Gorky's letter to me of September 8, 1908. He wrote, "Burenin was here a few days ago, and he had much to say about you."

I can also cite other evidence. In the spring of 1909, I took advantage of Holy Week and Easter Week to realize my old dream of seeing Italy. After deducting the time needed to travel both directions, I was left with nine or ten days at my disposal. Of course, given this amount of time, my getting to know Italy was reduced to checking Bedeker's guide and seeing if everything in the major cities was where it belonged. There was really no time left for a trip to Capri, especially since I pictured Capri as just a tiny button on the royal robe of Italy. However, I felt ashamed, for it was not right to be in Italy without visiting an old friend. My wife and I arrived on Capri late in the evening, checked into a hotel, and at ten o'clock the next morning set off for Gorky's place. Soon we were gazing at the peeling exterior of a rented

[10] [Gorky was one of a group that held shares in and managed the "Znanie" Publishing House in St. Petersburg. He was also its leading literary contributor.]

house, about which his Petersburg "friends" talked and wrote in the newspapers, as they would about a luxurious private villa. But one cannot fault them for doing so, because out of love for Gorky they probably considered that a great writer needs to "delight in fasting and bask in privations."[11]

The "villa" was poorly furnished. In the dining room stood a long, unpainted table on sawhorses, where Gorky, may God forgive him, fed us rather badly. We encountered many people at the "villa": his adopted son, Zinovy Alexeevich (a brother of Sverdlov, the future chairman of VTsIK[12]), Lunacharsky, Shalyapin, and Malinovsky-Bogdanov, the widely educated and intelligent philosopher-sociologist, who for some reason came to nothing. After breakfast we went out onto the terrace. At first, Shalyapin, who was rather frivolous, as are all highly gifted persons, and the adopted Sverdlov clowned around, imitating circus wrestlers making their entrance. Then, Gorky started a conversation with Lunacharsky. He talked about his plan to establish a school for propagandists on Capri and was calculating how much it would cost him. I listened gloomily and thought: This is all we need now. We've just barely avoided a trial for his "appeal,"[13] the examining magistrate's office is filled with literary cases awaiting prosecution according to the stringent Article 129 of the Criminal Code, and here he is with a new and even more dangerous venture. It will be a long time until Gorky sees Russia again.

The accusation that Gorky only feigned to be a Bolshevik is a malicious lie. Why should it be so surprising that he was a Bolshevik? I can understand that if I had suddenly become a Bolshevik at the age of seventy, without ever having been a socialist, this would have been strange indeed. Gorky, however, had joined the Bolsheviks early in his life. His only mistake was that he did not emigrate with us after the victory of his party.

Let me return now to the question of Gorky's faith. My insistence that he believed in God from his early youth is substantiated also by a page in his story *The Confession*. There he describes a religious procession of peasants with an enthusiasm and depth of

---

[11] [See p. 3.]

[12] [The Russian abbreviation for the All-Russian Central Executive Committee of the Congress of Soviets, a major organ of state power following the Bolshevik revolution. Ya. M. Sverdlov served as its chairman from November, 1917, until his death in 1919.]

[13] [See p. 202.]

emotion that cannot be explained by talent alone. It must be that the scars of a wound closed long ago had begun to ache again.

Then, as I have already noted, it was Man that became the object of Gorky's faith. This faith was strong, and he never abandoned it. It runs through all his work. According to Gorky's faith, a "Godlike man" can do anything if he really desires it.

As always happens after an unsuccessful war, whether foreign or domestic—Russia had to survive both at the same time in 1904–1906—the stress reveals itself most sharply in sensual manifestations. There were the *ogarochniks* and *ogarochny* evenings,[14] which crippled the lives of many innocent young women. The sensualist writers, led by Artsybashev, reared their heads and behaved insolently. Artsybashev's filthy novel, *Sanin*, in which a woman is treated like a mare, met with great public success. When the book was seized and a criminal investigation was begun, according to an article on pornography in the Code, Artsybashev asked me to defend him. I remember his astonishment and even resentment when I told him that I had read only a few chapters of his novel when it was being published in one of the journals and suggested that he send me the book, so I could look through it.

I immediately asked Gorky what I should do. In reply I received a letter from him indicating his surprise. At the same time, the letter was remarkably well thought out and sincere. It read:

You surprised me with your question as to whether you should defend Artsybashev. It seems to me that in this case there is no question. From my point of view it doesn't matter that someone has written a justification of the bestial nature in man, but that the fools who order us about consider themselves to have the right to judge a person for his opinions, violate his freedom of thought, and punish him. And for what? What is a writer? He is this or that arrangement of nerves, organized in some way or another by the pressure of the psychological atmosphere that surrounds him. A person of our time is agonizingly defenseless from the influence of society, which is frequently hostile toward him. He is defenseless because he is psychologically impoverished, helpless. The choice of

[14] [Literally, the term *ogarochniks* means "those with candle stubs," in this case young intellectuals of the sensualist school, who extolled the gratification of the senses and advocated living for the moment, or "burning the candle at both ends." The "evenings" were those such as the all-night receptions at the flat of the mystical poet, Vyacheslav Ivanov, in St. Petersburg.]

impressions entering the soul, the receptacle of experience, does not depend on the will of Artsybashev, Timofeev, or Ivanov. It may be that Timofeev is a very chaste and pure fellow, but the quantity and quality of his observations of reality forced him unwittingly to choose Duloup* as his hero; and it is very possible that Sanin is as repulsive to Artsybashev as he is to me. Perhaps Sanin is poorly depicted, but can we maintain that he is not real?

Forgive me for making a crude comparison, but much of our contemporary literature resembles vomit. People are poisoned by the impressions of their existence, and they become sick. In the vast majority of those who are presently writing, the ability of the organism to resist the social poisons that penetrate it is not sufficiently developed, and in many writers this ability is lacking altogether. They are psychologically unstable, always wavering. Moreover, they are extremely impressionable and they lack any kind of corrective device for sorting out their impressions and organizing them. It seems to me that this corrective device is a *perception* of the world as an active and dynamic process, in which everything is temporal and only motion is eternal. I know that there are people who contend that this motion is meaningless and insulting to human dignity, but I also know that those who talk the most about human dignity actually possess the least amount of it. For me, however, life is full of meaning; it is a most magnificient process of accumulating psychological energy, a process which is obvious and undeniable, and perhaps even capable of turning dead matter into that which feels and thinks.

But my views are irrelevant in this case, and I apologize for getting off the track. Your question, I repeat, surprised me very much. It disturbs me because I hear in it the sad sound of alienation, of psychological paralysis and estrangement that ruins so many of us in our prime.

Forgive me once more, but I must say that we would be acting more intelligently and more decently if we were to unite in defending one of our own. And it would not make any difference whether it were Artsybashev, as in this case, or someone else. Our enemy is banality, in which our feet are mired up to our knees. This banality in life is cleverly and diligently cultivated by those for whom it is essential, like a dirty moat which blocks access to their fortress. The trial against Artsybashev is banal and impertinent, as are all these so-called "literary trials."

While we were exchanging letters, I also had time to become more familiar with the novel *Sanin* and its author. Artsybashev repelled me with his complacency and ridiculous conceit that he

---

* Duloup was the hero of a criminal case dealing with the seduction of minors. It created a great sensation in Petersburg at the time.

was not a Russian but a Tartar, and that he did not love Russia. If that were so, why did he live there and eat its bread? And once, for no reason, he bared his arm and showed me an intricate tattoo.

I replied to Gorky that I could not agree with him, that the government was not involved here and the question pertained not to the freedom of creativity but to the freedom of publishing trash. I told him that when I read the last line of *Sanin* ("He jumped from the railroad car to meet the rising sun") even my dentures began to ache. He did not need to jump from the car to meet the rising sun while the train was moving. He jumped, in fact, as a ticketless passenger (in every sense of the word), when he noticed the approach of the conductor.

Let me dwell, at least for a few lines, on conversations I had with Gorky. At first I avoided touching on the Jewish question, which at that time so troubled the conscience of the Russian intellectuals. Was it out of fear of encountering a hidden anti-Semitism that I hesitated? Certainly not. Gorky was not that sort. I feared instead that he might try to assure me of his pro-Semitism.

Whether because of pride or for some other reason, I have always abhorred programmed pro-Semitism and have considered it more insulting than anti-Semitism. Who is an anti-Semite? Either a lazy fool, who has never bothered to examine his prejudices, or some malignant person, who hates others generally and displays his hatred along the line of least resistance. But the trouble with a conventional pro-Semite is that he speaks of Jews as if he were a member of the Society for the Protection of Animals. Usually I cut short such sugar-coated oratory with a casual remark: Is it worth talking about such trifles? A people is not like a loose woman, who needs sympathy because of her profession. What a people needs is for others to realize that it must be reckoned with and that it will respond to the slightest kick with a sound slap in the face.

What, then, was Gorky's attitude toward the Jewish question? In my opinion, it was the soundest attitude of all, the same as that held by Korolenko, Milyukov, or Mikhailovsky, for whom a question simply did not exist. As far as they were concerned, the Jews were deprived of rights, and therefore all decent people must come to their defense.

I recall that when Gorky was reading a new play to some friends in Kuokkala, my attention was drawn to a passage in which the hero remarks with horror about someone, "But, you know, he's an anti-Semite."

I said to Gorky, "Better take this passage out, or else everyone will make fun of it, for Russia's not the place to reproach someone with anti-Semitism. It's an everyday thing here, an *article de Saint-Petersbourg*."* Gorky looked at me in surprise, but he did not delete the passage.

It turned out that I was right. When that passage came along during the premiere, it drew some politely restrained, good-natured laughter from the audience.

I recall how Gorky described to me the pogrom in Nizhny Novgorod. Some thirty years have passed, but the sound of his voice and the expression of his face live within me as though it were yesterday. He spoke quietly and deliberately, gazing into the distance as we walked along, trying to overcome his emotions. His voice was filled with a mixture of pain and shame.

He finished the story with a shocking episode. A crowd was attacking a house inhabited by Jews. A small gang left the crowd and burst into the house itself. From the third story they threw out a coffin containing the body of a Jew dressed in ceremonial funeral garb. The attackers drew back in horror and scattered.

"Now, understand this," added Gorky. "One part of the crowd did not spare even the dead; but the other part, a much larger one, found that the very presence of a corpse quelled its malice and savage mischievousness."

No less typical of Gorky was his attitude toward women and children. The question of attitudes toward women is significant, not only because it pertains to half of the human race, but also because it provides a reliable measure of male conscientiousness. What a disgrace it is to add social and legal injustice to the gross unfairness of nature, which has burdened a woman with the pangs of pregnancy and childbirth, as well as the task of nursing these hungry little freeloaders. In family life it is not important who is guilty of what. All that is important is who suffers more. With rare exception it is the woman. Therefore, she is in the right, even when she is guilty of something.

In depicting women Gorky was always chaste and compassionate. He never chose to write about bedroom scenes, and he never encouraged the use of brothels. He did not produce a single obscene page. In his story *Mother*, he gave a touching portrait of a

* "Specialty of St. Petersburg."

woman, not merely of childbearer or mistress of the kitchen.

The elderly, old-fashioned women whom Gorky described loved their children so much that they also came to love their children's starry dreams. They often went hungry and were always fearful that the children would not return home after going out in the evening. They would listen night after night, anxiously awaiting the sweet music of those precious steps on the stairway. These mothers never complained, nor cursed, nor made reproaches. Timid, modest shadows, why have so few songs been composed about them? Why so few stories about their invisible deeds of valor?

In our folk wisdom we have the scornful expression: "Love is blind." What a monstrous absurdity! I am certain that this wisdom was first proclaimed by some proprietor of a pawnshop, who made a mistake in appraising an item that he coveted. No, love is not blind. It is the only thing in the whole world that indeed can see. Love alone has an eye that is sharp and true. It sees that which indifference will never discern.

Gorky also loved children, and his love for them was unbounded. He probably realized our great responsibility toward them. Of course, first of all he loved his own "Maximka." He loved him not only with a fatherly love, but a motherly love as well, a love that was watchful and concerned. At night he frequently took him to his own bed and entertained him with stories, either those of others or those he made up himself.

I recall Gorky's amusing account of something that Maximka once pulled on him. Gorky had just finished telling Maximka a story he had made up, and the boy's face shone with excitement. "Did you like the story?" Gorky asked. "Do you want me to tell you another one?"

The boy answered, cuddling up, "No, I'd rather have twenty kopeks for a pretty little top I saw."

Later on I saw Maxim Alexeevich for a few moments in the summer of 1922 at Gorky's place abroad. He was already married. A few years ago, I read in the newspaper a short notice of his death in Moscow. I sensed painfully what a loss this was for Gorky. On the spur of the moment, I wrote to him, but then I tore up the letter, for not long before this I myself had experienced the futility of words of consolation.[15]

[15] [Gorky's son died in May, 1934. Two years previously, Gruzenberg's only daughter, Sofia, had died in Berlin.]

Let me proceed now to Gorky's court cases and to clarifying certain passages in our correspondence. Between the third and the sixth of January, 1905, rumors began to circulate among the public and in the press that a priest named Gapon, from the prison administration, was organizing the working masses for a procession to the Winter Palace, with the aim of presenting their needs directly to the Emperor. These rumors were confirmed, and the Ministry of Justice called in Gapon for an explanation. Gapon acknowledged the rumors and declared categorically that the procession would take place and that it was fully within the law, since there were supposed to be no barriers between the monarch and his people.

Some civic groups began to worry, anticipating needless bloodshed. During the night of the eighth and ninth of January, a delegation was organized by a number of prominent public and political figures, including Gorky, I. V. Hessen, Professor Kareev, A. V. Peshekhonov, V. A. Myakotin, E. I. Kedrin, Professor V. I. Semevsky, N. N. Shnitnikov, and Ivanchin-Pisarev. The delegation called on the Minister of Internal Affairs, Svyatopolk-Mirsky, State Secretary Witte, and Major-General Rydzevsky, who was in charge of the police; but its concern resulted only in the departure of the Emperor and his family to Tsarskoe Selo, while massive military units were called out and ordered to use their weapons without leniency.

The morning of January 9 arrived, and the procession began, with several thousand workers carrying icons, banners, and portraits of the Emperor. Just as the crowd started to cross the Troitsky Bridge, it met with gunfire; and old men, women, and children, not to mention the young workers, fell to the ground.

The autocracy taught the people a firm lesson, but in doing so it also dealt itself a death blow. In my opinion, the visible events leading to both of our revolutions, those of 1905 and 1917, began with January 9, 1905, when the callousness of the autocracy aroused the anger of those who hitherto had been like gentle lambs.

The delegation felt obligated to inform the country about what had occurred and decided that it was appropriate to do so by issuing an appeal, which Gorky was entrusted with drawing up. During its searches the police found a draft of Gorky's appeal at the home of one of the members of the delegation. All the delegates were arrested and imprisoned in the Peter and Paul Fortress. However, after a short time they were released, all except Gorky, who was legally charged with drawing up the draft of the appeal.

The charge that was formulated read: "The Nizhny Novgorod guildsman, A. M. Peshkov,[16] age 35, is charged with drawing up an appeal on January 9, 1905, in St. Petersburg, calling for the overthrow of the existing regime; and with intent to circulate this appeal, such circulation having not taken place due to circumstances independent of his volition."

After looking over the indictment, I was convinced that the prosecutor's office of the Chamber of Justice, acting under the direction of the Minister of Justice, had committed a gross judicial error, mainly because it was not yet familiar with the partially revised criminal code that had been recently introduced. I shall not burden those readers who are not jurists with my juridical considerations, but shall limit myself to pointing out that the new criminal code allowed a person to be punished for intent to commit a crime only in special cases specified in the law. And the crime with which Gorky was charged did not belong to this category.

Taking advantage of the right of petitioning that witnesses be called, I included in my petition all the circumstances of the case, as well as my whole legal argumentation, and I also quoted Gorky's appeal in its entirety. I gave a copy of the petition to representatives of the press, and it appeared in the newspapers the day after it was submitted to the Chamber of Justice.

The Ministry and the prosecutor's office could not help but recognize their error after it had been pointed out to them. However, there is a great difference between realizing an error and admitting it. For the Chamber of Justice to retreat now was all the more difficult, since it had already officially scheduled Gorky's case to be heard on May 3, 1905, and had posted an announcement to this effect on the gates of the court building.

The Chamber of Justice had to turn to the Ministry for help. Finally, a general meeting of the Chamber was called, and the following naive solution was devised: The scheduled hearing of the case would be cancelled and turned over to the examining magistrate's office for preliminary investigation "in order to question the witnesses designated by Counsellor Gruzenberg." Since all the witnesses lived in St. Petersburg, their appearance in court was mandatory, which in itself indicated that a *preliminary* investigation was superfluous.

[16] [This was Gorky's real name. He adopted the pseudonym Maxim Gorky at the beginning of his literary career in 1892.]

For several months the case remained in the hands of the examining magistrate without any action being taken. It was finally disposed of by placing it under one of the manifestos on amnesty.

Because of my inherent pugnacity in those days, I did not want to "grant amnesty" to the Ministry; and I wrote to Gorky, asking him whether we should not decline amnesty ourselves and demand a hearing of the case. I thought of the line, "It's amusing to beat you, honorable bears."[17] Gorky replied to me with the following letter: "I think that it is now no longer worthwhile for me to squabble with the prosecutors. Let's grant them amnesty and may they disappear. My state of health is not good. I've had a bad case of pleurisy. For about a month now I've been sitting at home with compresses, blister flies, and various other unpleasantries. My skin is irritated and my nerves even more. I'm as cross as the devil. But I think the doctor will release me soon, and then I'll come to Petersburg and see you."

Gorky presented me with his copy of a five-volume collection of his works in an unusually elegant binding. On the inside of each cover was an artistic inlay of small multi-colored pieces of leather. One of these inlays was even a reproduction of Beklin's *Isle of the Dead*. Gorky cherished this copy because an amateur bookbinder, who had gone to the Crimea to escape death from consumption, had spent many months working on it. I was particularly touched by the dedication and the following verses, which may or may not have been included later somewhere else.

Like sparks in a cloud of black smoke,
Amidst this life we are alone.
But we are also the seeds of tomorrow;
We are also the flames of the future.

With honor we serve in the bright temple
Of Liberty, Truth, and Beauty,
So that a blind mole
May grow to be a proud eagle.

Let me say a few words now about Gorky's story *Mother*, at least in regard to the administrative and legal ordeals it endured. Hardly had the story appeared when it was seized by the censor. This action was immediately confirmed by a ruling from the Chamber of Justice, which brought criminal proceedings against Gorky. It

[17] ["Bears" in this instance means clumsy people.]

was indeed unfortunate that this could be happening to a good book.

I went to the head of the Main Administration for Affairs of the Press, Senator Belgard, whom I had not known previously. I found him to be quite attentive as I expressed my view that the book was a good one and should certainly not be subject to the criminal law. Belgard replied that he had not seen the book, because such seizures were made by the Censorship Committee and not by the Main Administration for Affairs of the Press. However, he promised that he would look through the book, and, if he agreed with my opinion about it, he would see that it was not destroyed. He gave instructions while I was still there to have the book delivered to his home. When I stopped to see him about three days later, I was very happy to hear him say, "I have already ordered the Censorship Committee to release the book." On this basis it was possible to stop the court proceedings that had been initiated.

In answer to my report to Gorky, who was in Italy, I received the following letter: "Please accept my hearty and most sincere thanks. I think that *Mother* is a realistic piece of work, and perhaps a few persons, having read it, will breathe a bit more easily. If such people find enjoyment, I would like them to know how you have so kindly helped them at this difficult time, when life for everyone is so sad. To put it more simply, you have helped me accomplish my task of bolstering the faltering spirit of resistance to the dark and hostile forces of life. I value your assistance highly. With sincere friendship and gratitude, I extend my hand to you."

I was of the opinion that Gorky's prolonged stay abroad, due to the aggravation of his tuberculosis, was seriously affecting both the reputation he deserved and his creative process. If one remains away too long, people will begin to malign him.

I also had an even more important concern. A writer of fiction cannot stay long outside his homeland, for no matter how great his store of impressions and information about his native land, it will never take the place of rubbing shoulders with his own people.

Insistently I began to call Gorky home. At first he agreed with me, and he wrote:

Thank you for your kind letter and your gracious readiness to help me in my affairs. I have decided to return to Russia, but I don't know yet when I'll do so, because I am burdened with a variety of business that must be finished here. I also don't feel very well. My cough is getting the best of me. It is imperative that I get better, and I am diligently trying to do so. The possibility of a trial and other unpleasantries does not bother me in the least, just as it has not in the past, but I would like to be in good health and spirits when I arrive. All the same, I think we'll see each other soon, and I'll be able to shake your hand again. I'll be very glad to see you.

However, after a few months he changed his mind and wrote me a long, candid letter. It compares favorably with the best pages of his literary works, and in a biographical sense it contributes much to an understanding of Gorky's life and character. I shall omit the introductory part of the letter, which deals only with business matters, but I feel that it is imperative to quote a long excerpt from the rest of it.

Allow me to express my sincere gratitude for your kind attitude toward me. I value it very highly and am genuinely touched by it. You ask why I don't write to you about myself and my thoughts and feelings. There are at least three reasons. First of all, I have no way of knowing that my thoughts and feelings are of interest to you. Second, I can't speak and write about myself without thinking after each phrase that I said it wrong, that I wrote it incorrectly. And finally, I do not consider it my right to let my personal affairs occupy the attention of others, particularly of someone who is working as hard as you.

Life is interesting for me, but then it seems to be my custom to be interested in life, a custom given to me by nature itself. I see many wonderful people and often get infatuated with them. Sometimes disappointments come along, and I feel depressed, but then, like a woman, I get infatuated again. I like Italy more and more. It is a country of great people, wonderful tales, and terrible legends, a festive and abundant land, one that is good to its people. I love it with sadness and with envy, and I believe that slowly but surely it is marching toward a new Renaissance. Just recently I visited Florence, Pisa, Lucca, Siena, and some small towns in Tuscany. I stood in awe before the riches of the past; and observing the vigorous and harmonious activity of the present, I thought of our Kologrivs and Arzamases, of Poshekhonie and other towns of our lazy, tottering, unhappy homeland.

You write, "It seems to me that things have become boring for you." Life is not boring, but I find it unbearably distressing to think of Russia and to read Russian newspapers, journals, and books. It is terribly painful and disappointing for me to see my spiritually destitute countrymen adorn themselves in the gaudy rags of foreign words and foreign ideas, trying to cover their own sad impoverishment, their spiritual ugliness, their lack of strength and pitiful weakness of spirit.

For four years the masquerade of the defeated has been going on. For four years the survivors, hiding their wounds and pains from one another, have pretended to be merry; and hiding the swelling of their endlessly slapped faces, they have puffed out their cheeks and whistled, as if to say, "See how gay we are, how carefree." All this makes me furious. But, of course, I know that not everything is bad. I'd even say that I know this better, I believe, than many of those who live in our homeland. Is this self-deceit? No, Oskar Osipovich, it is the result of numerous reports from all the pits and crevices of Russia. I am deeply grateful to you for your proposal to intercede on behalf of my return. I am confident that you would undoubtedly succeed—but don't do it.

It is good for me to remain here awhile. There is much I need to learn, and gradually I am learning. I have more than three thousand books, and I read eight newspapers and all the journals. I do not feel torn away from my homeland. There are good people around me, and my respect for man is not diminishing, but growing and becoming even more distinct. No, it is too early for me to return to Russia. And even if I wanted to do so or for some reason considered it necessary, I would return to Irkutsk or Archangel, or even to prison, if this is what the most pitiful, the most giftless of all the European governments wished.

I have many problems. Perhaps they are trivial, but they are *my* problems, and I must solve them. I believe in myself. I believe that my work is useful, and it makes no difference at all where I work. I am thoroughly Russian and primed with enough powder from my youth to last for a long time to come. Let the grave diggers bury me alive, but to the end I'll say what I consider has to be said. And, finally, let me assure you that is not important what attitude people have toward me, but only what attitude I have toward them.

Your kind and gracious idea of interceding for my return to Russia probably occurred to you because of the strange newspaper report about my alleged homesickness and about the steps I had taken to return to Russia. This is pure invention. It goes without saying that I have not taken any such steps.

For thirty-five years Gorky's name has been on everyone's lips. Thirty-five impatient years, which have swept away not only what was obsolete but what was just beginning to take shape. Yet, Gorky has remained intact, a feat that cannot be explained alone by the fascination of his talent.

What, then, is the secret of his exceptionally durable influence?

Surely the answer lies in the fact that he was a faithful spokesman for those who had been neglected by an unjust social order and had not yet truly lived. He spoke for those who knew no joy, the millions whose mothers felt the same suffering and anxious hopes for happiness as did our mothers in giving birth to us who are now departing.

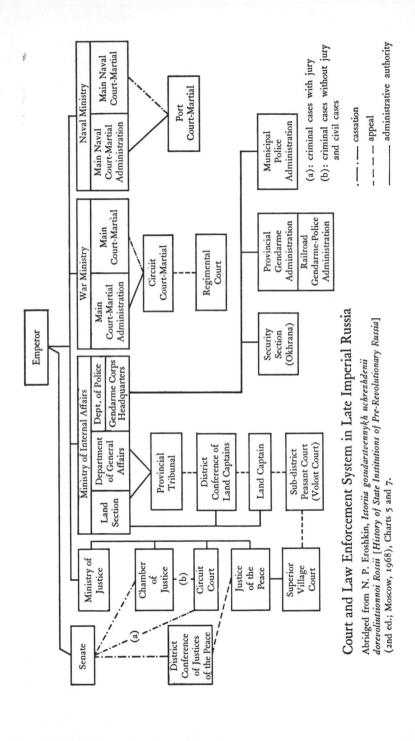

Court and Law Enforcement System in Late Imperial Russia

Abridged from N. P. Eroshkin, *Istoriia gosudarstvennykh uchrezhdenii dorevoliutsionnoi Rossii* [*History of State Institutions of Pre-Revolutionary Russia*] (2nd ed.; Moscow, 1968), Charts 5 and 7.

Chart contents:

Emperor

Ministry of Internal Affairs
- Department of General Affairs
- Land Section
- Dept. of Police
- Gendarme Corps Headquarters

War Ministry
- Main Court-Martial Administration
- Main Court-Martial

Naval Ministry
- Main Naval Court-Martial Administration
- Main Naval Court-Martial

Ministry of Justice

Senate

Provincial Tribunal
District Conference of Land Captains
Land Captain
Sub-district Peasant Court (Volost Court)

Circuit Court-Martial
Regimental Court

Port Court-Martial

Chamber of Justice
Circuit Court
Justice of the Peace
Superior Village Court

District Conference of Justices of the Peace

Security Section (Okhrana)
Provincial Gendarme Administration
Railroad Gendarme-Police Administration
Municipal Police Administration

(a): criminal cases with jury
(b): criminal cases without jury and civil cases

— · — cassation
— — — appeal
———— administrative authority

Glossary of Names

This glossary contains the names of persons mentioned by Gruzenberg who seem important enough for further comment. Especially
well-known political and literary figures are not included.

Aksakov, Ivan Sergeevich (1823–86). Leading publicist and popu-
larizer of the Slavophiles. Graduated from the Imperial School
of Jurisprudence in St. Petersburg in 1842. Entered government
service and remained for several years before turning to
journalism. Edited *Den* [*Day*], 1861–66; and *Rus* [*Russia*],
1880–86. Quite conservative, especially toward the end of his
career, but often critical of the government. Was frequently
censored and forbidden to publish at all during the 1870s.

Alexandrov, Peter Akimovich (1836–93). Lawyer. Held various
posts in the Ministry of Justice. Appointed an examining
magistrate in 1859, an Assistant Prosecutor of the St. Petersburg
Circuit Court in 1866, a Prosecutor of the Pskov Circuit Court
later in 1866, an Assistant Prosecutor of the St. Petersburg
Chamber of Justice in 1869, and then Assistant Chief Prosecutor
of the Criminal Cassation Department of the Senate. Left
government service because of a conflict with his superiors in
1876 and became an advocate. Gained prominence as the
defense counsel in the Vera Zasulich case in 1878.

Andreevsky, Sergey Arkadievich (1847–1918). Lawyer, writer, and
critic. Best known of the so-called "literary lawyers." Held
various posts in the Ministry of Justice, including an Assistant
Prosecutor of the St. Petersburg Circuit Court. Became a
defense lawyer in 1878, after refusing to prosecute the Vera
Zasulich case. Wrote much poetry but was more competent in
his critical literary essays.

Annenkov, Paul Vasilievich (1812–87). Literary critic. Closely
acquainted with many writers and other critics. Especially
influential in the 1850s. Lived much of his life abroad. Produced
several volumes of essays, memoirs, and biographical sketches.

Artsybashev, Mikhail Petrovich (1878–1927). Writer and essayist. Wrote short stories and novels depicting violent emotions, sexual license, bloodshed, and death. Dealt with carnal desire in his sensational novel *Sanin* (1907) and with suicide in *At the Brink* (1911–12). Expelled from the Soviet Union in 1923. Settled in Warsaw as a political journalist.

Avksentiev, Nikolay Dmitrievich (1878–1943). Moderate Socialist Revolutionary leader. Active in the first Soviet of Workers' Deputies. Minister of Internal Affairs in the Provisional Government, August–September, 1917. Emigrated to France after the Civil War, and to the United States in 1940.

Blok, Alexander Alexandrovich (1880–1921). Leading symbolist poet. Expressed his contemplative response to mystical love in much of his early poetry. Later became more concerned with a cosmic vision of contemporary events, his best known poem being *The Twelve* (1918), on the inexorable march of the revolution.

Bogdanov, Alexander Alexandrovich (pseud. Malinovsky) (1873–1928). Physician, philosopher, economist, sociologist, and revolutionary figure. Joined the Bolsheviks in 1904 but broke with Lenin in 1909. Helped Gorky and Lunacharsky organize a Party school on Capri in 1909. Published books on Marxist economics, as well as works on philosophy and science, but was regarded by the Bolsheviks as a revisionist. After 1923, spent most of his time on problems of blood transfusion.

Bonch-Bruevich, Mikhail Dmitrievich (1870–1956). Quartermaster-general of the Northwestern Front, 1914–15. Chief-of-Staff of the Northern Front, 1915–16. Briefly commanded the Northern Front in 1917. After the October Revolution, was appointed by the Soviet government as Chief-of-Staff of the Supreme Commander-in-Chief of the Russian forces. Member of the Supreme Military Council, February–November, 1918. Later became a member of the State Geodetic Administration and a specialist in aerial photography.

Bonch-Bruevich, Vladimir Dmitrievich (1873–1955). Literary specialist, ethnographer, and historian. Joined the revolutionary movement in the 1880s. Sided with the Bolsheviks in 1903. After the October Revolution, became secretary of the Council of People's Commissars. Founder and first director of the State Literary Museum in 1930. Published works on literature and Russian religious sects from the 1890s through the 1930s. Brother of General M. D. Bonch-Bruevich.

Bulatsel, Paul Fyodorovich (1867–1919). Lawyer. One of the founders of the Union of the Russian People in 1905 and a member of its

Central Council. Defended various pogromists and members of the Union on other charges, most notably those accused of assassinating M. Ya. Herzenstein, a liberal member of the First Duma. Published articles in *Svet* [*Light*], *Rossia* [*Russia*], and other rightist journals.

Chernov, Viktor Mikhailovich (1873–1952). One of the leaders of the Socialist Revolutionary Party. Wrote the Party platform in 1905–06. Minister of Agriculture in the Provisional Government, May–August, 1917. Chairman of the Constituent Assembly, January, 1918. Emigrated to Western Europe in 1920 and later to New York.

Dobrolyubov, Nikolay Alexandrovich (1836–61). Chief literary critic for *Sovremennik* [*The Contemporary*], 1856–61. During his brief career became highly regarded by the radical intelligentsia for his literary, philosophical, and social views. Expressed his faith in progress and emphasized service to society.

Dubrovin, Alexander Ivanovich (1855–1918). A St. Petersburg physician and main founder of the Union of the Russian People in 1905. Served as its president and editor of its organ, *Russkoe znamie* [*The Russian Banner*]. Wrote *The Secret of Destiny* in 1907, an anti-liberal, anti-Semitic prophecy of Russia's future. Inspired pogroms and political assassination through the Union. Shot by the Bolsheviks.

Dukhonin, Nikolay Nikolaevich (1876–1917). Chief-of-Staff of the Supreme Commander-in-Chief, September–November, 1917. Acting Commander-in-Chief, November, 1917. Refused orders by the Bolsheviks to initiate armistice negotiations with the Germans. Was discharged by the government and killed by mutinying soldiers at military headquarters at Mogilev in November, 1917.

Durnovo, Peter Nikolaevich (1844–1915). Joined the Department of Police in 1872. Director of the Department, 1884–93. Assistant Minister of Internal Affairs, 1900–05. Minister of Internal Affairs, 1905–06. Appointed to the State Council in 1906.

Gerard, Vladimir Nikolaevich (1839–1903). Lawyer. Entered the Ministry of Justice in 1859. Served on various commissions including the one preparing the introduction of the Judicial Statutes of 1864 into Poland. Appointed chief secretary of the Senate in 1866. Became an advocate in 1868. Specialized in criminal cases. Elected to the St. Petersburg Council of the Bar in 1869. Served on the Council for many years, part of the time as vice-president and from 1901 until his death as president.

Gogel, Sergey Konstantinovich (1860–1933). Lawyer and legal scholar. Held various posts in the Ministry of Justice in the 1880s and

1890s, including an Assistant Prosecutor of the St. Petersburg Circuit Court and member of the editorial staff of *Zhurnal Ministerstva Iustitsii* [*Journal of the Ministry of Justice*]. Lecturer in criminal law at St. Petersburg University, 1904–11. Rector of the St. Petersburg Psycho-Neurological Institute, 1911–17. Published several books on the sociological aspects of crime and the administration of justice. After the October Revolution, emigrated to Berlin.

Gorky, Maxim (pseudonym of Alexander Maximovich Peshkov) (1868–1936). Noted novelist, short story writer, dramatist, poet, and publicist. Gained popularity in depicting the life of the lower classes. Best-known works include *Twenty-Six Men and a Girl* (1899), *Song of the Petrel* (1901), *The Lower Depths* (1902), *Mother* (1907), and his autobiographical *Childhood* (1913). Was associated with the Bolsheviks and closely acquainted with Lenin, though critical of some Bolshevik policies. Lived on Capri, 1906–13, and in western Europe during most of the 1920s. Died in the U.S.S.R.

Granovsky, Timofey Nikolaevich (1813–55). Professor of general history at Moscow University, 1839–55. Also gave public lectures in European history, 1843–44, 1845–46, and 1851. A member of the Stankevich philosophical circle in Moscow in the 1830s and closely acquainted with Herzen. Was a moderate westernizer.

Guchkov, Alexander Ivanovich (1862–1936). A leader of the Union of the 17th of October. Chairman of the Third Duma, 1910–11. Minister of War and Navy in the Provisional Government, March–May, 1917. Emigrated to Paris after the October Revolution.

Herzen, Alexander Ivanovich (1812–70). Radical journalist and literary and social critic. Emigrated in 1847 and spent the rest of his life in Western Europe, much of it in London. Professed a rather romantic socialism; called for greater political and social liberty in Russia. Published *Kolokol* [*The Bell*], 1857–67, in London, which was smuggled into Russia, where it was widely read. Wrote a series of critical essays in 1847–50, collected under the title *From the Other Shore*; and incisive memoirs, *My Past and Thought*, in the 1850s.

Herzenstein, Mikhail Yakovlevich (1859–1906). Professor of economics at Moscow University. Member of the Moscow Municipal Duma and Moscow Zemstvo. Authority on agrarian affairs for the Constitutional Democratic Party in the First Duma. Assassinated in Finland by the Union of the Russian People in July, 1906.

Hessen, Iosif Vladimirovich (1866–1943). Lawyer, journalist, and political figure. One of the founders of the Constitutional Democratic Party in 1905. Deputy in the Second Duma. Co-editor (with P. N. Milyukov) of *Rech* [*Speech*], 1906–17. On the editorial staff of *Pravo* [*Law*], 1898–1917. After the October Revolution, emigrated to Berlin.

Iollos, Grigory Borisovich (1859–1907). For many years was a specialist in economics on the staff of the moderately liberal Moscow newspaper *Russkiia vedomosti* [*Russian Gazette*] and served as co-editor, 1906–07. Received a doctorate in political economy from Heidelberg University. Was a Jewish convert to Christianity but advocated Jewish emancipation. Deputy in the First Duma. Assassinated in Moscow by the Union of the Russian People in March, 1907.

Ivanov, Vyacheslav Ivanovich (1866–1949). A leading symbolist poet in St. Petersburg. Published several volumes of rather erudite, philosophical verses between 1903 and 1920. Interested in religious myths and cosmic phenomena. Emigrated to Italy in 1924.

Karabchevsky, Nikolay Platonovich (1851–1925). Lawyer. Participated in a number of important criminal and political cases. Was one of the counsels for the defense in the Multan Votyak trials in the 1890s; for the plaintiffs in the Kishinev pogrom trial in 1903; for the defense in the trial of Egor Sazonov, the assassin of the Minister of Internal Affairs Plehve in 1904; and for the defense in the Beilis ritual murder trial in 1913. Emigrated to France after the October Revolution. Published various legal articles.

Ketcher, Nikolay Khristoforovich (1809–86). Physician and literary figure. Served as a government medical inspector but also translated Shakespeare's plays into Russian, 1841–50 and 1862–79, as well as other English literary works. Joined the Stankevich philosophical circle in Moscow in the 1830s, and throughout the years maintained a close association with writers and other intellectuals.

Kokovtsov, Paul Konstantinovich (1861–1942). Scholar in Oriental studies. Appointed professor of Hebrew at St. Petersburg University in 1894. Wrote many works on Hebrew, Aramaic, Syriac, Turkic, and Ethiopic philology and literature. Was elected to the Academy of Sciences in 1909. Acted as expert witness for the defense in the Beilis trial in 1913.

Koni, Anatoly Fyodorovich (1844–1927). Prominent jurist. Prosecutor in the St. Petersburg Circuit Court, 1871–75. Assistant director of one of the departments in the Ministry of Justice, 1875–77. Presiding judge in the St. Petersburg Circuit Court, 1877–81. Presided at the Vera Zasulich trial in 1878. Presiding judge in the Civil Department of the St. Petersburg Chamber of Justice, 1881–85. Chief Prosecutor of the Cassation Department of the Senate, 1885–91, 1892–97. Served on various legal commissions. Appointed to the State Council in 1907. Professor of criminal law at Petrograd University, 1918–22.

Korolenko, Vladimir Galaktionovich (1853–1921). Well-known novelist, short story writer, and publicist. Possessed a strong sense of humaneness and justice. Was exiled in his student days for his populist views. Best-known works include *Makar's Dream* (1885), *The Blind Musician* (1886), and the autobiography of his early life, *The History of My Contemporary* (1906–22). Editor of the literary and scholarly journal *Russkoe bogatstvo* [*Russian Wealth*], 1895–1914.

Kosorotov, Dmitry Petrovich (1856– ?). Physician. Specialist in forensic medicine. Appointed assistant in the St. Petersburg Military Clinical Hospital in 1887; lecturer at St. Petersburg University in 1895. Edited *Russkaya meditsina* [*Russian Medicine*], 1889–94. Published many articles on toxicology and infectious diseases. Acted as an expert witness for the prosecution in the Beilis ritual murder trial in 1913.

Krushevan, Paul Alexandrovich (1860– ?). Journalist and writer. Editor of the anti-Semitic newspaper *Bessarabets* [*The Bessarabian*] in Kishinev, 1897–1903. Initiated the 1903 pogrom in Kishinev. Founded another anti-Semitic newspaper, *Drug* [*The Friend*], in Kishinev in 1905 and served as its editor. Wrote short stories and a novel in the 1890s. Deputy in the Second Duma.

Kuropatkin, Alexey Nikolaevich (1848–1925). Minister of War, 1898–1904. Supreme Commander-in-Chief of all forces during the Russo-Japanese War, 1904–05. During World War I was Commander-in-Chief of the Northern Front, February-August, 1916. After the February Revolution, was arrested but was soon released and settled on his provincial estate.

von der Launitz, Vladimir Fyodorovich (1855–1906) Military career since 1873. Appointed governor of Tambov province in 1902 and of St. Petersburg in 1905. Supported the Union of the Russian People and its Fighting Brotherhood. Assassinated by a Socialist Revolutionary.

Lopukhin, Alexey Alexandrovich (1864–1927). Entered service in the Ministry of Justice in 1886. Assistant prosecutor and prosecutor in various circuit courts and chambers of justice, 1890–1902. Director of the Department of Police in the Ministry of Internal Affairs, 1902–05. Governor of Estonia, 1905. In 1908, revealed to the Socialist Revolutionary Party that one of the key members of its terroristic organization, E. F. Azef, was a police agent. Sentenced to five years' exile in 1909. Granted amnesty in 1912.

Lunacharsky, Anatoly Vasilievich (1875–1933). Literary historian and critic; dramatist. Joined the revolutionary movement in 1892. Sided with Lenin after the 1903 congress of the Social Democratic Party. Became Commissar of Education after the October Revolution and held this post until 1929.

Maklakov, Vasily Alexeevich (1870–1957). Lawyer. Especially active in political cases. One of the defense counsels in the Beilis ritual murder trial in 1913. Member of the Central Committee of the Constitutional Democratic Party. Deputy in the Second, Third, and Fourth Dumas. Ambassador to France under the Provisional Government in 1917. After the October Revolution, remained in Paris.

Malinovsky-Bogdanov, Alexander Alexandrovich. (See Bogdanov).

Margolin, Arnold Davidovich (1877–1956). Lawyer in Kiev. One of the defense counsels at the beginning of the Beilis ritual murder trial in 1913 but withdrew and served as a witness for the defense. A leader in the Jewish Territorialist Organization in Russia. Active in the Ukrainian Rada in late 1917–early 1918 and a justice in the Ukrainian General Court. A deputy foreign minister under the Petliura government, 1919–20. Member of the Ukrainian delegation to the Paris Peace Conference in 1919 and head of the Ukrainian diplomatic mission to London in 1919–20. Emigrated to the United States in 1922.

Mazeh, Yakov (1859–1924). Graduated from the law faculty at Moscow University in 1886. Became a member of the Zionist movement in the 1880s. Appointed Chief Rabbi of the Moscow Jewish community in 1893. Promoted Hebrew culture. Acted as an expert witness for the defense in the Beilis trial in 1913. Deputy in the Constituent Assembly in 1918. Participated in the last Zionist Council in Russia in 1920.

Merezhkovsky, Dmitry Sergeevich (1865–1941). Poet, novelist, dramatist, critic, and publicist. One of the most influential advocates of symbolism. Interested in religious mysticism. Wrote essays on early and modern Russian authors, a trilogy dealing with the spiritual aspects of the ancient world, the Renaissance, and modern Russia, and many other historical novels, poems, and dramas. Emigrated in 1919, first to Warsaw and then to Paris.

Mikhailovsky, Nikolay Konstantinovich (1842–1904). Sociologist, journalist, and literary critic. One of the most articulate advocates of populism. Wrote for *Otechestvennyia zapiski* [*Notes of the Fatherland*], 1868–84; and *Russkoe bogatstvo* [*Russian Wealth*] after 1892. Also published books.

Milyukov, Paul Nikolaevich (1859–1943). Historian and political figure. Lectured at Moscow University, 1886–95, until dismissed on political grounds. One of the organizers of the Union of Liberation in 1903 and the Constitutional Democratic Party in 1905. First chairman of the Party's Central Committee and leader of its deputies in the Third and Fourth Dumas. Minister of Foreign Affairs in the Provisional Government, March–May, 1917. Emigrated to Western Europe after the October Revolution. Wrote several important works on Russian cultural, economic, and political history.

Mukhanov, Alexey Alexeevich (1860– ?). Graduated from the law faculty of St. Petersburg University and served for several years in the Ministry of Justice. Was also a Chernigov provincial marshal of the gentry. Left government service and joined the Constitutional Democratic Party. Deputy in the First Duma and chairman of its Agrarian Commission.

Muraviev, Nikolay Valerianovich (1850–1908). Held various posts in the Ministry of Justice and lectured on criminal legal procedure at Moscow University during the 1870s. Appointed an Assistant Prosecutor of the St. Petersburg Chamber of Justice in 1879, a Prosecutor in 1881, a Prosecutor of the Moscow Chamber of Justice in 1884, and Chief Prosecutor of the Criminal Cassation Department of the Senate in 1891. Minister of Justice, 1894–1905. Headed a commission for revising the laws, 1894–1904. Published many legal articles.

Myasoedov, Sergey Nikolaevich (1867–1915). Officer in the Gendarme Corps, 1892–1907. Commander of the gendarmerie at Verzhbolovo [Virbalis], 1901–07. Put on the reserve list in 1907 but restored to active duty in 1909. Suspected of being a German agent and dismissed in 1912. Assigned to the Tenth Army as an interpreter in 1914. Again came under suspicion and was tried and executed.

Nabokov, Vladimir Dmitrievich (1869–1922). Lawyer and political figure. Wrote books and articles on criminal law, 1896–1904, as well as political articles after that date. Co-publisher of *Rech* [*Speech*], 1908–14. Member of the Central Committee of the Constitutional Democratic Party. Deputy in the First Duma. Head of the Chancellery of the Provisional Government and member of the Juridical Council in 1917. Emigrated to Berlin in 1919. Killed there by a Russian monarchist who was intending to shoot P. N. Milyukov.

Nadson, Semyon Yakovlevich (1862–87). Minor poet. Was very

popular in the late nineteenth century. Wrote in lyrical style.
Stressed love of homeland and faith in the future.

Nekrasov, Nikolay Alexeevich (1821–78). Well-known poet and
journalist. Mainly depicted the peasantry in his poems, the most
famous of which are *Red-Nose Frost* (1863) and *Who Is
Happy in Russia?* (1879). Co-editor of *Sovremennik* [*The
Contemporary*] from 1847 until it was closed by the government
in 1866. Co-editor (with Saltykov-Shchedrin) of *Otechestvennyia zapiski* [*Notes of the Fatherland*] from 1868 until his
death.

Nikitin, Ivan Savvich (1824–61). Poet. Wrote realistic and often
poignant poems of the hopeless plight of the poor, especially the
peasantry. Best known works are *Kulak, Night Rest of the
Drivers, The Tailor,* and *The Village Pauper.*

Nikolay Nikolaevich (1859–1929). Grand Prince. An uncle-once-
removed of Emperor Nicholas II. Supreme Commander-in-Chief
of Russian forces from August, 1914, to September, 1915.
Commander-in-Chief of the Caucasus Front from September,
1915, to March, 1917. Emigrated after the February Revolution.

Nosar-Khrustalev, Georgy Stepanovich (1879–1918). Lawyer and
political figure. Chairman of the first Soviet of Workers' Deputies
from October 14 to November 26, 1905, when arrested. Not
affiliated with a political party in October but joined the
Mensheviks in November. Was tried and exiled to Siberia in
1907. Escaped to Western Europe but returned to Russia in 1914.
Imprisoned 1914–17. After the October Revolution, was active
against the Bolsheviks, who arrested and shot him.

Passover, Alexander Yakovlevich (1840–1910). Lawyer. Refused
conversion from Judaism to Christianity in order to obtain a
university professorship. Served in the Ministry of Justice at
various provincial posts during the 1860s. Became a practicing
attorney in St. Petersburg in 1872 and remained there until
his death. Specialist in civil law and a prominent leader of
judicial conferences for lawyers-in-training. Belonged to the St.
Petersburg Council of the Bar for a number of years.

Petrunkevich, Ivan Ilich (1844–1928). Political figure. Active in
zemstvo work, 1868–1905. One of the founders of the Union of
Liberation in 1903 and the Constitutional Democratic Party in
1905. Chairman of the Party's Central Committee, 1909–15.
Leader of the Party's faction in the First Duma. Co-publisher of
Rech [*Speech*], 1908–14, and publisher, 1914–17. Emigrated
to the United States in 1920 and then to France in 1921.

Pikhno, Dmitry Ivanovich (1853–1913). Journalist and economist.
Appointed professor at Kiev University in 1877. Editor of

Kievlyanin [*The Kievan*], 1879–1907, but was associated with the newspaper until his death. Expressed a conservative editorial policy. Member of the State Council.

Plevako, Fyodor Nikiforovich (1843–1908). Lawyer. Best known for his defenses in criminal cases. Noted for his eloquence. Member of the Union of the 17th of October. Deputy in the Third Duma.

Polivanov, Alexey Andreevich (1855–1920). Chief of the General Staff, 1905–06. Assistant Minister of War, 1906–12. Appointed to the State Council in 1912. Minister of War from June, 1915, to March, 1916. Served in the Red Army after the October Revolution. Member of the delegation sent to Riga to negotiate a peace treaty with Poland in 1920. Died there of typhus.

Polonsky, Yakov Petrovich (1819–98). Poet. Wrote simple, lyrical verses, many of which were set to music. Expressed an affinity with nature but also a civic concern for individual freedom and progress. Published several volumes of poetry from the mid-1840s through the early 1890s. Best known works are *The Grasshopper Musician* and *The Sun and the Moon.*

Potekhin, Paul Antipovich (1839–1916). Lawyer. Became an attorney attached to the commercial courts in 1862 according to the procedures that existed before the judicial reform of 1864. Began to plead cases before the new St. Petersburg Chamber of Justice in 1867. Specialized in civil cases. Became a member of the St. Petersburg Council of the Bar in 1870 and remained for many years. Elected president in 1900. Served several times on the St. Petersburg Municipal Duma's education commission. Known for his eloquence.

Pranaitis, Justin Bonaventura (? –1917). Roman Catholic priest. Considered himself an expert in Jewish history and beliefs. Wrote a monograph, *The Christian in the Jewish Talmud,* or *Secrets of the Teaching of the Rabbis About Christianity,* in the early 1890s, which purported to be proof of ritual murder. Acted as an expert witness for the prosecution in the Beilis trial in 1913. Died in St. Petersburg.

Pugachev, Emelyan Ivanovich (ca. 1742–75). Cossack leader of a major peasant uprising, 1773–75. Captured a number of government fortresses and cities including Kazan, Penza, and Saratov, and was marching toward Moscow. Defeated by government forces and executed in Moscow.

Rachkovsky, Peter Ivanovich (1853–1911). Foreign agent of the Department of Police in Paris, 1885–1902. Subsequently held various posts in the Department in St. Petersburg including head of the political section. Encouraged A. I. Dubrovin to organize the Union of the Russian People in 1905.

Razin, Stepan Timofeevich (ca. 1630–71). Cossack leader of a major
peasant rebellion, 1667–71. Captured Tsaritsyn, Astrakhan,
and Saratov, and was besieging Simbirsk, when defeated by
government troops. Executed in Moscow.

von Rennenkampf, Paul Karlovich (1854–1918). First appointed to
General Staff in 1882. Held various command posts over the
years. Served with distinction in the Russo-Japanese War,
1904–05. Commander of the First Army, 1914–15. Blamed for
the Russian defeat at Tannenberg in 1915 and dismissed from
his command. Killed by the Bolsheviks.

Rodichev, Fyodor Izmaylovich (1856–1933). A leading member of
the Union of Liberation, 1903–05. One of the founders of
the Constitutional Democratic Party in 1905 and a member of
its Central Committee. Deputy in all four Dumas. Commissar
for Finnish affairs in the Provisional Government in 1917.
Emigrated after the October Revolution.

Ruzsky, Nikolay Vladimirovich (1854–1918). Member of the Military
Council before World War I. Appointed Commander of the
Third Army, then Commander-in-Chief of the Northern Front
from August to December, 1915, and again from August,
1916, to May, 1917. Shot by the Bolsheviks.

Saltykov-Shchedrin, Mikhail Evgrafovich (1826–89). Satirist and
journalist. Held various posts in the civil service, 1844–68.
Began writing in the late 1840s. Chose M. Shchedrin as his
pseudonym. Mainly portrayed the life of the provincial gentry.
Best known works are *Provincial Sketches* (1856–57), *The
History of a Town* (1869–70), *Gentlemen of Tashkent* (1869–
72), and *The Golovlyov Family* (1872–76). Co-editor (with
N. A. Nekrasov) of *Otechestvennyia zapiski* [*Notes of the
Fatherland*], 1868–78, and, editor, 1878–84, when the journal
was closed by the government.

Shalyapin, Fyodor Ivanovich (1873–1938). Singer. Began his musical
career in Tiflis (Tbilisi) in 1893. Sang leading operatic roles in
St. Petersburg from 1894 and in Moscow from 1899. Also
made foreign tours. Best known for his roles in Glinka's *Life
for the Tsar*, Rimsky-Korsakov's *Maid of Pskov*, and Mussorg-
sky's *Boris Godunov*. A close friend of Gorky, who influenced
his artistic development. Emigrated to Western Europe in 1922.
Died in Paris.

Shcheglovitov, Ivan Grigorievich (1861–1918). Held various posts
in the Senate and Ministry of Justice, 1890–1906. Minister of
Justice, 1906–1915. Member of the State Council, 1907–17;
appointed chairman in 1916. Arrested by the Provisional Government in 1917. Shot by the Bolsheviks.

Shmakov, Alexey Semyonovich (? –1916). Moscow lawyer and

journalist. Wrote several anti-Semitic books between 1897 and 1912. Acted as counsel for the defense in the Kishinev pogrom trial in 1903 and private attorney for the prosecution in the Beilis ritual murder trial in 1913.

Spasowicz, Włodzimierz (Spasovich, Vladimir Danilovich) (1829–1906). Renowned lawyer and writer. Lectured on criminal law at St. Petersburg University, 1857–61. Retired when the university was temporarily closed and became an advocate. Member of the St. Petersburg Council of the Bar for many years. Wrote books on contemporary criminal law, contract law, ancient Polish law, and the history of Polish literature and general Slavic literature.

Stolypin, Peter Arkadevich (1862–1911). Entered the Ministry of State Domains in 1885. Appointed governor of Grodno in 1901 and Saratov in 1903. Minister of Internal Affairs and Chairman of the Council of Ministers, 1906–11. Noted mainly for curtailing the Duma, suppressing the revolutionary movement, and introducing agrarian reforms. Assassinated in Kiev by a revolutionary.

Sukhomlinov, Vladimir Alexandrovich (1848–1926). Chief of the General Staff, 1908–09. Minister of War, 1909–15. Dismissed and placed under house arrest on the charge of failure to provide adequate supplies for the army. Tried and sentenced to hard labor by the Provisional Government in 1917. Released by the Bolsheviks under the amnesty of May 1, 1918. Emigrated to Finland and then to Germany.

Sverdlov, Yakov Mikhailovich (1885–1919). Revolutionary figure. Joined the Social Democratic Party in 1901 and sided with the Bolsheviks at the 1903 congress. After the October Revolution, became Secretary of the Central Committee of the Bolshevik Party and Chairman of the Central Executive Committee of the Congress of Soviets. Was a close associate of Lenin.

Svyatopolk-Mirsky, Peter Danilovich (1857–1914). Assistant Minister of Internal Affairs and head of the Gendarme Corps, 1900–02. Served as a provincial governor, 1902–04. Minister of Internal Affairs from August, 1904, to January, 1905. Considered somewhat liberal but aroused popular indignation by suppressing the Bloody Sunday demonstration.

Tagantsev, Nikolay Stepanovich (1843–1923). Professor of criminal law at St. Petersburg University, 1868–82. Lectured at the Imperial School of Jurisprudence in St. Petersburg for many years. Appointed to the government commission for drafting a new criminal code in 1881. Became a member of the Criminal Cassation Department of the Senate in 1887. Editor of

Zhurnal grazhdanskago i ugolovnago prava [*Journal of Civil and Criminal Law*], 1873–78. Published many articles.

Trepov, Fyodor Fyodorovich (1803–89). Chief of police in Warsaw in the early 1860s. Suppressed the demonstration there in 1861 with considerable brutality. Transferred to St. Petersburg in 1866. Served as governor-general and chief of police. Was shot and wounded by Vera Zasulich in 1878 for ordering the flogging of a political prisoner.

Troitsky, Ivan Gavrilovich (1858– ?). Professor of Hebrew language and literature at the St. Petersburg Theological Academy. Between 1885 and 1913, published several books on the Jewish language, ancient Jewish history, teachings of the Talmud, and Biblical archeology. Acted as an expert witness for the defense in the Beilis ritual murder trial in 1913.

Tyutchev, Fyodor Ivanovich (1803–73). Noted poet. First published in the 1830s but gained greatest renown in the 1850s. Wrote in a rather archaic lyrical style. Expressed romantic sentiments at times but also metaphysical concepts, inclined toward pessimism. Published some conservative nationalistic poetry toward the end of his life.

Unkovsky, Alexey Mikhailovich (1828–93). Lawyer. Elected provincial marshal of the gentry in Tver in 1857. Advocated a liberal emancipation of the serfs and became a defender of peasant interests during the land settlement. Moved to St. Petersburg in 1866 and established an excellent reputation in civil cases. Took occasional criminal cases when appointed by the court, for example in the trial of the assassins of Alexander II in 1881. Member of the St. Petersburg Council of the Bar until he withdrew because of illness in 1885. Elected president of the Council of the Bar for part of this period.

Witte, Sergey Yulievich (1849–1915). Railway official, 1870–92. Minister of Ways and Communications, 1892–93. Minister of Finance, 1893–1903, during which time promoted industrialization. Chairman of the Committee of Ministers, 1903–05, and of the Council of Ministers, 1905–06. Drafted the October Manifesto in 1905. Member of the State Council from 1906.

Yanushkevich, Nikolay Nikolaevich (1868–1918). Taught in the General Staff Academy, 1910–14, and served as head of the Academy, 1913–14. Chief of the General Staff, March–August, 1914. Chief-of-Staff of the Supreme Commander-in-Chief, 1914–15. Quartermaster General of the Caucasus Front, 1915–17. Retired in 1917. After the October Revolution, was arrested and killed under unclear circumstances while being taken to Petrograd.

Zamyslovsky, Georgy Georgievich (1872– ?). Lawyer and rightist leader in the Third and Fourth Dumas. Member of the Union of the Russian People. Wrote pogromist brochures. Acted as private attorney for the prosecution in the Beilis trial in 1913. Published a book shortly before the February Revolution in 1917 alleging that Beilis was guilty of ritual murder despite his acquittal.

Zasulich, Vera Ivanovna (1851–1919). Became associated with the revolutionary movement in the late 1860s. Was arrested, imprisoned for two years, and banished to the provinces. Returned to St. Petersburg in 1878. Shot and wounded the governor-general of St. Petersburg, F. F. Trepov, in 1878, but was acquitted by a jury. Fled to Western Europe. Joined the Social Democrats and served on the board of *Iskra* [*The Spark*]. At the 1903 congress, sided with the Mensheviks. Returned to Russia in 1905, remaining there until her death.

Zhukovsky, Vladimir Ivanovich (1836–1901). Lawyer. Held various posts in the Ministry of Justice. Appointed an Assistant Prosecutor of the St. Petersburg Circuit Court in 1870. Refused to act as prosecutor in the Vera Zasulich trial in 1878 and became a defense lawyer.

Bibliography

Works by Gruzenberg

Vchera: vospominaniia [*Yesterday*: *Memoirs*]. Paris, 1938. The basis of the present translation. Chapters previously or subsequently published elsewhere:

"Bred voiny" [The Delirium of War], *Sovremennyia zapiski* [*Contemporary Notes*], *24* (1925), 268–84; *25* (1925), 288–315.

"O Maksime Gor'kom" [Maxim Gorky], *Posledniia novosti* [*Latest News*], July 25, 1936, 3; July 27, 1936, 3.

"O V. G. Korolenko" [V. G. Korolenko], *Na chuzhoi storone* [*In Foreign Parts*], *13* (1925), 70–85.

"Poruchik Pirogov" [Lieutenant Pirogov], *Sovremennyia zapiski* [*Contemporary Notes*], *21* (1924), 230–46.

"Sram. Vospominaniia o dele Beilisa" [Shame. Memoirs of the Beilis Case], included in the *samizdat* publication, *Obshchestvennye problemy* [*Social Problems*], No. 9 (January-February, 1971), as reported in *Posev* [*Sowing*], Special issue No. 9 (October, 1971), 21.

Ocherki i rechi [*Essays and Speeches*]. New York, 1944. A collection of articles, speeches, and letters prepared by a group of Gruzenberg's friends.

"Iz dnevnika iurista" [From a Jurist's Journal], *Zakon i sud* [*Law and Court*]. A regular column on various legal topics, including occasional reminiscences, written during the period 1929–1933, when Gruzenberg edited this monthly journal in Riga.

"K voprosu o smertnoi kazni v Rossii" [On the Question of the Death Penalty in Russia], *Pravo* [*Law*], June 6, 1910, 1431–39. A critique of the huge number of death sentences from 1905 through 1909, especially those imposed on civilians by Circuit Courts-Martial and often arbitrarily administered.

"Literaturno-kriticheskiia zametki" [Critical Literary Notes], *Nauchno–literaturnyi sbornik* "Budushchnosti" [*Scholarly and Literary Collection from* "The Future"] (1900), 367–78. A review of two books of Jewish stories, together with personal reflections on understanding one's identity as a Jew. Part of this article served as the basis for the chapter entitled "My Jewish Heritage" in Gruzenberg's memoirs.

"O 'zapisnykh knizhkakh' V. G. Korolenko" [On the Notebooks of V. G. Korolenko], *Posledniia novosti* [*Latest News*], March 8, 1936, 2. Comments on Korolenko's published notebooks, covering the period 1880–1900, as well as on Korolenko's personal qualities.

"Pamiati G. B. Sliozberga" [In Memory of G. B. Sliozberg], *Posledniia novosti* [*Latest News*], June 13, 1937, 2. A tribute to a well-known Russian Jewish lawyer.

O petrogradskoi advokatskoi gromade [*On the Petrograd Bar*]. Petrograd, 1916. A speech to the jubilee assembly of Petrograd lawyers and lawyers-in-training on the fiftieth anniversary of the creation of the Petrograd Bar. Included in *Ocherki i rechi*, 76–91.

Works about Gruzenberg

Gol'denveizer, A. A. "Advokat-boets: pamiati O. O. Gruzenberga" [Lawyer and Fighter: In Memory of O. O. Gruzenberg], in Gol'denveizer's book, *V zashchitu prava* [*In Defense of the Law*], 241–49. New York, 1952. Characterization of Gruzenberg.

Gorshun, B. L. "Gruzenberg kak ugolovnyi zashchitnik" [Gruzenberg as a Criminal Defense Counsel], *Posledniia novosti* [*Latest News*], September 1, 1938, 4. Review of Gruzenberg's memoirs, *Vchera: vospominaniia*, as well as an assessment of his career.

"Grusenberg, Oscar Osipovich," *Encyclopaedia Judica*, 7, 952–53. 16 vols. Jerusalem, 1971–72. Biographical sketch, emphasizing Gruzenberg's association with Jewish affairs.

Kucherov, S. L. "Evrei v russkoi advokature" [Jews in the Russian Bar]. In *Kniga o russkom evreistve ot 1860–kh godov do revoliutsii 1917 g.* [*Book of Russian Jewry from the 1860s to the Revolution of 1917*], 400–37. New York, 1960. Edited by Ia. G. Frumkin and others. (In translation in *Russian Jewry, 1860–1917*, 219–52. New York, 1969.) Includes a biographical sketch of Gruzenberg, concentrating on his defense of Jews.

Kulisher, E. M. "Gruzenberg kak advokat" [Gruzenberg as a Lawyer], in *Ocherki i rechi*, 8–20. Interpretive commentary on Gruzenberg's talent as a trial lawyer.

Naidich, I. A. "Gruzenberg i russkoe evreistvo" [Gruzenberg and Russian Jewry], in *Ocherki i rechi*, 32–44. Summary of Gruzenberg's participation in cases involving Jews and his views on Jewish rights, assimilation, and Zionism.

Stolkind, A. Ia. "Pamiati O. O. Gruzenberga: vospominaniia iz zaly suda" [In Memory of O. O. Gruzenberg: Memoirs from the Courtroom], in *Ocherki i rechi*, 21–31. Personal recollections of Gruzenberg in Russia and as an émigré.

Tsitron, I. L. "Zhiznennyi put' O. O. Gruzenberga" [The Course of O. O. Gruzenberg's Life], in *Ocherki i rechi*, 45–57. Informative account of Gruzenberg's life and career.

The Russian Judiciary

Atwell, John W., Jr. "The Russian Jury," *Slavonic and East European Review*, 53 (January, 1975), 44–61. An examination of the establishment and functioning of the Russian jury from 1864 to 1914.

Foinitskii, I. Ia. *Kurs ugolovnago sudoproizvodstva* [*A Course in Criminal Legal Procedure*]. 2 vols. St. Petersburg, 1896–99. History, organization, and functioning of criminal legal procedure: prosecution, defense, evidence, witnesses, verdict, appeal, cassation.

Gessen, I. V. (ed.). *Istoriia russkoi advokatury, 1864–1916* [*History of the Russian Bar, 1864–1916*]. 3 vols. Moscow, 1914–16. Published by the Russian Councils of the Bar. Contains much information, including statistics.

Gogel', S. K. *Voprosy ugolovnago prava, protsessa i tiur'movedeniia* [*Problems of Criminal Law, Legal Proceedings, and Imprisonment*]. St. Petersburg, 1906. A collection of essays arguing for more humane means of dealing with crime and treating prisoners.

Gold'man, L. I. (ed.). *Politicheskie protsessy v Rossii, 1901–1917* [*Political Trials in Russia, 1901–1917*]. Moscow, 1932. Brief descriptions of 498 political cases.

Kaiser, F. B. *Die russische Justizreform von 1864* [*The Russian Judicial Reform of 1864*]. Leiden, 1972. Detailed explanation of the genesis and drafting of the reform. Extensive bibliography.

Karabchevskii, N. P. *Rechi, 1882–1914* [*Speeches, 1882–1914*]. 3rd ed. Petrograd, 1916. Courtroom speeches of a prominent defense lawyer.

Koni, A. F. *Sobranie sochinenii* [*Collected Works*]. 8 vols. Moscow, 1966–69. Memoirs, speeches, and essays of a distinguished jurist.

Kucherov, Samuel. "The Jury As Part of the Russian Judicial Reform of 1864," *American Slavic and East European Review*, 9

(April, 1950), 77–90. An investigation of the origin and implementation of the Russian jury system.

Kucherov, Samuel. *Courts, Lawyers and Trials Under the Last Three Tsars.* New York, 1953. The major work in English on the Russian judiciary between 1864 and 1917. Extensive bibliography.

Samuel, Maurice. *Blood Accusation: The Strange History of the Beiliss Case.* New York, 1966. A detailed and interpretive account of this notorious ritual murder case, in which Gruzenberg was chief defense counsel.

Sliozberg, G. B. *Dela minuvshikh dnei: zapiski russkago evreia [In Bygone Days: Notes of a Russian Jew].* 3 vols. Paris, 1933–34. Memoirs of a well-known lawyer during the last two decades of tsarist rule.

Spasovich, V. D. (Spasowicz, W. D.). *Sochineniia [Works].* 3 vols. St. Petersburg, 1889–1902. Writings and speeches of one of the most capable late-nineteenth century lawyers in Russia.

Szeftel, Marc. "Personal Inviolability in the Legislation of the Russian Absolute Monarchy," *American Slavic and East European Review, 17* (1958), 1–24. A study of the discrepancy between the safeguards of individual rights specified in the Judicial Statutes of 1864 and the extensive powers of the police.

Tager, A. S. *The Decay of Czarism: The Beiliss Trial.* Philadelphia, 1935. A history of the trial with emphasis on the social and political context. Translated from the Russian.

Vilenskii, B. V. *Sudebnaia reforma i kontrreforma v Rossii [Judicial Reform and Counter-reform in Russia].* Saratov, 1969. A Marxist-Leninist interpretation of the judicial reform of 1864 and subsequent decrees that seemed designed to preserve class privileges.

Vinaver, M. M. *Nedavnee: vospominaniia i kharateristiki [Recent Times: Memoirs and Testimonials].* 2nd ed. Paris, 1926. Memoirs of a Russian Jewish lawyer during the last years of tsarist rule.

Wagner, William G. "Tsarist Legal Policies at the End of the Nineteenth Century: A Study in Inconsistencies," *Slavonic and East European Review, 54* (July, 1976), 371–94. An examination of the Russian government's efforts to create and maintain an independent judiciary while simultaneously circumventing its jurisdiction.

Wortman, Richard. "Judicial Personnel and the Court Reform of 1864," *Canadian Slavic Studies, 3* (Summer, 1969), 224–34. A study of the recruitment of qualified personnel by the Ministry of Justice prior to the judicial reform of 1864.

Wortman, Richard. *The Development of a Russian Legal Con-*

226

BIBLIOGRAPHY

sciousness. Chicago, 1976. A comprehensive investigation of changes in composition and attitudes of judicial personnel during the several decades preceding the reform of 1864, with emphasis on the relationship of law and autocratic authority, professionalization of the judiciary, and the concept of judicial independence.

Legal Periodicals

Iurist [*The Jurist*]. St. Petersburg, 1902–1905. Weekly. Editors: N. P. Karabchevskii and L. D. Liakhovetskii. Articles on legal topics; news of legislation, trials, courtroom speeches; register of cases before the Senate; chronicle of foreign judicial news.

Pravo [*Law*]. St. Petersburg, 1898–1916. Weekly. Editors: V. M. Gessen, N. I. Lazarevskii, and others. Articles on legal topics; decisions of cassation cases in the Senate; news of legislation, trials, courtroom speeches, activities of the St. Petersburg Juridical Society.

Sudebnaia Gazeta [*Judicial Gazette*]. St. Petersburg, 1882–1905. Weekly. Editor: F. V. de-Veki. Decisions of cases before the Senate; news of legislation.

Trudy Iuridicheskago Obshchestva pri Imperatorskom S.-Peterburgskom Universitete [*Transactions of the Juridical Society of the Imperial University of St. Petersburg*]. St. Petersburg, 1908–14. Annual. Editor: M. M. Vinaver. Articles and speeches.

Zakon i sud [*Law and Court*]. Riga, 1929–38. Monthly. Organ of the Russian Juridical Society. Editors: O. O. Gruzenberg and others. Articles on legal topics; news of émigré juridical activities, as well as legal developments in the Soviet Union.

Zhurnal Iuridicheskago Obshchestva pri Imperatorskom S.-Peterburgskom Universitete [*Journal of the Juridical Society of the Imperial University of St. Petersburg*]. St. Petersburg, 1871–1906. (Title varies.) Monthly. Editors: V. N. Lamkin and others. Articles and news.

Zhurnal Ministerstva Iustitsii [*Journal of the Ministry of Justice*]. St. Petersburg, 1859–1917. Monthly. Editors: V. F. Deriuzhinskii and others. Official publication on criminal, administrative, and international law and legal proceedings.

Jews in Russia (to 1917)

Baron, Salo W. *The Russian Jew Under Tsars and Soviets.* New York, 1964. A well-balanced survey of social and cultural life, economic conditions, and government policy.

Cohen, Israel. *Jewish Life in Modern Times.* 2nd rev. ed. New York,

227

1929. Sketches of cultural and religious life, economic status, and family relationships of European Jews in the early twentieth century.

Dawidowicz, Lucy S. (ed.). *The Golden Tradition: Jewish Life and Thought in Eastern Europe.* New York, 1967. Excerpts from autobiographies, memoirs, and letters of some sixty Eastern European Jewish intellectuals in the nineteenth and early twentieth centuries on religion, education, literature, the arts, political movements, and Zionism. Useful introductory essay.

Dubnow, S. M. *History of the Jews in Russia and Poland.* 3 vols. Philadelphia, 1916–20. For years the best-known account of Jewish life in Russia and Poland, especially in the nineteenth and early twentieth centuries.

Frumkin, Ia. G. and others (eds.). *Kniga o russkom evreistve ot 1860–kh godov do revoliutsii 1917 g.* [*Book of Russian Jewry from the 1860s to the Revolution of 1917*]. New York, 1960. Essays by various Russian Jewish émigrés on such topics as the legal status of Jews in Russia, economic life, education, participation in the professions, arts, and literature, Zionism, and emigration.

Frumkin, Jacob, and others (eds.). *Russian Jewry, 1860–1917.* New York, 1969. Translation of *Kniga o russkom evreistve.*

Gessen, Iu. I. *Evrei v Rossii* [*The Jews in Russia*]. St. Petersburg, 1906. Social, legal, and economic conditions of Russian Jews in the early nineteenth century.

Greenberg, Louis. *The Jews in Russia.* 2 vols. New Haven, 1944–51. A scholarly examination of the status of Jews in Russia during the nineteenth and early twentieth centuries with emphasis on the struggle for emancipation.

Margolin, A. D. *The Jews in Eastern Europe.* New York, 1926. Mainly memoirs of a Russian Jewish lawyer during the late tsarist period with commentary on Jewish political and economic life, pogroms, and Jews in emigration, and a section on the author's participation in the Beilis ritual murder case.

Raisin, Jacob S. *The Haskalah Movement in Russia.* Philadelphia, 1913. A thorough inquiry into the origins and development of the Jewish "Enlightenment" in Russia with attention to Jewish achievements in art, music, literature, and science.

Vital, David. *The Origins of Zionism.* Oxford, 1975. Includes a sound exposition and assessment of the early stages of the Zionist movement in Russia in the late nineteenth century.

Zborowski, Mark, and Herzog, Elizabeth. *Life is With People: The Jewish Little-Town of Eastern Europe.* New York, 1952. An informative reconstruction of Jewish life in Eastern Europe before World War I, much of the information being based on interviews with immigrants to the United States.

Russian Jewish Periodicals

Budushchnost' [*The Future*]. St. Petersburg, 1900–04. Weekly. Editor: S. O. Gruzenberg. Articles on legal, economic, and cultural aspects of Jewish life in Russia. Annual supplement: *Nauchno-literaturnyi sbornik* "Budushchnosti" [*Scholarly and Literary Collection from* "The Future"].

Evreiskaia starina [*Jewish Antiquities*]. St. Petersburg, 1909–30. Quarterly. Editors: S. M. Dubnov and others. History and ethnography of the Jews in Russia and Poland.

Voskhod [*The Dawn*]. St. Petersburg, 1881–1906. Monthly until 1899. Editor: A. E. Landau. Scholarly, literary, and political journal directed toward Jewish cultural advancement and emancipation. Weekly supplement: *Nedel'naia khronika* "Voskhoda" [*Weekly Chronicle* of "The Dawn"], edited by S. O. Gruzenberg. After 1899, semi-weekly, then weekly. Editor: M. G. Syrkin. Similar format but greater emphasis on Zionism. Supplement: Knizhki "Voskhoda" [*Booklet of* "The Dawn"], 1901–06.

Index

Iollos, G. B., 76
*Is Everything at Peace among the
People?* (Blok), 187
It Cannot Be (Polonsky), 15
Ivanov, V. I., 196*n*, 197

Jewish beliefs and customs, xi–xx,
12–14, 18–22
Judges: civilian, xxi–xxii, 36–37, 39,
45–46, 54–58 *passim*, 60, 66–67,
72, 85–86, 92, 113–23 *passim*, 127–
29, 173, 176, 186; military, 92–102
passim, 141–54 *passim*, 168. *See
also* Justices of the peace
Judicial Statutes of 1864, xx–xxii, 36,
164
Juridical Society, St. Petersburg, 79
Juries, xxi, 36, 60, 107–108, 112–13,
123, 185–86
Justice, Minister or Ministry of, xvi,
xxi, 34, 38, 52, 66, 78–83, 83–84,
86–87, 109–21 *passim*, 201, 202
Justices of the peace, xxi, 36, 55

Kadets. *See* Constitutional Demo-
crats
Kahal, 112, 119
Kamashansky, P. K., 85–87
Karabchevsky, N. P., 43, 51–52, 113
Kazetsky case, 127
Ketcher, N. Kh., 35
Khomenko case, 60–62
Kiev University, xvi, 3, 28–32
Kievlyanin (*The Kievan*), 114
Knight for an Hour, A (Nekrasov),
15
Kokovtsov, P. K., 108, 117, 118
Koni, A. F., 127
Konstantin Konstantinovich, 191
Korolenko, V. G., xxviii, 103, 105,
114, 119, 162, 169–88, 191, 198
Kosorotov, D. P., 116
Krushevan, P. A., 81
Kuropatkin, A. N., 127

Launitz, V. F. von der, 76, 88
Lawyers: attorneys for civil plaintiffs,
40, 86, 113, 116–17; defense coun-

sels (other than Gruzenberg),
xxii, 2–3, 37–44, 51–52, 93, 111–23
passim, 125, 133–34, 141, 145, 147,
164, 182; private attorneys, xxii,
34, 182. *See also* Prosecutors
Lawyers-in-training, xvi–xvii, xxii,
34–35, 37–38
Lenin, V. I., 49, 69, 70
Le Temps (*The Times*), 69
Lilienblum, Moses Lieb, xiv–xv
Literary cases, 111, 172–73, 175–77,
196–98, 203–204
Lopukhin, A. A., 71
Louis XVI, 65
Lower Depths, The (Gorky), 190*n*,
191
Lunacharsky, A. V., 195

Main Administration for Affairs of
the Press. *See* Press, Main Admin-
istration for Affairs of the
Main Court-Martial. *See* Courts
Makarenko, A. S., 131–68 *passim*
Maklakov, V. A., 113
Malinovsky-Bogdanov, A. A. *See*
Bogdanov
Margolin, A. D., 109, 111*n*
Marx, Karl, 69, 73
Maxwell case, 48–58
Mazeh, Yakov, 108
Merezhkovsky, D. S., 192*n*, 193*n*
Mikhailovsky, N. K., 4, 198
Milyukov, P. N., xxiv, xxvii, 76, 82,
88, 105, 198
Ministers or Ministries. *See* Internal
Affairs; Justice; War
Mironov, P. G., 34, 38, 43–44, 106
Misfortune of Being Wise, The
(Griboedov), 41*n*
Mother (Gorky), 199, 203–204
Mukhanov, A. A., 82–83
Muraviev, N. V., 38, 83–84
Muraviev Commission, 79
Myasoedov, S. N., 126–40 *passim*

Na chuzhoi storone (*In Foreign
Parts*), 169*n*
Nabokov, V. D., 114